Persons, Powers, and Pluralities

Princeton Theological Monograph Series

K. C. Hanson, Charles M. Collier, D. Christopher Spinks,
and Robin Parry, Series Editors

Recent volumes in the series:

Lisa E. Dahill
*Reading from the Underside of Selfhood:
Bonhoeffer and Spiritual Formation*

Paul Ingram, editor
Constructing a Relational Cosmology

Chris Budden
*Following Jesus in Invaded Space:
Doing Theology on Aboriginal Land*

Philip Ruge-Jones
Cross in Tensions

Christian T. Collins Winn
*"Jesus Is Victor":
The Significance of the Blumhardts for the Theology of Karl Barth*

Charles Bellinger
*The Trinitarian Self:
The Key to the Puzzle of Violence*

Mary Clark Moschella
*Living Devotions:
Reflections on Immigration, Identity, and Religious Imagination*

Caryn D. Riswold
*Coram Deo:
Human Life in the Vision of God*

Guttesen, Poul F.
*Leaning into the Future:
The Kingdom of God in the Theology of Jürgen Moltmann
and the Book of Revelation*

Persons, Powers, and Pluralities
Toward a Trinitarian Theology of Culture

Eric G. Flett

◆PICKWICK *Publications* · Eugene, Oregon

PERSONS, POWERS, AND PLURALITIES
Toward a Trinitarian Theology of Culture

Princeton Theological Monograph Series 158

Copyright © 2011 Eric G. Flett. All rights reserved. Except for brief quotations in critical publications or reviews, no part of this book may be reproduced in any manner without prior written permission from the publisher. Write: Permissions, Wipf and Stock Publishers, 199 W. 8th Ave., Suite 3, Eugene, OR 97401.

Pickwick Publications
An Imprint of Wipf and Stock Publishers
199 W. 8th Ave., Suite 3
Eugene, OR 97401

www.wipfandstock.com

ISBN 13: 978-1-60608-658-2

Cataloging-in-Publication data:

Flett, Eric G.

    Persons, powers, and pluralities : toward a trinitarian theology of culture / Eric G. Flett.

    Princeton Theological Monograph Series 158

    xii + 254 p. ; 23 cm. Includes bibliographical references.

    ISBN 13: 978-1-60608-658-2

    1. Torrance, T. F. (Thomas Forsythe), 1913–2007. 2. Trinity. 3. Theology. I. Title. II. Series.

BX4827 T67 F40 2011

Manufactured in the U.S.A.

Chapter 4 appeared as "Priests of Creation, Mediators of Order: The Human Person as a Cultural Being in Thomas F. Torrance's Theological Anthropology." © 2005 *Scottish Journal of Theology*. Originally published in *Scottish Journal of Theology* 58:2 (2005) 161–83. Reprinted with permission.

Portions of chapter 5 were presented at the 2007 meeting of the Thomas F. Torrance Theological Fellowship and subsequently published as "Culture as a Social Coefficient: Toward a Trinitarian Theology of Culture." © 2009 *Cultural Encounters*. Originally published in *Cultural Encounters* 5:1 (2009) 53–74. Reprinted with permission.

To JoAnn

Contents

Acknowledgments / ix

Introduction / 1

1. Torrance's Doctrine of God: The Triune Creator / 5

2. Torrance's Doctrine of Creation I: Order as Contingent / 60

3. Torrance's Doctrine of Creation II: Order as Redeemed / 84

4. Torrance's Doctrine of Humanity: Priests of Creation, Mediators of Order / 116

5. Torrance's Theology of Culture: A Social Coefficient of Knowledge / 139

6. Toward a Trinitarian Theology of Culture: Persons, Powers, and Pluralities / 217

Appendix: Project Outline / 241

Bibliography / 247

Acknowledgments

THIS BOOK IS THE RESULT OF DOCTORAL WORK I UNDERTOOK AT King's College, University of London—a course of research that ended in 2004. I am glad that the initial work, bound in blue and submitted to the King's examination board, will now get a chance to see a wider audience thanks to the willingness of Wipf and Stock Publishers to add this volume to its Princeton Theological Monographs series.

It is my happy task to offer thanks to the many persons and institutions who have extended their generosity and friendship to my family and myself while this project was being completed, and while I conducted the light revisions necessary in order to prepare it for publication.

My greatest theological debt is to the late Ray S. Anderson, former Professor of Theology and Ministry at Fuller Theological Seminary. The seeds for this project were sown while my wife and I studied under Ray's guidance as MA students at Fuller. When I told Ray of my growing interest in the field of theological anthropology and theology of culture he recommended I spend time at King's pursuing these interests. His support has continued throughout, both academically and pastorally, reading numerous drafts of chapters and guiding me through the peculiarities of academic research in the UK. For his friendship, advocacy, and willingness to take risks in the name of Jesus Christ I am deeply grateful. His passing is a personal loss, and a loss to the broader Christian community he served so faithfully.

I would also like to thank Elmer Colyer, Professor of Historical Theology at The University of Dubuque Theological Seminary. Consistently enthusiastic and constructively critical, Elmer has been a valued dialogue partner during the research and writing of this project.

A handful of institutions have made this research possible. In particular I would like to thank Rotary International and the Rotary Clubs of Woodinville, Washington, and Hammersmith, England, for their financial sponsorship and hospitality. During the 1998–1999 academic year I had the privilege of serving as a Rotary Ambassadorial Scholar in

London. This was an immensely enjoyable period of time for my family and I, and their support made the transition from the United States to the United Kingdom lighter than it otherwise would have been.

While in London my family and I were residents of The London Goodenough Trust for Overseas Postgraduates. Then Warden Noelle Vickers welcomed us into this community with a solemn charge that we would receive from this rich community only as much as we put ourselves into it. Never have we felt more at home in our lives. This project has been enriched in numerous and intangible ways through the cultural and intellectual diversity represented there, particularly by the many international friendships we developed, friendships The Goodenough College so eagerly and generously encourages. In particular, I would like to thank Noelle Vickers, Mandy Backhouse, and Ashley Null for making the Goodenough Trust a unique place to live and conduct research, and my most immediate theological conversation partners as we walked Southampton Row to the weekly postgraduate seminar at King's: Randall Rauser, Kelly Kapic, and Brian Brock.

The final stages of this project were completed while serving for two years as Visiting Instructor in Christian Foundations at Seattle Pacific University. I consider myself fortunate to have entered the teaching profession at this institution, and for the opportunity to work alongside colleagues who understand teaching and scholarship as a sacramental act. Kerry Dearborn welcomed me into SPU with her fullest trust and support, while Rick Steele bore much of the burden of orienting me to the demands of this particular vocation and in the process has come to define for me the essence of what a teacher-scholar is. I shall long be grateful for their fellowship and encouragement. Finally, thanks to the many students I had the privilege of teaching during my time at SPU. You entertained numerous stories about the progress of this project, and my career, with interest and good humor.

The research for this project began at the same time Murray Rae came to join the faculty in the Department of Theology and Religious Studies at King's College, London. I consider myself fortunate that our careers have overlapped. Murray's supervision of this project has improved it vastly. He has been incisive in his comments and recommendations, consistently available and has extended himself in ways that have taken him far beyond his job description or any cultural expectations. Thanks are also due to the Rae family as a whole, for their hospitality and friendship during our time in London.

Final thanks are due to Eastern University, the academic institution where my wife and I have both found a hospitable place for teaching and research. Oriented as it is by a focus on the integration of faith and learning in the service of social justice, Eastern is an environment conducive to the kinds of work, both intellectual and practical, that the theology of culture articulated here envisions. A special thanks to my colleagues in the Christian Studies department, in particular Kent Sparks, Dwight Peterson, and Steve Boyer; and in the Business department, like-minded deviant and friend Lindy Backues, and my wife, JoAnn.

It is to JoAnn, and my sons, Miles and Elliot, that I owe my greatest debt. The sheer joy of watching my sons grow and develop as persons frequently overwhelmed me, all the while sustaining me when my passions for this project stagnated or were non-existent.

JoAnn has scattered her vocational and educational pursuits, and many friendships, over a number of years and many countries, in order to make this project possible. Such is the tangible evidence of her belief in its value and her love for me. Her support has gone far beyond the emotional or the monetary, and many of the chapters here are improved in style and content because of her feedback. Her interests and teaching in the field of business and social enterprise have generated numerous conversations that have served to test many of the assertions made in this project, and will serve to extend its implications even further into areas where my expertise is woefully lacking, and where the conclusions here will serve the poor more faithfully and tangibly. Not so affectionately referred to as her 'third child', she has long waited for the labor involved in the delivery of this project to cease. Now, with gratitude and joy, I dedicate this book to her.

E. G. F.
Newtown Square, PA

Introduction

KATHRYN TANNER, PROFESSOR OF THEOLOGY AT THE UNIVERSITY OF Chicago Divinity School, notes in her recent book *Theories of Culture* that "although less than one hundred years old, the modern anthropological meaning of 'culture' now enjoys a remarkable influence within the humanistic disciplines of the academy and within commonsense discussions of daily life."[1]

She continues, citing the observations of anthropologists Alfred A. Kroeber and Klyde Kluckhohn: "In explanatory importance and in generality of application it [the concept of culture] is comparable to such categories as gravity in physics, disease in medicine, evolution in biology."[2]

The pervasiveness of the concept, and its explanatory power, are due in no small part to the broad range of meanings associated with the term. To speak of culture is to speak also, in some sense, of "context," "community," "ideology," and "tradition." The breadth of semantic reference the term carries is a plus, for it can be used to explain just about anything, from beliefs, to products, to social movements. In fact, the term "culture" has been so qualified by the adjectives placed in front of it (institutional culture, world culture, personal culture, sports culture, etc.) that one can no longer be certain about exactly what it refers to. I have often found that my endeavors to use the term with a precision beyond the popular or generic are met with confusion, resistance, and numerous requests for clarification. On the rare occasion I am able to qualify the term to the satisfaction of my audience, I am frequently asked why, in light of all the fuss, the term is even used at all. James Clifford explains both the popularity and predicament of the term when he observes that "culture is a deeply compromised idea I cannot yet do without."[3] Sociologist Robert Wuthnow makes the same point when he

1. Tanner, *Theories of Culture*, ix.
2. Kroeber and Kluckhohn, *Culture*, 3.
3. Clifford, *Predicament of Culture*, 10.

notes that culture is a concept "which remains subject to ambiguities of treatment but which retains value as a sensitizing concept for investigations into the symbolic-expressive dimensions of social life."[4]

Two things in particular seem clear from Clifford's pithy observation: the term "culture" *is* a deeply compromised idea that seems to have no clear center of meaning. Like Sisyphus and his stone, our renewed efforts to give concrete shape to the term consistently fall back on us at the point when we seem closest to success. It would seem the most reasonable thing to do, after relentlessly qualifying the idea, would be to give up. And yet, again in agreement with Clifford, this term is one we cannot do without, for it refers to a reality that plays a decisive role in the sustenance and subversion of human life. For whatever reason we simply cannot walk away from the stone.

This project is an attempt to clarify the meaning of the term further in my own mind. As one whose life has been fundamentally reoriented by the triune God of Jesus Christ, and immeasurably enriched through cross-cultural experience, it is an attempt to bring the two realms of experience and thought together into a coherent and integrated whole. The point of focus for this task is the thought of the Scottish Reformed theologian Thomas F. Torrance

"Following the Line"

In an interview given in March of 1999 Pat Metheny, guitarist, composer, and founder of The Pat Metheny Group, one of the most successful and innovative jazz groups of the past thirty years, was asked to comment upon his musical philosophy and improvisational method.

---

4. Wuthnow et al., *Cultural Analysis*, viii. Wuthnow goes on to note that "the social sciences are in danger of abandoning culture entirely as a field of inquiry" due largely in part to the fact that the stuff of which culture is made: feelings, beliefs and values, cannot be empirically examined without a great deal of difficulty and expense (3). I imagine Torrance would say that here we have a case where the method of inquiry has been defined before the object of study has been engaged. Consequently, the object of study (culture) is either abandoned or turned into something else that is more conducive to the method of investigation we wish to employ. Conceptual tools that may be appropriate to another field of inquiry or other scientific goals will not suffice here. New conceptual tools must be developed to accommodate a different object of inquiry. We offer here some conceptual tools drawn from Torrance's thought that may grant us further insight into the reality we ambiguously refer to as "culture."

Metheny described his improvisational technique as linear and narrative. When improvising he is focused upon telling a story that has a beginning, middle, and end. Consequently, his improvisational technique is not based upon the random selection of individual notes but rather upon the progressive development of a single idea—whether that idea is melodic, harmonic, or rhythmic. Metheny's objective is to let that single idea be itself and to follow it to its natural conclusion, weaving it in and out of his improvisation, using it as a touchstone or organizing motif, with the goal of telling a story where that single idea holds center stage and impacts every other note he plays. Metheny calls this "following the line."

We find the same dynamic present in Torrance's thought when he refers to the Trinity as "the ground and grammar of theology."[5] "Following the line" seems an accurate and accessible way of describing the origin and goal of all theological reflection that seeks to be determined by the reality of God as triune. In order to gather the resources necessary for the development of a trinitarian theology of culture we will follow this line through three areas of Torrance's thought. Torrance suggests those areas himself when he notes the essential boundaries and dynamics of what he calls "theological science": "So far as theological science is concerned it is imperative that we operate with a *triadic relation* between God, man and world, or God, world and man: for it is this world unfolding its mysteries to our scientific questioning which is the medium of God's revelation and of man's responsible knowledge of him."[6]

Torrance refers to this "triadic relation" throughout his writings.[7] It provides the anchor that both grounds and integrates Torrance's theological project. The theological content of each pole, and how they are related, is essential to the integrity of the theological reflection based upon them. Torrance's thought is rigorously and consistently trinitarian. The work he has done integrating these three poles and filling them with content will be an asset to the project we are about to develop. The line we will follow will touch upon each of these areas and then

---

5. Torrance, *Ground and Grammar of Theology*.
6. Torrance, *Reality and Scientific Theology*, 69.
7. The most explicit and extended development of this "triadic relation" may be found in Torrance, *Reality and Evangelical Theology*, 21–30.

conclude by exploring a concept in Torrance's thought that assumes and incorporates his thinking in each of these areas.[8]

We begin this study with a consideration of Torrance's doctrine of God as triune Creator in chapter 1. Here we will specifically note how God's activity as Creator is conditioned and determined by his Being as triune. We will then follow the line originating in Torrance's doctrine of God through his doctrine of creation, noting its influence on this aspect of his thought. We will develop this particular area of his thought in two chapters. Chapter 2 will consider the created order specifically as "contingent," while chapter 3 will consider that same order as both fallen and redeemed. Chapter 4 will take us into a consideration of Torrance's theological anthropology and his understanding of human persons as "priests of creation" and "mediators of order", created in continuity with the contingent order, but also in distinction from it, as creatures given a unique constitution and identity and entrusted with a cultural task that is doxologically motivated. Our final task, in chapter 5, will be to "improvise" a theology of culture, something Torrance did not explicitly develop, that continues the trajectory of this line by rooting the origin, *telos,* and transformation of human culture in the triune being of God. We will be helped toward this final destination through a consideration of Torrance's concept of "the social coefficient of knowledge", a concept that is different from the components that have led us to it, but also profoundly integrated with, and founded upon, them. The argument of the final chapter will be to suggest the following: 1) This concept continues the trinitarian logic and line we have been following through Torrance's thought; 2) This concept, and the dynamics it seeks to describe, are based upon, and integrated with, Torrance's doctrines of God, creation, and humanity as developed in the preceding chapters; and 3) This concept may thus serve as a heuristic basis for the development of a theology of culture that is trinitarian in nature and congruent with Torrance's overall theological project.

---

8. The three areas mentioned by Torrance, and their interrelationships, are not unique to his thought. Many authors employ the doctrines of God, creation, and humanity to frame their reflections on the nature and goals of human cultural activity, even if the content of each area, and the dynamics between them, are variously defined.

Torrance's Doctrine of God
The Triune Creator

THIS STUDY BEGINS WITH A CONSIDERATION OF TORRANCE'S DOCTRINE of the triune Creator. We do so for the following reasons: First, for *pragmatic reasons*. Torrance rarely considers the doctrines of God or creation in isolation from each other.[1] To separate two doctrines so intimately linked in his thinking would not only be difficult, but also counterproductive for anyone seeking an accurate grasp of his thought.

Secondly, these two doctrines are intimately linked in Torrance's thought for *theological reasons*. This is not because Torrance understands the relation between these realities to be a necessary one, but because he understands the relation between Creator and creation to be a contingent one, where the rationality of one order refers us *analogically* to the other.[2] Torrance describes the contingent relationship between the divine and creaturely when he notes that "the reason for the creation is theologically traced back to the free, ungrudging will of God's love to create a reality other than himself which he correlates so closely with himself that it is made to reflect and shadow forth on its contingent level his own inner rationality and order."[3] Creator and creation cannot be considered in isolation from each other if we are to have accurate knowledge of either.

---

1. Torrance's doctrine of the triune Creator receives its most concentrated and systematic treatments in Torrance, *Ground and Grammar*, chapters 3 and 4; *Trinitarian Faith*, chapter 3, and *Christian Doctrine of God*, chapter 8. These treatments are dominated by Torrance's fundamental concern: how the uniqueness of the triune Creator qualifies the character of the created order.

2. We will develop Torrance's concept of "contingency" in chapter 2.

3. Torrance, *Divine and Contingent Order*, 35.

Third, we consider this aspect of Torrance's thought at the outset of this study for *methodological reasons*. This project develops a theology of culture based upon a trinitarian understanding of the doctrines of God, creation, and humanity. The intimate and integrated understanding of triune God, contingent creation, and humanity as a "priest of creation" presented in Torrance's work makes his thought attractive to those seeking to understand any aspect of the created order from a trinitarian perspective. Little effort is required to integrate what Torrance has consistently and intimately joined together over the length of his career. This makes Torrance's doctrine of God as triune Creator a particularly fitting cornerstone upon which to develop a trinitarian theology of culture.

The Tri-unity of God as the Basis for the Creativity of God

Torrance frequently begins his theological reflections with the divine order, and with the doctrine of creation this is no exception. God cannot be known with accuracy, even as Creator, from an examination of that which is external to his being. One must move in a different direction and begin at that point where God himself has entered the boundaries of space and time and offered knowledge of himself, primarily as Father and subsequently as Creator. At the forefront of Torrance's mind is a concern that the divine and contingent orders not be confused, and that the former provide the controlling ground for understanding the latter, while the latter properly reflects the purposes of the former. For Torrance, the balance between these two orders can only be properly configured and maintained within a trinitarian framework. Torrance would fully agree with the remarks of Colin Gunton: "The only satisfactory account of the relation between the Creator and the creation is a trinitarian one."[4] In our own attempt to unfold Torrance's doctrine of creation we will proceed in this chapter, and indeed this entire project, upon the advice of Robert Jenson, who comments that "any work of God is rightly interpreted only if it is construed by the mutual roles of the triune Persons."[5] After discussing the mutual roles of the triune

---

4. Gunton, *Christ and Creation*, 75.
5. Jenson, *Systematic Theology* 2:25.

Persons in relation to the created order, we will then continue with a consideration of the created order itself, its contingency and ordering, in chapters 2 and 3.

Since the way each of the divine Persons qualifies the created order is of particular interest, we will structure our exposition around a statement by St. Basil that Torrance refers to frequently. It will serve as a structural means of attending to Jenson's advice. In an essay titled "Spiritus Creator: A Consideration of the Teaching of St. Athanasius and St. Basil,"[6] Torrance notes that "Basil distinguishes the work of the Father as 'the original cause of all things that are made,' and the work of the Son as 'the operative cause,' and the work of the Spirit as 'the perfecting cause.'"[7]

The fellowship of the Father, Son, and Spirit serves as the basis for God's creative activity, since that activity flows from, and is conditioned by, the particular identities and functions of each divine Person. Torrance calls this "a fellowship in creative activity"[8] in order to emphasize the *nature* of God's creative agency. That agency is grounded in the perichoretic relationships between the Father, the Son, and the Holy Spirit as distinct *hypostases*, and it is upon the basis of these perichoretic relationships that the unity of God's agency is asserted. The very plurality of God serves as the basis for the unified and creative agency of God, exercised in bringing forth a reality external to Godself. To understand God as Creator, the created order as contingent, and the nature of the relation between them properly, we must first articulate why the triunity of God serves as the basis for the creativity of God. We will accomplish this goal through *a consideration of the identity and function of each divine Person as understood in relation to the created order*. Our interest is in how the particularity of each divine Person qualifies the created order, a created order that results from, and is sustained by, their "fellowship in creative activity."

---

6. This essay can be found in Torrance, *Theology in Reconstruction*.

7. Ibid., 221. A contemporary version of Basil's statement can be found in Robert Jenson's *Systematic Theology*, where he notes that "God the Father is the sheer given of creation; God the Spirit is the perfecting Freedom that animates creation; God the Son is the mediator of creation." See Jenson, *Systematic Theology* 2:25. This better captures the intent of Basil and eases the temptation to take his words here as denoting a causal chain of relations among the Persons of the Trinity, as opposed to equal, free and perichoretic ones.

8. Torrance, *Theology in Reconstruction*, 220.

The Creativity of God Is Signified by the Fatherhood of God

If one were to ask Torrance which of the triune persons we should begin our exploration of the created order with, his answer would be "the Father," for "knowledge of God as Creator is taken from knowledge of God as Father, and not the other way around."⁹ Although Torrance wants to focus on the Father first, for reasons we shall soon consider, he would also point out that focusing attention on the identity and work of one divine Person does not invalidate their perichoretic and consubstantial relations with the others:¹⁰ "The one being of God is whole and complete not in the Father alone but in the Son and in the Holy Spirit as much as in the Godhead. Each is the whole God and wholly all that God eternally is as God."¹¹

For Torrance, the creativity of God is signified by the Fatherhood of God, for it is as the Father Almighty that God is the Almighty Creator. This may be understood as the Patrological qualification of creation since it asserts that the created order originates in the love, freedom, and will of the triune God and not some necessary or generic creative action. God's creative activity flows from the Father as *the originate cause of creation*. This is to assert the primacy of the Father/Son relation over

---

9. Torrance, *Trinitarian Faith*, 76.

10. This is an assertion questioned by Colin Gunton. See Gunton, "Being and Person," where Gunton faults Torrance's doctrine of God as being overly Augustinian, in that it obscures the plurality of God's activity and identity by an overemphasis upon the unity of God's operations toward the created order. Torrance's rejoinder may be found in Colyer, *Promise of Trinitarian Theology*, 314–18.

There are areas in Torrance's thought where this critique is applicable; where Torrance's emphasis upon the unity of God's being overshadows and homogenizes the plurality of God's action. In particular, when Torrance is affirming the ontological unity between the Father and Son, and quotes with approval Athanasius's statement that everything that can be said about the Father can be said about the Son, except "Father." However, in defense of Torrance, he is careful to note that there are in fact distinctions between the Father, the Son, and the Holy Spirit that go beyond identity to agency. This is particularly clear in Torrance's *Christian Doctrine of God*, where Torrance asserts, not only that there is no priority of unity over plurality in God (they arise "concurrently"), but that particular actions may be ascribed to each divine Person upon the basis of the doctrine of *perichoresis*. This would seem to preserve the *unity* of God's Being and action, in that the divine Persons do not act in isolation, but also the *plurality* of God's Being and action, in that each divine Person also acts uniquely. This will be discussed further later in this chapter.

11. Torrance, *Trinitarian Faith*, 80.

the Creator/creation relation, the latter being grounded in the former, and the former being transcendent over the latter.

Torrance takes his lead from the Nicene Creed, where an affirmation of the Fatherhood of God precedes his activity as Almighty Creator.[12] Torrance understands this to be an intentional and theologically significant ordering of words, where primacy is given to the personal identity of God as Father over his activity as Creator, the former qualifying the agency involved in the latter and conferring upon the created order a unique character. The created order does not refer beyond itself to a God who is simply the "Creator," "First Cause" or "Unoriginate," but primarily to the God who is "Father"—the *triune Creator*.[13] The created order is meant to be a temporal analogue of his eternal being even while being maintained as a reality with its own distinctive being and rationality. Understanding God as Creator apart from God's identity as "Father" is to operate with a differentiation that tells us little about the identity and vocation of human persons in the created world.[14] Consequently, the resources for theological reflection and ethical guidance on the human activity of culture making are sparse. When the concept of Creator is qualified by that of "Father" however, we are offered truths, images and goals which provide boundaries for the ordering of social life, a social life that takes shape in the midst of creation, in the context of our relations with others, and before a triune God.

In addition, to reverse the order of these words by placing "Creator" prior to "Almighty Father" implies that the identity of God as Father is dependent upon his activity as Creator. This is to subvert the theologic of the Nicene Creed and consequently to suffer a profound loss of theological content. It is to signify the Father from his created works as opposed to signifying him from the Son *through* whom he works and

---

12. Ibid., 76.

13. "It is to the ultimate Love of God the Father that the 'reason' for the creation is to be traced, why it exists at all, but also why it is what it is and not something else" (Torrance, *Christian Doctrine of God*, 212).

14. Colin Gunton notes that "the tendency of all theology of creation after Augustine is to move from the abstract to the concrete: from abstract omnipotence or absolute power to the economy of creation and redemption." This is due in part to "a concentration on the concept of causality at the expense of a more personally conceived relation between God and the world." To focus exclusively or even primarily upon causality and abstractions is to "effectively by-pass the second and third persons of the Trinity." (Gunton, *The Triune Creator*, 147).

the Spirit *in* whom he works. Torrance's rationale for qualifying God's activity as Creator by asserting the primacy of his identity as Father is captured by Athanasius when he comments that "it would be more godly and true to signify God from the Son and call him Father, than to name him from his works and call him Unoriginate."[15] For Torrance, a truly scientific theology demands such a qualification. We must approach the object to be known on its own terms and in a manner congruent with what it has revealed itself to be.

For this reason the Fatherhood of God and the Father/Son relation serve as a more appropriate basis for understanding God's creative activity, and the created order that has resulted from it, than the Creator/creature relation. We signify the creativity of God from the Fatherhood of God for the following reasons:

The Father Signifies the Triune Being of God

Athanasius, and Torrance in concert with him, has just asserted that if we signify God from the Son we are confronted with God as Father. The Son stands as a concrete witness to, not only the reality of God as Creator, but also the identity of God as Father. As not only the Son of the Father but the eternal Logos or Word of God, the witness of the Son is in word as well as deed and as such assumes a particularity that cannot be achieved by the created order. It achieves this particularity because the Son shares a *personal relation* with the Father that is based not only upon a unity of being and action but of hypostatic differentiation as well. None of this can be said of God's relationship to the created order. Torrance's theological rule of thumb, and emphasis upon *a posteriori* knowing, leads him to posit that knowledge of particulars is prior to knowledge of generalities. A clear example of this rule of thumb at work is his concern to prioritize our knowing of the Father through the Son as opposed to our knowing the Creator from the creation.[16]

Torrance is concerned that to understand God primarily in terms of his function as Creator and to signify him from his works is not only to genericize God's identity and activity but, by so doing, open it up to the

---

15. Torrance, *Trinitarian Faith*, 76. Quoted from *Contra Arianos*, I.34.

16. This rule of thumb is noted by Colin Gunton in Gunton, *The Triune Creator*, 119 and may be found in Torrance, *Hermeneutics of John Calvin*, 4–5.

far greater dangers of anthropomorphizing God's identity and activity by understanding God only in relation to ourselves and our world.

While the created order functions as a witness to the creative power of God it is nonetheless a "mute witness."[17] This is because the created order is a reality that is external to the being of God and as such, its capacities to signify a concrete, particular, and personal reality beyond itself are severely limited. This remains true even as we acknowledge that the created order is a direct product of the divine will, created in freedom and love as the sphere of God's loving-kindness, and as a witness to God's reality and almighty power. It must still be maintained however, that while the created order may point to the creative power of God it can only do so in a generic sense and for that purpose relies heavily upon human perception and creativity to draw theological content out of its unique order. Humanity, in all its creative attempts to do so, has failed in its endeavors, constructing a Creator that is rarely worthy of worship, love or adoration and often serves to repulse and confuse rather than illumine and attract. Various forms of natural theology bear witness to the fact that more concrete guidance is needed for the human mind in order to save it from its in-turned and destructive anthropomorphic projections upon God as Creator.

Such guidance is generously given in the Son where we learn that God is not only Creator, but fundamentally Father. In the Son we have, not a setting aside of the created order as a witness to God, but a placing of the created order within the sphere of revelation, and as such illumined by the witness of the Son and, through his work, enabled to function according to its created *telos*. This is precisely what Torrance has in mind in advocating the role of the created order, not as an independent source of knowledge, but a source of knowledge properly based upon the witness of the Son to the Father. Torrance does this when he argues that there can be "no independent natural theology."[18]

Taking our cue from the Son then, we discover that before God was Creator, he was Father, and that the Fatherhood of God conditions the creative power of God, directing it toward a particular purpose (creation), thus enabling it to witness to him within certain boundaries and in the context of certain relations. The relation of fundamental

---

17. Torrance, *Christian Doctrine of God*, 213.
18. See Torrance, *Karl Barth: Biblical and Evangelical Theologian*, chapter 5.

importance is the relation of the Son to the Father. Such truths cannot be read off the surface of the created order.

However, the Son not only points to the identity of God as Father, but also to the reality of the Spirit and in so doing the tri-unity of God. God as Creator is triune and his tri-unity not only conditions his creativity but makes it both possible and purposeful as well, providing the basis for God's continuing relationship to the created order.

Colin Gunton captures this emphasis upon the fundamental role God's tri-unity plays in his creative activity by developing an emphasis of Irenaeus on the work of the Father taking place through his "two hands": namely, the Son and the Spirit.[19] The Father would not be Creator if his creative activity were not mediated through the Son and the Spirit. For that reason we signify the creativity of God from the Fatherhood of God because the Fatherhood of God points to the triunity of God, which in turn stands as the basis for the creativity of God.

The Father Signifies the Eternal Being of God

Signifying God from the Son and acknowledging him as Father is to acknowledge and know God as he is in his innermost being, and not simply as he appears to us. God is not simply *like* a Father to us in that he created us. Nor is he *like* a Father to us only in terms of the way he responds to us. Both statements are true as regards God's external relations with the world, but we are interested here to point out that even if God had no relation whatsoever to the created order he would still be "Father." The Fatherhood of God is grounded in the internal perichoretic relations of the Godhead, not in relations established with a created order external to the divine Being.[20]

For Torrance, this point is unambiguous: "while God was always Father, he was not always Creator or Maker."[21] Torrance's emphasis here is twofold: firstly, he emphasizes that God's internal and external rela-

---

19. See in particular his *Christ and Creation* and *The Triune Creator*.

20. Torrance contends that the confusion of the internal and external relations of God is at the basis of the Arian controversy. This confusion was inherited from Origen's doctrine of God. See Torrance, *Trinitarian Faith*, 84–89. For Torrance's thoughts on the function of metaphor and the language we use to refer to the divine Persons, see Torrance, "Christian Apprehension."

21. Torrance, *Trinitarian Faith*, 87. See also Torrance, *Christian Doctrine of God*, 207–10.

tions are distinct and are not to be confused. The latter are contingent upon the former. A single citation will be sufficient: "There is . . . a oneness in being and nature between the Father and the Son [internal relation], but a total otherness in being and a complete disparity in nature between the Creator and creature [external relation]. An entirely different relation obtains in each case, for one is ontological and belongs to the intrinsic life and eternal Being of God, and the other is contingent and relates to the temporal existence of the creature."[22]

Maintaining the distinctness of these two relations *preserves* the free relation between them. The Father is Creator because he is the eternal Father and has *freely* willed the existence of a reality other than himself. Consequently, the reality other than God is free to be distinctly itself. The relation between the Father and the world he has created is one of freedom because the fatherhood of God is not contingent upon the reality of a world external to him. It is not necessary for God to be Creator in order for him to be Father. That the Fatherhood of God signifies the eternal Being of God is not to uphold the eternity of God at the expense of the value of the temporal world. Rather, it is to preserve the distinctive reality of each and their proper relation to one another. God created the world and maintains relations with it, not because it is necessary to his being but precisely because it is not. Consequently, it is a relation of both freedom and love. In addition, the fact that the Fatherhood of God is grounded in his eternal Being, while his being Creator is not, also means that God's relation to the world is primarily personal in nature as opposed to simply causal. The imagery used to describe this relation therefore, should conform to this reality.

Secondly, Torrance wishes to emphasize that the eternal Fatherhood of God signifies not only the triunity of God, but also *the character and quality of God's creative power*. It is the power of freedom and love that is exchanged between Father and Son and is extended to the world through the Spirit. This is yet another reason why Torrance is eager to assert "it is as Father that God is Creator, not vice versa."[23]

Asserting the eternal Fatherhood of God therefore not only signifies that God is triune in his innermost being, but also that his Fatherhood is not dependent upon the external relation he has established with the world in freedom, love and grace. In addition, the creative power God

---

22. Torrance, *Christian Doctrine of God*, 207. Parentheses mine.
23. Ibid., 209.

exercises is not that of abstract omnipotence unconditioned by a personal or particular identity, but that flowing from the mutual relations of freedom and love between the Father, Son, and Spirit and graciously exercised in the formation of the world with a distinct character and *telos* as opposed to sheer createdness. Torrance's point is clear: "While the creation of the universe, in form and matter out of nothing, certainly involved omnipotent power, we must think of that power not in an abstract way as bare unlimited power in itself ... but as the living power of the eternal Father flowing from his intrinsic nature as Love, as the movement of Love that God is ever in himself as Father, Son, and Holy Spirit."[24]

There is an additional reason why Torrance is keen to point out that the reality of God as Creator is contingent upon his identity as Father. It means that *there is an aspect of becoming in God that is an eternal quality of his being as triune.* God was not always Creator but *became* Creator through a definite act of his will. Likewise, God was not always incarnate but became incarnate through an act of his will. This is also true of the Spirit's coming at Pentecost, for that event also signified a "radical change in the nature and mode of his [God's] presence in the world."[25]

The newness of God's acts in creation, incarnation and at Pentecost, even for God,[26] point to another truth that suggests we locate God's agency as Creator in his identity as the eternal Father.

The Father Signifies the Creative Being of God

The fact that the eternal Father became Creator, the eternal Son became incarnate, and the eternal Spirit is personally active in the world of space and time, point to the *dynamic being of God* as well as the unlimited freedom of God. Both God's internal relations and external relations point to the dynamic nature of his being. Internally, he is a living communion of three persons, each in relation with the other, unified

---

24. Ibid., 209.
25. Ibid., 208.
26. "While God was always Father and was Father independently of what he has created, as Creator he acted in a way that he had not done before, in bringing about absolutely new event—this means that the creation of the world out of nothing is something *new even for God.* God was always Father, but he became Creator" (ibid., 208).

in being and operation yet distinct in identity and agency. Externally, he becomes Creator of the world, he becomes a creature in the world, and he continually sustains and transforms the world through his Spirit "while nevertheless remaining eternally the God that he always was."[27] The freedom of God is the basis for the creative activity of God. This is perhaps Torrance's most interesting point, and it is here that he brings his concerns over confusing the internal and external relations of God, and his assertions that God is primarily Father and not Creator, together.

For Torrance, the fact that the Father is Begetter of the Son and subsequently Creator of the world points to the reality that it is as Father that God is Creator and not the other way around. By grounding the Fatherhood of God in God's eternal being as Begetter of the Son Torrance avoids confusing the external and internal relations of God, and preserves the priority of the Fatherhood of God in all of God's creative activity.

In developing this line of argument, Torrance first notes that "throughout the early Church the name 'Father' was understood in a twofold but indivisible way, as the one being (*mia ousia*) of the Godhead, and as the Father of the Son."[28] In the former sense "Father" was understood to be "identical with the personal Being or intrinsic Communion that the one God is in himself."[29] In the latter sense the meaning of "Father" fell more upon the identity of the Father in relation to the Son and the Spirit as a distinct *hypostasis*.[30]

God as Father=Godhead was understood in the early Church to refer to God in the totality of his being as the "one supreme almighty being, uncreated, self-sufficient, all-perfect, who is the transcendent Fount, Source, and Author of all other being."[31] It is important to note here that Torrance is not advocating any understanding of the *Monarchia* of the Father that would understand the deity and personhood of the Son and the Spirit as deriving from that of the *hypostasis* of the Father.[32] Here

---

27. Ibid., 208.

28. Torrance, *Trinitarian Faith*, 78; and Torrance, *Christian Doctrine of God*, 205.

29. Torrance, *Christian Doctrine of God*, 131.

30. A fuller discussion of these distinctions and their import may be found in ibid., 128–31.

31. Torrance, *Trinitarian Faith*, 79.

32. See Torrance, *Christian Doctrine of God*, 121, for a brief discussion. In an earlier

"Father" is understood to refer to the totality of God's being in communion, and it is only as such that he is Creator of all things.

Such an understanding of the Father is not particular enough even for Torrance, for he goes on to assert that "God is this ultimate Source or Fountain of being ... only as he is eternally Father of the Son and as such is the Fount of being intrinsically in his very nature as God."[33] The Son is begotten of the nature and being of God while the world is created by the will of God. This distinction between the internal and external relations of God is essential for Torrance as it locates the creative activity of God in God's very Being as a triune communion of love, not a particular Person or *hypostasis*.

The identity of God as Father must precede the activity of God as Creator, for it is only as the Father is the Father of the Son that he is Creator of the world. Central to God's creative activity are not the existence of a world external to himself (that would make a relation between the world and God necessary) but the reality of a Son begotten of himself (internal relation). This emphasis locates God's creative activity as an eternal aspect of his being and not something that arises from his relation to the world: "It is because God is inherently productive and creative in his very being as God, that he is Creator."[34] Athanasius, with characteristic clarity and conciseness, makes a complementary observation when he observes, "if God is without Offspring, then he is without work; for the Son is his Offspring through whom he works."[35] The *Father* is our Creator. He is not an unmoved mover, static in being and essence, but precisely the opposite. He is the Father of the Son and the Spirit and is essentially a dynamic being, free to do things never done before and free to become things never comprehended before. This is an inherent and eternal quality of his being and stands as the presupposition of his work in the creation of the world. For Torrance:

---

work Torrance notes, "it is the *triune God*, the undivided Trinity, who is the one [and] only ultimate Principle of all things" (Torrance, *Trinitarian Faith*, 80).

33. Torrance, *Trinitarian Faith*, 79.

34. Ibid., 79. Torrance emphasizes the inherent dynamism of God's being elsewhere when he speaks of God's Word and Act inhering in his Being and his Being in his Act. This signifies that "the being of God is not intrinsically empty of word or activity, not mute or static, but is essentially eloquent and dynamic ... for his being and activity inhere in one another" (Torrance, *Trinitarian Faith*, 131).

35. Cited in Torrance, *Trinitarian Faith*, 79.

"It is exclusively as almighty Father, the unlimited and ineffable Cause of all that is, that God is to be recognized as the almighty Creator."[36]

The Father Signifies the Personal Being of God

That God is Father, and as such Creator, is a vital assertion for Torrance, not only because it signifies that God's very being as such is *creative*, but also that God's very being is *personal*.[37]

For Torrance, the trinitarian nature of God and the personal nature of God are intimately intertwined. The one qualifies and defines the other. Indeed, "apart from the doctrine of God as Father, Son, and Holy Spirit . . . our conception of God quickly degenerates into an impersonal or nonpersonal one, or becomes merely the personification and deification of our own desires and ideals."[38]

Of particular interest to Torrance, in affirming that God is primarily Father and only subsequently Creator, is how God's personal and triune nature conditions the way God exercises creative power and toward what ends. In short, that power is exercised in a personal, intimate, and relational way and towards salvific and redemptive goals. This comes through clearly in Torrance's understanding of the nature and activity of the Holy Spirit, considered below.

Only as we understand God as Father, Son, and Holy Spirit will we be able to convey the truth that God is intrinsically personal, interpersonal, and personalizing. To name God according to his economic functions as Creator, Redeemer, and Sustainer would be to forfeit the personal, interpersonal, and personalizing nature of God, while also opening the door to the deification of human fears, desires, and projects. Not only is signifying the being of God from the Father theologically accurate, it also carries with it a critique of human social activity. The God who has created and redeemed the world is a personal God, who has created a contingent world and placed in its midst personal

---

36. Ibid., 81.

37. Torrance notes that the experience of God as personal had a profound impact on the cultural symbols available at the time for conceptualizing the nature and being of God. Greek terms signifying "being" and "essence" that were impersonal in nature were appropriated and, under the impact of divine revelation, given meanings that communicated the very personal nature of God as revealed through the incarnation. See Torrance, *Christian Doctrine of God*, 103.

38. Torrance, "Christian Apprehension," 141–42.

creatures, created in such a way that they would generate a social environment that would not only bear witness to the personal nature of their Creator, but that would also sustain them as personal beings. The triune God, as personal, provides a benchmark for making evaluations regarding what is personal and what is not, what sustains personal life and what subverts it. These dynamics are captured in a selection of Torrance's writing that we shall have opportunity to quote again later: "Within this trinitarian perspective, the power or almightiness of God is revealed to be essentially *personal*, defined by God's triune Nature and Being as Father, Son, and Holy Spirit. This personal power of God is not a power that overrules the creature but sustains the creature, not power that negates the freedom of the creature, but the power of the Love that God is, power therefore that sustains the relation and freedom of the creature before God, for it is always creative, and in relation to his human creatures always personalizing and humanizing power."[39]

The Identity of God as Father and Creator is Signified by God the Son

The Son signifies God as both Father and Creator, since it is only through the person and work of the Son that we may come to know God as Father, and because it is only through the mediation of the Son that the Father is Creator. This may be understood as the Christological qualification of creation. The Father's creative activity flows through the Son as *the mediate or operative cause of creation*. Torrance cites the thought of Hilary of Poitiers in this regard: "It is [the] understanding of the Fatherhood of God, mediated in and through the Person and Work of Jesus Christ, his beloved Son, that governs all that is truly thought and said of God as the Creator."[40]

God's creative activity is mediated in and through the person and work of Jesus Christ. With this affirmation an additional term is added to how we are to understand the nature, character, and purpose of the created order. The created order is not only qualified by the work of the Father but also by the Person and work of the Son as both Mediator and Redeemer. However, prior to considering the impact of the Person

---

39. Torrance, *Christian Doctrine of God*, 206.
40. Torrance, *Trinitarian Faith*, 77.

and work of the Son upon the created order we will note why it is that we may signify the Father as Creator from the Son as Mediator and Redeemer. We signify the Father from the Son for three reasons:

The Son's Unity in Being and Action with the Father: *Homoousion*

There is both a distinction and oneness in the creative activity of the Father and the Son. At this point emphasis will fall upon the oneness of that being and action and as such upon the fundamental importance of the doctrine of the *homoousion* in Torrance's thought.

All the *foci* of Torrance's thought rest firmly upon his understanding of what the *homoousion* doctrine means and what its implications are, not only for Christian faith and life, but for the entire range of human activity and understanding. Here we will draw out its particular importance for Torrance's understanding of the triune Creator.

Perhaps the most concise statement of Torrance's belief in the unity of being and activity between Father and Son comes from the assertion of Athanasius that "whatever is said of the Father is said of the Son, except Father."[41] This phrase certainly does get the point across, if perhaps in an exaggerated way. However, it is a point that needs to be made and maintained.

Much has been made of the epistemological significance of the *homoousion* and we will not go into detail here regarding its importance for Christian thought in general or Torrance's thought in particular.[42] Rather, we are interested here to point out briefly why this doctrine must be maintained if we are to go forward with the development of a trinitarian doctrine of creation as a contingent order in chapters 2 and 3. Indeed, Torrance asserts that the doctrine of the *homoousion* was placed in the Nicene Creed in such a way as to force its readers to identify the Son with the Creator.[43] We see here the importance of the Son in a doctrine of creation and that importance hinging upon a unity of act and being between Father and Son—this unity being signified by the phrase *homoousios to Patri*.

41. Ibid., 79.
42. Kang, "Epistemological Significance," 341–66 and, with reference to the doctrine of the Spirit, see Torrance's "Epistemological Relevance of the Holy Spirit."
43. Torrance, *Trinitarian Faith*, 117.

The Epistemological Significance of the Homoousion

The doctrine of the *homoousion* is epistemologically significant for a doctrine of creation because it enables us to ascertain that the eternal Father is the almighty Creator. For this very reason we should not discount the epistemological importance of the *homoousion* in the development of a theology of creation or culture. Our theological ideas often serve as the foundry in which we forge the conceptual tools we use to interpret and shape the created world as well as our relations within it. To revisit the argument above, it is for this reason that a knowledge of God as the Almighty Father must take priority over, and condition our understanding of, his role as Almighty Creator. The particular must condition the general and the simply causal must be relativized by the personal and relational.

Such a framework is impossible apart from the epistemological foundations provided by the doctrine of the *homoousion*, for apart from it we would have no avenue of knowledge that would take us from the created order to the eternal being of God as a personal communion of Father, Son, and Spirit; bound together in love and freedom. Nor would we have any idea how the power and responsibility given to human stewards by the Creator was to be exercised in relation to the created order. Knowledge of God as Father through the Son reveals to us the character of God's creative power as grounded in his love and freedom as a communion of persons. Conceptions of God as Creator, unconditioned by his identity as Father, cause us to fall back upon conceptions of God's power that are purely causal and have no *telos* beyond the event of creation. In a discussion of the providence of God Torrance notes that: "God does not exercise his sovereign Power upon us from above and beyond us like some impersonal *force majeure*, but in an intensely personal and patient way from below, by penetrating into the dark disordered depths of our alienated creaturely existence in order to work savingly, healingly and preservingly within it."[44]

---

44. Torrance, *Christian Doctrine of God*, 222. Torrance makes much the same point elsewhere when he says that the revelation of the Father as Almighty Creator through the Son that the *homoousion* secures "is a revelation of God's almightiness that conflicts with the ideas of limitless arbitrary power which we generate out of our this worldly experiences, make infinite, and attribute to God, for the divine power manifest in Jesus Christ is of an altogether different kind. It is not in terms of what we think God can do, but in terms of what God has done and continues to do in Jesus Christ that we may understand something of what divine almightiness really is." See Torrance, *Trinitarian Faith*, 82.

This should characterize both the way we exercise the power and responsibility given to us as stewards of the created order God upholds, as well as our relations within it. However, without the epistemological foundations provided by the doctrine of the *homoousion* "there would be no identity between God and the content of his revelation and no access for mankind to the Father through the Son and in the Spirit."[45]

In addition, upholding the unity of being and action between the Father and the Son in creation is to uphold a belief that the created order itself is a unified order with a single and distinct rationality and *telos*, with that rationality and *telos* being manifest in the Son. Torrance points to this fact, this assumption of a unified rational order, as the basis for all empirical science and indeed all life in the world.[46]

The Soteriological Significance of the Homoousion

The redemptive significance of the *homoousion* is given concentrated attention in *The Trinitarian Faith* where Torrance asks: "What would be implied if there were no oneness in being between the incarnate Son and God the Father?"[47] Torrance first considers the implications if there were no oneness in *being* between Father and Son and then moves on to the implications involved if there were no oneness in *act*.[48]

One of the implications we have already given attention to is the revelatory significance of the doctrine. Is God really who he appears to be in Jesus Christ? Without the *homoousion* we may never be sure. Without concrete and reliable knowledge of God a whole world is opened up where God's silence and hiddenness become a playground for human speculation and mythology, the formation of God after the image of humanity's ideals and fears as opposed to the transformation of the world after Christ the Image of God. Torrance's concern with the oneness of being between the Father and the Son is primarily to secure theological foundations for a doctrine of revelation—to assert that Christ is the *self*-revelation and *self*-communication of God; that,

---

45. Torrance, *Trinitarian Faith*, 133.
46. Torrance, *Ground and Grammar*, 52–53.
47. Torrance, *Trinitarian Faith*, 133.
48. Ibid., 133–45.

in the words of Basil "the Person of the Father is known in the Form of the Son."[49]

The oneness of being and act between the Father and the Son is not only vital for a doctrine of revelation but also a doctrine of reconciliation. As the Son reveals the Father through the humanity he has assumed, he also heals the humanity he has assumed and the created order along with it. Revelation and reconciliation are tied up in the Son's vicarious assumption of our humanity, and essential to both is a unity of being and act between the Father and the Son. As Torrance notes, "If Jesus Christ is not himself God, then there is no final authority or validity for anything he said or did for human beings. If he were not divine, he could not act divinely, and if he were not Creator, he would not be able to save and recreate humanity."[50]

Here Torrance, paraphrasing Athanasius, ties together Christ's role as Creator and Mediator of the created order with his redemptive work on behalf of humanity. If Christ is not understood as united to the Father in his creative activity then Christ's redemptive work has no ontological validity. For Christ to be our re-Creator he must also be our Creator, and as such divine. Only God can create and only God can redeem. Christ as an intermediary between God and humanity simply as a moral exemplar is explicitly ruled out. By so doing Torrance assumes a relation between the Father and the Son in God's creative work that necessitates both their *hypostatic* particularity and *homoousial* consubstantiality.

In *The Christian Doctrine of God* Torrance gives more explicit attention to the concept of *perichoresis* and its importance for understanding the being and activity of God.[51] It is enough to point out here that the doctrine of the *homoousion* is pivotal to our understanding of the redemption of humanity and the created order and their continuing place in the creative purposes of God. As Torrance notes: "The evangelical significance of the *homoousion* is very apparent in its direct bearing upon the saving acts of Jesus Christ, in healing, forgiving, reconciling and redeeming lost humanity, for it asserted in the strongest way that

---

49. St. Basil quoted in ibid., 135.
50. Ibid., 138.
51. See Torrance, *Christian Doctrine of God*, chapter 7.

they are all done out of a relation of unbroken oneness and communion between Jesus Christ and God the Father."[52]

However, the *homoousion* also has to do with the nature of Christ's assumption of our humanity, for he was not only *homoousios* with God, but with humanity as well. His revelatory and redemptive work relies on his oneness in being with us as well as his oneness in being with the Father.[53] The doctrine of the *homoousion* carries with it a dual significance when considered in the light of the Person and work of Christ, for his ministry is not only towards humanity on behalf of God but also towards God on behalf of humanity.

The Eschatological Significance of the Homoousion

The doctrine of the *homoousion* not only grants us accurate knowledge of who our Creator is, or what he has done on our behalf to redeem and reconcile us to himself, it also orients us toward our eternal destiny in him and empowers us to look for and work towards that destiny. The eschatological significance of the *homoousion* is found in its ability to demonstrate that not only the origin but also the end of the created order is bound together with the Person and work of Jesus Christ and that the created order is upheld by God for a purpose that will be realized due to Christ's work. Because of the oneness in act and being between the Father and the Son, the created order has been included in the eternal purposes of God.

Torrance also mentions that the *homoousion* has implications for the nature of divine judgment, for the Kingdom that Christ inaugurated has no end and will continue into eternity. This tells us that there is continuity as well as a discontinuity between the inauguration of Christ's kingdom on earth and its continuation into eternity. All that Christ assumed and affirmed regarding our humanity and the created order in general, through his assumption and redemption of it, will persist and be integrated into the Kingdom to come. This comes though strongly in Torrance: "What the Son of God became in Jesus Christ, experienced,

---

52. Torrance, *Trinitarian Faith*, 141.

53. "Only at that point where in Jesus Christ the Incarnate Word is *homoousios* with us in our human nature and *homoousios* with God in his divine Being, is there a real revelation and therefore a real knowing of God which really derives form the eternal Being of God as he is in himself" (Torrance, *Theology in Reconstruction*, 214).

said, and undertook for us and for our salvation, is grounded in God and has been assumed into God as his very own."[54]

Torrance bases such a statement upon the following truth: it is not only the eternal Logos who shares in the internal relations of the Holy Trinity, but the incarnate Christ as well. To affirm that the incarnate Son shares an internal relation to the one being of God, and was not simply created and favored by him, is to assert that the whole life of Jesus was to be regarded "as embraced within the coinherent relations of the Holy Trinity."[55] This is an affirmation more profound even than that of the opening chapters of Genesis where the created order is affirmed as "good." Now we discover more fully what that primal affirmation discloses; we learn that the created order is not only good, but will share in the eternal purposes of God due to Christ's participation in it and redemption of it.

The humanity that the eternal Son took upon himself was our humanity, and by taking it upon himself he revealed not only the depths of our corruption, but also the depths to which he would go to heal that corruption. However, his life for our life was more than simply an exchange, and it was more than an affirmation that creaturely life was "good," it was a revelation of what human life was meant to be as well as a call to form our lives after his in humble obedience to his command. It was a revelation of the purpose of creaturely life and the possibility of directing and orienting it properly. It was the placement of human life, in all its relations and contingencies, before us in all its perfection as the archetype of human life determined by God. With the inclusion of Jesus' humanity in the life of God the eschatological significance of the *homoousion* becomes clear—Jesus Christ is the Dominical Man in whom all humanity has been embraced and redeemed by God, and after whom all humanity is to be conformed.

The Son's Differentiation in Identity and Operation from the Father: *Perichoresis*

Torrance's emphasis upon the unity of being and act between Father and Son, signified by the *homoousion*, does not rule out the significance of the differentiation between them. In fact, the opposite is true. Torrance

---

54. Torrance, *Trinitarian Faith*, 143–44.
55. Ibid., 143.

briefly notes that distinction and particularity are the presuppositions upon which the concept of *homoousios* affirms unity and oneness of being: "*Homoousios*, however, has another important nuance. If the Son is eternally begotten of the Father *within* the being of the Godhead, then as well as expressing the oneness between the Son and the Father, (*homoousios*) expresses the distinction between them that obtains within that oneness."[56]

Torrance cites St. Basil and continues: "'For nothing can be (*homoousios*) with itself, but one thing is (*homoousios*) with another.' [This] implies that while the Father and the Son are the same being they are eternally distinct for the Father is unchangeably the Father and not the Son and the Son is unchangeably the Son and not the Father. The *homoousion* was thus a bulwark against Sabellianism and Arianism, against unitarianism and polytheism, alike."[57]

In *The Trinitarian Faith*, where Torrance makes this observation, there is no further development of the dual implications inherent in the doctrine of the *homoousion*. It does appear that while Torrance is interested in pointing out the particularity of the Persons as well as their consubstantiality, no direct links are made between their unique identities and functions in relation to the created order. When it comes to the created order consubstantiality appears to rule over particularity.[58]

However, Torrance seems to have noticed this overemphasis, and in his latest work *The Christian Doctrine of God*, much more attention is given to the particularity of the divine Persons and their relationship to the created order.[59] In this work he notes that "each divine Person retains his unique characteristics as Father, Son, or Holy Spirit, in a union without confusion, for the individual characteristics of each of the three Persons do not separate them, but constitute their deep and mutual belonging together . . . *Homoousially* and *hypostatically* they interpenetrate each other in such a way that each Person is distinctively who he is in relation to the other two."[60]

---

56. Ibid., 124–25.
57. Ibid., 125.
58. This is precisely Colin Gunton's critique. See Gunton, "Being and Person."
59. See in particular chapters 6–8.
60. Torrance, *Christian Doctrine of God*, 145.

Torrance develops the concept of *perichoresis* at greater length elsewhere.[61] We should note however, that while Torrance does pay far greater attention to the commonalities in identity and activity between the Father, Son, and Spirit in his earliest material, this hardly means he has ignored the importance of the *hypostatic* distinctions in order to do so. Torrance should not be faulted for highlighting the *homoousial* relations between the divine Persons when the issue under discussion requires it.[62] It seems apparent from both his most recent work, and even some of his earliest essays,[63] that the *hypostatic* relations between the divine Persons, and their particular operations toward the created world, are of equal importance to him as the *homoousial* relations.

Therefore, while the oneness of activity between the Father and the Son is grounded in the oneness of being between them, this does not prevent Torrance from asserting a distinctive identity and function for each divine Person: "Owing to this oneness of Nature between the Father, the Son and the Holy Spirit there is a oneness of Activity between them, *although each in accordance with his own hypostatic reality engages in the creative work of God in his own distinctive way.*"[64]

This statement asserts that the creative activity of the triune God cannot be properly conceived apart from a dual emphasis on 1) the unity of God's being and agency, and 2) the particular identities and operations of each divine Person. Both of these truths are essential for

---

61. See ibid., chapter 7.

62. We have noted Torrance's discussion of the concept in *Trinitarian Faith*, a book concerned with an exposition of the Nicene Creed and an elucidation of Patristic thought on the doctrine of the Trinity. During this period Arianism was the focal concern. Consequently, Torrance's emphasis falls upon the unity of Christ in act and being with God the Father. While it would have been accurate to point out that the Son is different from the Father in both identity and activity, in this case it may not have been altogether helpful in responding to Arius and his followers. We note from this that Torrance and the Patristic theologians were contextual thinkers. The other context in which Torrance relies heavily upon the doctrine of the *homoousion* is in his response to the pervasive epistemological dualism of Western scientific culture. Torrance's "preoccupation" with the doctrine of the *homoousion* is more a reflection of the issues and contexts he engages than a weakness in his doctrine of God or a lack of interest in the particularity of the divine Persons.

63. We think here of one of Torrance's earliest essays "Spiritus Creator," where his entire discussion is dominated by the particularity of the Spirit: his relationship to the world, and his work within it. See Torrance, *Theology in Reconstruction*, 209–28.

64. Torrance, *Christian Doctrine of God*, 212. Italics mine.

a proper understanding of the origin, character, and destiny of the created order and, by inference, human cultural activity within it.

Previously we considered the mutual relationships between the divine Persons as grounded in a unity of being and act between them. Presently we will consider that mutuality as grounded in their *hypostatic* and functional particularity. Specifically, we are concerned with the particularity of the Son and his relation to the created order as Mediator. We briefly point out his unique function as a consubstantial member of the Holy Trinity in three spheres:

1. *Mediator in creation* as the eternal *Logos*: Mediator of the created order
2. *Mediator in revelation and reconciliation* as the incarnate Savior: Redeemer of the created order
3. *Mediator in consummation* as the coming One: *Telos* of the created order[65]

The particularity of Christ's identity, and his unique relation to the created order, are highlighted by the above titles and activities. These activities are attributed uniquely to Christ, even though carried out in *perichoretic* communion with the Father and the Spirit.

As the begotten One, the Son is the eternal Logos of God and as such the means through which the created order was brought into being and given its own unique reality, rationality, order, and *telos*. Its reality and rationality are bound up with him and it is in him that all things hold together. Though the Father and the Spirit are inseparably bound together with the Son in this activity, it is the Son to whom these truths are ascribed.

Indeed, Wolfhart Pannenberg holds that the very differentiation of the Son from the Father stands as the basis for the differentiation between God and the created order. Therefore, Christ stands as not only the means through which the created order is brought into being, but

---

65. Torrance notes the centrality of Christ's person and work in interrelating creation, redemption and consummation when he comments that "In the incarnation the order of redemption has been made to intersect with and overlap the order of creation in such a way that the whole history of mankind and the universe comes under the Kingdom of Christ as the First and the Last, the *Protos* and the *Eschatos*, the origin and goal of creation—and so we have the Christological and soteriological interrelation between eschatology and cosmology" (ibid., 214).

also the basis upon which the distinction between the two realities is upheld.

It was the eternal Son who was begotten of the Father, and not the Father or the Spirit, who became flesh in the person of Jesus Christ and by doing so bound the created order to himself in love, redeeming it from its bondage to sin. As the eternal Word Christ mediated the creation of the world, and as the incarnate Savior Christ heals and re-creates the world.

Finally, it is the eternal Logos through whom all things were made and it is for him and in him that all things will be brought to their destined end and design. Christ is the coming One who will return to consummate the order he both created and redeemed and who will offer all things before the feet of the Father for his honor and glory.

Pointing out the differentiation in identity and operation between the Father and the Son qualifies both the nature (based upon otherness) and character (love, freedom) of their communion as well as their relationship with the created order (based upon otherness, love, and freedom). They are distinct persons and their relation to the created world is personal in nature.

The Work of God the Father, Mediated through God the Son, Is Signified by God the Holy Spirit

The creative work of the Father, mediated through the Son of God, is signified by the Spirit of God, for it is through the Spirit of God that God is free to be present to the created order; binding it to himself in love while sustaining, orienting, and perfecting it according to his purposes. Torrance, developing the thought of Athanasius, says as much when he notes that "the Spirit is the creative activity of God."[66] The creative activity of God, signified by the Spirit, "applies to the original works of creation and to all God's works and gifts in sanctification and recreation."[67] This may be understood as the Pneumatological qualification of creation. Here we have to do with the Spirit as the *perfecting cause of creation* in whom all things are oriented to their proper *telos* and brought to completion. It is the particular function of the Spirit

---

66. Torrance, *Theology in Reconstruction*, 215.
67. Ibid., 215.

to complete, perfect, and consummate what has been initiated by the Father and secured by the Son.[68] However, such an emphasis is not meant to imply that the creative activity of God is divided among the Persons of the Trinity, only that there is a proper distinction between them in terms of their mode of operation, those distinctions being signified by the prepositions *from* the Father, *through* the Son, and *in* the Holy Spirit.[69]

In the previous section, we relied heavily upon Torrance's work in *Trinitarian Faith* and *Christian Doctrine of God*. In this section we will draw once again upon those sources, but primarily from an essay Torrance published in 1965 entitled "*Spiritus Creator: A Consideration of the Teaching of St Athanasius and St Basil*."[70] The reason for this focus is that in Torrance's other treatments of the Person and work of the Holy Spirit the majority of attention is given to discussion regarding the historical development of the doctrine of the Spirit along with an exploration of the Spirit's *homoousial* and *hypostatic* relations with the Father and the Son. Consequently, mention of the Spirit's relation to the created order is made only in passing. Since that is our primary interest here, we will draw most of our thoughts from Torrance's reflections in "*Spiritus Creator*."[71]

Torrance's doctrine of the Spirit will be developed under two main headings: the being and identity of the Spirit and, secondly, the agency and activity of the Spirit, with particular emphasis upon the Spirit as "the perfecting cause" of creation.[72] This particular emphasis alone will

---

68. Torrance notes that through the economy of the Son and the Spirit "God in his sovereign freedom condescends in incredible mercy to enter man's creaturely existence as one of us . . . in order to fulfill his purposes of redemption and sanctification in us" (ibid., 212–13).

69. Ibid., 216.

70. This essay may be found in ibid., 209–28.

71. We should note here the helpful essays by Gary Deddo and Elmer Colyer on this subject. Deddo's essay, "The Holy Spirit in the Thought of T. F. Torrance" sketches the contours of Torrance's doctrine of the Spirit by considering the Spirit in relation to the other persons of the Trinity (*ad intra*) and in relation to the created order (*ad extra*). Elmer Colyer provides a condensed and thorough account placed within the context of Torrance's thought as a whole. See his *How to Read T. F. Torrance*, chapter 6

72. Torrance rarely treats the being and identity of the Spirit in isolation from the activity of the Spirit. When Torrance does focus specifically upon the *work* of the Spirit, his interests are primarily epistemological, Christological, ecclesiological and ecumenical. However, while developing these themes Torrance makes rich and provocative

require us to consider the identity and work of the Spirit from a number of different angles; however, this is exactly as it should be. As Torrance notes, citing Cyril of Jerusalem, "learn then that this Holy Spirit is one and indivisible, yet of manifold powers, working with many operations, yet not himself broken into parts."[73] The points developed under the main headings will be parallel with each other and together will point out why we signify the creative work of the Father, mediated through the Son, by the Person and work of the Holy Spirit.

The Being and Identity of the Spirit

The Spirit Is Divine: The Spirit of God

For Torrance, it is absolutely essential and appropriate that an exposition of the doctrine of the Spirit begin with an affirmation of the divinity and objectivity of the Spirit *contra* any understanding of the Spirit as emanation, immanent principle, or as a creative force, whether generically human or specifically ecclesial. As Torrance notes: "The Spirit is not just something divine or something akin to God emanating from him, not some sort of action at a distance or some kind of gift detachable from himself, for in the Holy Spirit God acts directly upon us himself, and in giving us the Holy Spirit God gives us nothing less than himself."[74]

In *Trinitarian Faith* Torrance spends some time developing both how and why the early church came to extend the affirmation of *homoousios* to the Spirit as well as the Son, and in particular the epistemological and soteriological reasons for doing so. We will not cover that ground here.[75]

What is important to note is that when we have to do with the Spirit, we have to do with "the utter godness of God" in all his glory and transcendence.[76] Without this affirmation in place, the door is opened to the confusion and conflation of the human spirit with the

---

statements about the activity of the Spirit in relation to the created order that we would like to note and explore further with this section. We understand his more explicit work on the being and agency of the Spirit to underpin the more suggestive comments developed here.

73. Torrance, *Theology in Reconstruction*, 210.
74. Torrance, *Trinitarian Faith*, 191.
75. See in particular ibid., 191–205.
76. Torrance, *Theology in Reconstruction*, 242.

Holy Spirit; God's sovereign involvement with the created order with the natural laws that guide and sustain it; God's agency and will with our experiences of subjectivity and inwardness; and finally, we confuse the kingdom of God with the kingdoms of this world. To affirm the Spirit as divine is to affirm not only that the Spirit is the means by which God dwells in us, but also the means by which we are transformed out of ourselves toward a divine *telos* not discernible in ourselves. We do not possess the Spirit, but rather the Spirit possesses us.

This shift from a center in the human subject to a center in the objectivity of the Spirit underlies Torrance's repeated assertions that the Holy Spirit is the *eternal* Spirit and as such the Spirit *of God*. This is entirely in keeping with emphases found throughout Torrance's thought, emphases that assert both the transcendence and freedom of God. In particular, Torrance speaks of a transcendence not bound by human or creaturely limitations, or a freedom that prohibits that transcendence from being embodied historically or socially.[77] This is because both the transcendence and freedom of God are concretely and Christologically understood in Torrance's thought. Recent proposals by Ted Peters[78], Phillip Clayton[79] and Catherine Mowry LaCugna[80] seeking to elucidate the relation of the triune God to the created order seem to collapse the fine balance Torrance intends by sacrificing the transcendence and freedom of God in order to emphasize God's intimate involvement in the created order. Paul D. Molnar, building upon the thought of Barth, proposes a more constructive way forward in his appeals for the development of a doctrine of the immanent Trinity, which I understand as a call to affirm the transcendence and freedom of the triune God as prior to, and unconditioned by, the created order.[81] For Torrance, divinity entails both transcendence and freedom in relation to the created order. In addition, to affirm the transcendence and freedom of God is to also affirm the goodness and integrity of the created order. This is precisely why Torrance asserts the divinity of the Spirit, for the distinctive work of the Spirit is the sustenance and consummation of the created order,

---

77. See Anderson, *Historical Transcendence*.
78. Peters, *God as Trinity*.
79. Clayton, *God and Contemporary Science*.
80. LaCugna, *God for Us*.
81. See in particular Molnar, "Toward a Contemporary Doctrine."

and this can only be achieved if the Spirit who acts is both transcendent and free; in sum, if the Spirit is the Spirit of God.

Torrance notes that in Holy Scripture and in the writings of the Church Fathers "the word 'spirit' was often used in an absolute sense of God, in respect of his infinite, transcendent, invisible, immaterial, and immutable nature." So, referring to God as "spirit" in this sense carried with it a reference to the nature of God as divine and, as divine, both perfect and transcendent.[82] However, the word "spirit" when applied to God not only referred to what God is *in himself*, but also "characterizes what God is in his limitless freedom toward everything that is not God." Consequently, to affirm that the Spirit is divine just as God is divine is not only to assert the Spirit's transcendence, but also, concurrently, the freedom of God to "sustain it [everything that is not God] in creaturely relation to himself, and in sovereign interaction with it."[83] A fine example of this is Torrance's understanding of the Greek Fathers use of *theosis*.[84]

In a discussion and clarification of the concept of *theosis*, Torrance points out the importance of the objectivity of the Spirit in relation to the human subject.[85] The integrity and goodness of the human subject is protected and elevated only when the radical objectivity and divinity of the Spirit is upheld. Any other move divinizes the creature or materializes the divine by collapsing one into the other instead of enabling the one to participate in the other. Colin Gunton makes a similar point when he discusses the importance of the doctrine of the Trinity for an understanding of creation and culture.[86] For Torrance, God's tran-

---

82. See Torrance, *Christian Doctrine of God*, 147–48 where Torrance distinguishes between "thinking of the Spirit absolutely and thinking of him relatively."

83. Torrance, *Trinitarian Faith*, 205.

84. See the recent work on this subject by Myk Habets, *Theosis in the Theology of Thomas Torrance*; and that of my colleague at Eastern University, Carl Mosser in "The Greatest Possible Blessing: Calvin and Deification"; and Mosser, "The Earliest Patristic Interpretations of Psalm 82, Jewish Antecedents, and the Origin of Christian Deification."

85. Torrance, *Theology in Reconstruction*, 243.

86. See Gunton, *The One, the Three and the Many*, 71 where Gunton asserts that the transcendence of God in relation to creation, and the three Persons of the Trinity in relation to each other, "creates space" for the other to be "itself." So, Torrance's emphasis here is not meant to crush the fragility of the created order or to override its distinctiveness, but just the opposite, to affirm it in its difference and uniqueness.

scendence becomes the basis for his intimate activity in and among persons:

> It is from the free ground of that transcendent otherness in himself in his Triune Being, that God freely and spontaneously creates others outwith himself for fellowship with himself and brings them into actual communion with himself. This freeflowing unconditioned outgoing movement of his Being means that God refuses to be shut off from us in his unapproachable Majesty, infinite otherness and incomprehensibility. He makes himself really accessible to us, and does so not only in communicating himself to us in the incarnation of his Son, but in imparting to us his Holy Spirit."[87]

That the divine is free to uphold the creature and the creature is able to participate in the divine is a reality made possible by the nature and identity of God and the nature and identity of the Holy Spirit. This truth finds expression in Torrance's comment that "God is Spirit and the Holy Spirit is God."[88] The being of God as Spirit flows directly into the distinctive activity of God the Holy Spirit as the one who not only protects the transcendence and ineffability of God, but also sustains and orients the creature in relation to God. Consequently, to affirm that "God is Spirit" in an absolute sense is to affirm the divinity of God and to affirm it equally to all Persons of the Trinity, while reference to the "Holy Spirit as God" is an affirmation of the divinity of the particular Person of the Spirit and the Spirit's distinctive work.

A final epistemological point should be noted. Since the Holy Spirit is divine, and thus both transcendent and free, accurate knowledge of the Spirit cannot be acquired through intent focus upon the Holy Spirit's work in creation, but only by reference to the Spirit in relation to the Son and the Father. It is axiomatic for Torrance that God can only be known through God. Therefore, an affirmation of the divinity of the Spirit is also an affirmation that the Spirit cannot be known accurately in isolation from the work of the Father and the Son. As Torrance notes: "The devout and accurate way to know the Holy Spirit is not by beginning with manifestations or operations of the Spirit in creaturely existence . . . but from the propriety of the Spirit to the eternal being of

---

87. Torrance, *Christian Doctrine of God*, 150.
88. Torrance, *Trinitarian Faith*, 205.

God, as the Spirit of the Father and the Son, and thus from his *internal relations within the Godhead.*"[89]

This is a way of saying that the Spirit is *translucent* in his very nature as spirit, but also that the Spirit's work is to bear a translucent witness to the Person of the Son, through whom we encounter the Father. This distinctive work of the Spirit will have implications not only for his relation to the Son, but also for his relation to the created order. These implications will be explored more fully when we focus in particular on the *activity* of the Spirit below.

The Spirit Is Translucent: The Spirit of Christ

Having just noted that God is spirit and the Holy Spirit is God, we now turn from a quality that characterizes the divine Being as a whole to a quality that characterizes the Holy Spirit as a particular *hypostasis*. Torrance refers to this quality as the "translucence" of the Spirit. Translucence is a quality not only of the Spirit's *being* as divine and as "spirit," but also of the Spirit's distinctive *work*, in particular as the Spirit of Jesus Christ.

George Hendry, in his book *The Holy Spirit in Christian Theology*,[90] gives voice to the frustrations experienced by those who seek to describe the particular identity and activity of the Holy Spirit, concluding that these frustrations are rooted in the doctrine itself: "It has almost become a convention that those who undertake to write about the Holy Spirit should begin by deploring the neglect of the doctrine in the life and thought of the Church today. [The chief reason for this neglect is rooted in the doctrine itself] for it is beset with difficulties and obscurities which baffle the mind."[91]

One of the chief "difficulties" is the fact that the Holy Spirit cannot be known in himself, for the Spirit of God, the translucent Spirit, is the Spirit of Jesus Christ. This is repeatedly noted by Torrance in his discussions of the nature and activity of the Spirit. Cardinal Yves Congar has sought to recognize this intimate relation between the Spirit and Christ by referring to the Spirit as the "Person without a face."[92] This designa-

---

89. Ibid., 208. Italics original.
90. Hendry, *The Holy Spirit*.
91. Ibid., 11.
92. Quoted in Smail, *The Giving Gift*, 30; and from Congar, *I Believe in the Holy Spirit*, 3:5.

tion seeks to negotiate the peculiar difficulties presented by the unique identity and agency of the Spirit as the Spirit sent *by* Jesus Christ to bear witness *to* Jesus Christ. The Spirit as a distinct *hypostasis* is upheld by Congar's affirmation that the Spirit is a "Person," while the inseparability and unknowability of the Spirit apart from Christ is affirmed with Congar's phrase "without a face." Congar's designation strives to recognize the unique identity and agency of the Spirit as the Spirit of Jesus Christ.

Torrance, in agreement with the assessment of Hendry, notes that the difficulty lies not only in the uniqueness of the Spirit as translucent, but also in "our wrong movement of thought" as we attempt to understand the Spirit: "The difficulty of the doctrine of the Spirit derives from this hiding of himself on the part of the Spirit behind the Face of the Father in the Son; or rather, the difficulty lies with our wrong movement of thought in trying to think of him after the mode of Being of the Father or after the mode of Being of the Son, instead of knowing him in accordance with his own mode of Being as *Spirit*, of the Father and of the Son."[93]

For Torrance, understanding the Spirit as translucent clarifies both the peculiar identity and agency of the Spirit as well as the movement of thought necessary to honor the Spirit and to properly recognize the Spirit's work. To consider the Spirit directly we must "look through" the Spirit, and to look through the Spirit and see Christ is to give the Spirit our full attention, consideration, and honor. When the Spirit confronts us with the Person of Jesus Christ (and through him, with the Father) we witness the most forceful declaration of the Spirit's unique identity and agency. As Torrance notes: "In the nature of the case the Spirit hides, as it were, his own *hypostasis* from us and reveals himself to us by revealing the Father through the Son."[94]

Of particular interest to Torrance, in asserting that the Spirit is translucent,[95] is to highlight the intimate relation between the Spirit and the Son. This intimate relation belongs to the essential nature and peculiar agency of the Spirit: "It belongs to the nature of his operation, and

---

93. Torrance, *Theology in Reconstruction*, 226–27. Italics original.

94. Ibid., 226.

95. Torrance also understands the translucency of the Spirit to be essential to the Spirit's creativity. This means that the creativity of the Spirit is boundless, but at the same time bound to the Person and work of the Son. See ibid., 254.

to the mode of his Being that the Holy Spirit comes to us not in his own Name, but in the Name of Christ."[96] Or again, in *The Trinitarian Faith*:

> The Holy Spirit is not directly known in his own *hypostasis* for he remains veiled by the very revelation of the Father and the Son which he brings... He does not show us himself, and so the world cannot receive him or know him. He shows us the face of the Father in the Son, and shows us the face of the Son in the Father. Thus it could be said of the Holy Spirit that he is the Face of the Father, in that he makes the Face of the Father to be seen in the Son.[97]

This is not to say that the Spirit is being marginalized or relativized by the Father or the Son, nor is it to suggest that the Spirit is not present among us or active in the created order, rather it is to recognize that "the Holy Spirit is indeed personally present among us, but in his *transparent and translucent mode of being*."[98] Torrance's emphasis upon the translucence of the Spirit is a result of his interest in doing "scientific theology" which requires the object to be known (in this case the Spirit) to determine the way in which it is both known and described. His language does not betray an interest in downplaying the unique identity of the Spirit, nor a difficulty in conceptualizing the Spirit's unique work.

Let us develop in a bit more detail how Torrance understands this relationship between the Spirit and Jesus Christ. For Torrance, the Spirit and the Son are bound together, not only eternally and ontologically, but also in the economic activity of God in creation, redemption, and consummation. This is seen most clearly in Torrance's emphasis that "the Holy Spirit is mediated by Christ and at the same time mediates Christ to us."[99]

The Holy Spirit is mediated to us through the incarnate Person of the Son, specifically "through Christ in his divine and human natures."[100] The *hypostatic* union of the divine and human in Christ are essential to a full understanding of the Spirit. For Torrance, only God can give God, and therefore, if human persons are to receive the Spirit the Son must not only be human but also divine. However, human persons are

---

96. Ibid., 227.
97. Torrance, *Trinitarian Faith*, 211–12.
98. Ibid., 212. Italics original.
99. Torrance, *Theology in Reconstruction*, 245.
100. Ibid.

not capable of receiving the Spirit, even if God is capable of giving the Spirit. Therefore, it is essential that Christ also be fully human, so that in Christ our human nature also receives the Spirit of God. Both the giving and receiving of the Spirit take place in the life of the incarnate Son and through his vicarious humanity. While the Spirit is present and at work in the created order prior to the incarnation, it is only through the Person and work of the Son that the Spirit is present to us in an unprecedented, personal, and transforming way: "Jesus Christ, true God and true Man, is thus the Mediator of the Holy Spirit."[101] For this reason it is "in the Name of Jesus Christ that the Holy Spirit comes to us, and in no other name."[102]

However, the Spirit is not only mediated to us through the incarnate and crucified Christ, but is sent by the ascended and glorified Christ. Indeed, the work of the Spirit is grounded in the life of the incarnate Son, for it was through the work of the Spirit that the Son was born and baptized, went through travail and temptation, and finally defeated the powers of sin, suffering, and death. But it was also by the Spirit that the Son was raised from the dead and, upon the request of the ascended Word, the Spirit was poured out upon all flesh. So, the Spirit is mediated to us through the entire vocation of the Son, born, crucified, raised, and glorified, and is not to be identified or known apart from him. As Torrance notes, the Spirit came [on Pentecost] "not as isolated and naked Spirit, but as Spirit charged with all the experience of Jesus as he shared to the full our mortal nature and weakness."[103]

It does not seem a stretch in light of this to assert that not only is the Spirit the Spirit of Jesus Christ, but precisely as such is also the Spirit of history, creation, and culture, for through the agency of the Spirit the created order is brought into being, sustained, redeemed, and perfected, and all of these things are done upon the basis of Christ's work and in concert with God's purposes revealed in him. These truths are manifest in the particular vocation of Jesus (his deity and vicarious humanity) and may be appropriately extended to the rest of creation as abiding characteristics of the Spirit's being and work. Indeed, this is a suggestion offered by Torrance himself: "The Holy Spirit is God in his freedom not

---

101. Ibid., 246.
102. Ibid., 247.
103. Ibid.

only to give being to the creation but through his presence in it to bring its relations with himself to perfection."[104]

What this brief treatment demonstrates is that Torrance understands the work of the Spirit, from beginning to end, to be fundamentally and materially related to the Person and work of the Son, eternal and incarnate. The creativity and translucency of the Spirit, therefore, are for the purposes of glorifying the Father in the Son in such as way as to enable the created order to refer beyond itself to its reason for being—to serve as a witness to its triune Creator: "The Holy Spirit does not bring to us any independent knowledge of God or add any new content to God's self-revelation, but while the knowledge of the Spirit himself as well as of the Father is derived through the Son, it is mediated and actualized within us through the presence and activity of the Holy Spirit."[105]

The Spirit is the Spirit of mediation and actualization, and both of those works take place in a profound engagement with the material world, with history, with time, and with culture. As Torrance affirms: "God really does impart himself to us and actually makes himself known to us *within the conditions of our creaturely forms of thought and speech.*" The italics are mine, and the point is made, however, it would be inappropriate to leave out the second half of Torrance's statement: "but without any compromise of his sheer Godness or any diminution of the Mystery of his transcendent Being."[106] This is profoundly true, not only of the Spirit's activity in the vocation of the Son, but also in the birth of the Church and the progress of her mission.

The Spirit Is Lord: The Holy Spirit

The intimate relationship between Christ and the Spirit just described means that the transformation initiated and sustained by the Spirit has as its ground and goal the holiness of Christ. As Torrance notes: "The Holy Spirit comes to us only through him as the Spirit of Holiness, the Spirit of Redemption, and the Spirit of Glory... as the Spirit in which he brought the divine holiness to bear upon our flesh of sin, sanctifying and perfecting in himself the very nature which he took

---

104. Ibid., 248.
105. Torrance, *Christian Doctrine of God*, 147.
106. Ibid., 151.

from us, and therefore he comes in all the richness of the divine human holiness of Christ."[107]

Since the holiness brought to bear upon the created order through the presence and ministry of the Spirit is the holiness of Christ, it is a form of power that perfects and sustains personal life in accordance with its original purpose, while also passing judgment upon and resisting features of the created order that stand contrary to God's purposes revealed in Christ. This is the work of the Spirit in sanctification.

God's sanctifying presence in the Spirit is, as Torrance has noted, the very coming of God into the world and the very presence of God to us in all his holiness and transcendence. However, while the Spirit protects the mystery and transcendence of God's being, the Spirit also makes the very being of God accessible to us and opens us up to his transforming presence. There is a genuine dialogical relation created and sustained by the Spirit of God—a relation between a holy and transcendent Creator and a fallen and sinful creature. However, the relation established by the Spirit does not crush the creature, or the creaturely forms that sustain and give expression to its life, but rather affirms and sustains the creature "within the space-time structures of existence in which he [God] has placed us."[108] Through this dialogical relation with the creature history is opened out to the transcendence and holiness of God while the self-giving of God is actualized within the boundaries of history.[109] The transformation and perfection of the created order is rooted in the power, freedom, and holiness of God, as that power, freedom, and holiness is extended to us through the Son and in the Spirit.

Torrance uses the words "humanization" and "personalization" when speaking specifically of the human person as the locus of God's sanctifying work. This is yet another reminder that Torrance is centrally concerned with the human person and the forms of life necessary for its healing and sustenance. The Spirit of God as the Holy Spirit comes to us to establish a dialogical relation that brings the holiness of God to bear upon human life in such a way as to draw the human into a personalizing relationship with the triune God. That relationship is then embodied and reflected in socio-cultural forms. As Torrance notes, cultural forms are not inconsequential to the sanctifying/personalizing

107. Torrance, *Theology in Reconstruction*, 248.
108. Ibid., 100.
109. Ibid., 102.

work of the Spirit: "Far from crushing our creaturely nature or damaging our personal existence, the indwelling presence of God through Jesus Christ and in the Holy Spirit has the effect of healing and restoring and deepening human personal being.[110] [This takes place] within the personal and social structures of human life where the Spirit is at work as *personalizing Spirit*."[111]

For Torrance, the terms personalization, humanization, and sanctification are nearly synonymous. Thus, the work of the Spirit as the Holy Spirit is the work of healing and sustaining personal life, and since personal life is historical life, this activity takes place within the context of culture and transforms those aspects of culture that subvert personal life. Gary Deddo, developing the thought of Torrance, notes: "In the Spirit God does not overwhelm us. Rather than a loss of self the Spirit provides its completion (*theosis, theopoiesis, teleiosis*). The Spirit perfects our humanity *in our humanity* on the basis of the humanity of Jesus Christ."[112]

Torrance, through his doctrine of the Spirit as *Holy* Spirit, is careful to articulate the fact that the Holy Spirit brings the holiness of God to bear upon creaturely life in a powerfully delicate fashion, with the result being that creaturely life is sanctified without crushing or subverting the ecology of that life. This is God's *modus operandi* because God has come to our historical humanity through the vicarious humanity of Jesus Christ. A trinitarian understanding of the sanctifying work of the Spirit is essential to Torrance's doctrine of God, as is the historical integrity of human life. Both are held together in his doctrine of God as *Holy* Spirit.

We may say that the Spirit is both personal and free and as such we can expect to find the Spirit at work in different ways in both the church and the world, however upon the same ground and toward the same goals in each sphere. The Spirit is poured out upon all flesh, upon the basis of Christ's objective work, with a mission to consummate and actualize that work historically. However, it is appropriate to note that the Spirit's work takes on a different shape and form relative to the sphere where that work is taking place. This would seem to be a direct implication of Torrance's assertion that God, through the Spirit, does not crush

---

110. Torrance, *Trinitarian Faith*, 230.
111. Torrance, *God and Rationality*, 188. Italics original.
112. Deddo, "The Holy Spirit," 95. Italics mine.

creaturely forms, but works in and through them to heal and perfect them. Though two spheres and modes of operation can be identified, they are as intimately interconnected in Torrance's thought as the objective and subjective, the mediate and immediate, the provisional and the universal, the intensive and extensive, the focal and the tacit. As Gary Deddo notes: "The Church ... is the immediate sphere of the Spirit's operation, but the world is nevertheless the mediate sphere. The Church is the community where reconciliation is intensively actualized through the Spirit. But this is done in order that it may be fulfilled extensively in all mankind and creation. The Church is the new humanity within the world, the provisional manifestation of the new creation within the old."[113] The Holy Spirit accomplishes his sanctifying work in the following two interrelated spheres:

THE SPIRIT IS PERSONAL: THE PERSONALIZING SPIRIT—For Torrance the Spirit represents, along with the Son, "the acute personalization of the nature and activity of God."[114] This truth was secured firstly through the affirmation that the Son is *homoousios* with the Father, and then, by extension, to the Spirit who is *homoousios* with both the Father and the Son. This made it impossible to think of the Spirit as an impersonal force or immanent principle detachable from God and independently operative in the world. The Spirit was the personal presence of the whole and holy God to creation.

The Spirit as the personal and intimate presence of God to us was made even more acute upon the giving of the gift of the Spirit at Pentecost, which, as Torrance notes, was predicated upon the atonement and glorification of Jesus Christ: "Until atonement was made and the Spirit was poured out they [the disciples] were incapable of becoming the habitation of the Holy One, and Christ could not open up their minds to grasp him for he could not be in them."[115]

Through the gift of the Spirit human persons are not only confronted with the holy presence of God, but are enabled to participate in God through the intimate presence of the Holy Spirit. It is this acutely personal presence of the Spirit that binds us to God, to one another, and to the created order in such a way that our personhood is properly

---

113. Ibid., 99.
114. Torrance, *Trinitarian Faith*, 216.
115. Torrance, *Theology in Reconstruction*, 252.

oriented, sustained, and healed and our cultural activity in the world is directed in such a way as to bring into being an environment that bears witness to the triune God, thus fostering the flourishing of human life created in the divine image.

The Holy Spirit is the personal Spirit, for the work of this Spirit is to bind us to God and to one another in such a way as to advance the purposes of God for creation. This work takes place normatively in and through the Christian community, for it is this particular community that the Spirit indwells in a unique fashion and equips for a unique mission. The focal point of God's work in the world is the community called the Church, the social-historical form of his presence in the world.

THE SPIRIT IS FREE: THE ROYAL SPIRIT—However, the work of the Spirit cannot be exclusively located there, for the Spirit is not only personal, but also free, and brings the transforming holiness of Christ to bear upon the world in extraordinary ways. There is also a tacit basis for the work of the Spirit for the Christian community arises out of, and is influenced by, other forms of human community. These other forms of human community are also products of the Spirit's work in creation. Torrance himself notes this when he asserts, not only that the Church may never possess the Sprit, but that "the Church was not founded with Pentecost; nor indeed was it first founded with the incarnation. It was founded with creation."[116] So, although "the Church does not derive from below but from above, it [also] does not exist apart from the people who make up its membership." Those who make up the membership of the Church participate in a number of human communities outside of the Church. It is their tacit participation in these communities that make the focal work/mission of the Church possible.[117] The focal work of the

---

116. Torrance, *The School of Faith*, cxix.

117. The nature and mission of the Church is rooted in the fact that it is a historical community composed of those who follow Jesus Christ within the context of other human communities: "It is therefore the mission of the Church by the witness of its word and life to bring all nations and races the message of hope in the darkness of our times, and to summon them to the obedience of the Gospel, that the love of God may be poured out upon them by the Spirit, breaking down all barriers, healing all divisions and gathering them together as one universal flock." Torrance, *Theology in Reconstruction*, 193. The very nature and mission of the Church, as historical and rooted in specific human communities, means that its witness will always take place "in the power of the Spirit" and "through the ambiguous forms of this age." The power of the Spirit does not eradicate or homogenize those forms (if this occurred, there would

Spirit in the Church assumes the tacit work of the Spirit in the formation and sustenance of all forms of human community. In the case of the former, the *personal* nature of the Spirit is focal as the Spirit who indwells the Church. In the case of the latter, the nature of the Spirit as *free* is focal as the *Spiritus Creator* who is at work throughout the created order. Both the nature of the Spirit (as personal and free) and the work of the Spirit (forming all human community and a specific human Community) bear witness to the triune Creator.

Having considered the being and nature of the Spirit we will now go on to consider briefly the agency and activity of the Spirit, specifically in relation to the created order. The Spirit creates, orients, transforms, and consummates the created order in ways congruent with his being and nature as described above.

The Agency and Activity of the Spirit

The Spirit Creates and Sustains the Created Order: The Creative Work of the Spirit

Throughout his writings, Torrance is unambiguous in his affirmation that the relation of the Spirit to the created order is a relation between Creator and creation. Consequently, the Spirit is not to be confused with the contingent laws of the created order, nor are we permitted to assert that the Spirit is contained by the created order or bound by it in any way. The Spirit as Creator is divine, and thus both transcendent and free. However, the creative action of the Spirit is not only characterized by his divine nature, but by the particularities of his Person as well: "The Holy Spirit is also Creator in union with the Father and the Son, no less than they, and in perfect communion and conjunction with them, but Creator *in his distinctive nature and activity as Spirit.*"[118]

There is indeed a fellowship in creative activity between the Father, Son, and Spirit, but it is appropriate to note that, even though the Spirit works in inseparable unity with the Father and the Son, the Spirit is nev-

---

be no Church, for a truly "universal flock" must include in its membership a plurality of representatives), but rather sanctifies them by enabling them to serve as translucent and transparent media for the glorification of God, which results in the personalization of human persons and progress toward the *telos* of the created order.

118. Torrance, *Christian Doctrine of God*, 216. Italics mine.

ertheless present to the world and creatively active in it "*of his own will*"[119] and "according to his own distinctive nature and activity as Spirit."[120]

As a way of signifying this unity in distinction St. Basil notes that all three Persons of the Trinity are the creative cause of all that is: "This extends to the creation of perceptible things, invisible powers, the dispensing and distributing of gifts, and the control of human affairs, from creation to the final judgment,"[121] but that this unified, singular agency is also characterized by an appropriate plurality and particularity, corresponding to each divine Person. Consequently, the Father, for St. Basil, is referred to as the "original cause," the Son the "operative cause," and the Spirit as the "perfecting cause."[122] This is one trinitarian model for reconciling the unity and plurality involved in God's creative work. Following Irenaeus, Colin Gunton was fond of noting that the Father works through his "two hands": the Son and the Spirit; while Torrance believes there to be one action of God mediated through two distinctive, though inseparable forms: through Christ and in the Spirit.[123]

As Creator, in union with the Father and the Son, the Spirit is both transcendent and free. However, the transcendence and freedom of the Spirit are exercised in a distinctive way according to the particular *hypostasis* of the Spirit. For this reason, the Church has referred to the Spirit in particular as the "Lord and Giver of life," referring to the transcendence and freedom of the Spirit respectively. The Spirit as Lord is *transcendent* over the created order, but not in such a way as to prohibit the *freedom* of the Spirit in giving life to the creature and sustaining the contingent created order, from both within and without. As noted in the previous section on the being and nature of the Spirit, the Spirit exercises his freedom by bearing a translucent witness to the Person of the Son (the Spirit *of Christ*), while exercising his transcendence by bringing the holiness of Christ to bear redemptively and transformingly upon the created order (the *Holy* Spirit). Torrance speaks of this work of the Spirit as "sanctification" when referring to the created order in general, and as "humanization" or "personalization" when speaking of human creatures in particular. In both cases, the creative work of the

119. Torrance, *Theology in Reconstruction*, 220. Italics original.
120. Torrance, *Christian Doctrine of God*, 216.
121. Torrance, *Theology in Reconstruction*, 220.
122. Ibid., 221.
123. Deddo, "The Holy Spirit," 84.

Spirit, as transcendent and free, is exercised in such a way as to affirm and heal the goodness and integrity of the created order while at the same time moving it toward its *telos* as revealed and secured in Christ. The Spirit accomplishes this work by orienting the created order toward its specific *telos* and, by so doing, transforming and perfecting the created order upon the basis of Christ's redemptive work. We will now consider in detail these two aspects of the Spirit's work as understood by Torrance.

The Spirit Orients and Directs the Created Order: The Eschatological Work of the Spirit

Torrance, developing the work of St. Basil, notes that "the creative and redemptive work of the Holy Spirit is to be thought of in terms of his inseparable relation from Christ . . . Not only does the Spirit have *koinonia kata physin* with the Father and the Son, but he is peculiarly closely related to the nature of the Son, and it is in this connection that his operations are to be discerned and understood."[124]

The creative and redemptive operations of the Spirit in relation to the created order cannot be understood apart from the Person and work of the Son. For Torrance, "the continuing existence of the universe is ontologically bound to the crucified and risen Jesus and destined to partake in the consummation of God's eternal purpose in him . . . [For, through the Son and in the Spirit] God irreversibly binds the created universe to his own Existence and his own Existence to the universe."[125]

This ongoing, contingent relationship has been secured by the Son, as just noted, but is oriented and sustained through the "perfecting" or "sanctifying" work of the Holy Spirit, particularly "through the liberating and quickening activity of the *Spiritus Creator* whereby the creature is creatively upheld and sustained in its existence beyond its own power in an *open-ended relation* toward God in whom its true end and purpose as creature are lodged."[126]

---

124. Torrance, *Theology in Reconstruction*, 221.

125. Torrance, *Christian Doctrine of God*, 217. If it were not for his repeated assertions of the unqualified transcendence and freedom of God throughout his works, one could conclude from this remark that Torrance is a panentheist. Such is the risk he is willing to take in asserting the intimate nature of God's involvement with his creation and the subtlety of his understanding of its contingence.

126. Ibid., 217. Italics original.

For Torrance "there is an inherent relation of Being and Act between the Spirit and the Son,"[127] to the extent that "the creative work of the Spirit is proleptically conditioned by that of redemption."[128] In other words, the sanctifying work of the Spirit presupposes the redemptive work of the Son at all points, and both the agency of the Son and that of the Spirit operate according to a single creative logic—towards the realization of God's *telos*, design, and purpose for the created order. This is made possible, not only because the created order is contingent, but because the Son and the Spirit continue to sustain this contingency ("open-ended relation"), and they do so toward a particular *telos* or goal ("toward God").[129] The work of the Spirit is conducted upon the basis of what Christ has secured through his Person and work and is oriented toward what Christ has declared and embodied as the purposes of God for creation.

A particular emphasis on this aspect of the Spirit's work may be found in Athanasius, who emphasized the "creative work of the Spirit in *renewing or sanctifying* the creature and consummating the relation of the creature to the Godhead."[130] This particular work of the Spirit does not occur in isolation from that of the Father and the Son, for all the activity of God is *from* the Father, *through* the Son and *in* the Holy Spirit. However, though there is a singular logic in God's creative activity, that singular logic requires us to note three distinct modes of operation by which it is carried out. The pluriformity of God's singular creative agency is indicated by the prepositions *ek, dia,* and *en*.[131] However, for Torrance "the special work of the Holy Sprit [in distinction from the Father and the Son] is to be discerned in that he brings the life giving power of God to bear upon the creature in such a way that through his

127. Ibid.. 148.

128. Torrance, *Theology in Reconstruction*, 217.

129. We will ultimately come to speak of the importance of "social coefficients of truth" in Torrance's thought. There are a number of factors that determine the character of a given social coefficient, but primary to each is what Torrance calls its "Archimedean point." Since the "continuing existence of the universe is ontologically bound to the crucified and risen Jesus," the Archimedean point for all social coefficients is ultimately Jesus Christ. This is already true in an objective and ontological sense; the work of the Spirit through the Church is to make that ontological truth a subjective reality within the coordinates of space and time, or, within the boundaries of culture.

130. Torrance, *Theology in Reconstruction*, 216. Italics original.

131. Ibid., 216.

immediate presence to the creature and in spite of its creaturely difference from God he sustains it in its being and brings its relation to the Creator to its true end in him."[132]

Our interest here is in pointing out the particular mode of operation signified by the fact that the creative work of God is fulfilled "*in* the Spirit." We take our cue from Athanasius in affirming that the Spirit's unique mode of operation is in orienting the created order toward its *telos* and, through his transforming power, directing the created order toward that end. By so doing, the created order is "consummated," "perfected," and "sanctified" upon the basis of Christ's work and according to the divine purpose and will.

Three things may now be said, in order to provide the basis for suggesting a fourth:

- The work of the Spirit presupposes and interpenetrates the work of the Son at all points.
- The work of the Son was the work of the *incarnate Son*, born, crucified, risen, and ascended, as the embodiment of God's purposes for the world. The vicarious humanity of Christ is a distinguishing mark of Torrance's Christology.
- The work of the Spirit is to sustain a relationship between the God revealed in the incarnate Son and the contingent created order, and the Spirit does so in order to transform the created order to its true end.

If, upon the basis of these truths, we may suggest that the incarnation is not only a union with human nature *per se*, but also *the entire ecology of human life*, we find the basis for a theology of culture emerging from Torrance's doctrine of God as triune, and particularly his understanding of the vicarious humanity of Christ.

The incarnation is a union, not only with *human* life, but with the entire ecology of human life, through the vicarious humanity of Christ. The Spirit unites us to *this* human, and unites all creation to *this* humanity. Through this union, the future of the created order is both revealed and secured, and the goal and basis of human cultural activity established. Through the work of the Spirit an open-ended relationship between Creator and creation is sustained and directed toward the *telos*

---

132. Torrance, *Christian Doctrine of God*, 218.

revealed and secured through the vicarious humanity of Christ—a *telos* having to do with the entire ecology of human life, and not simply that form of life we call "human." Torrance suggests such a connection himself in developing the thought of Athanasius:

> This [deeper reflection on the relation between the Spirit and the incarnation] resulted in a twofold doctrine: (a) an ontological relation between all men and the human nature of Christ, for the Incarnation of the creating Word posited a creative relation between Christ and all creation; and (b) the presence of the Spirit throughout all creation consummating its relation to God through the Word, and therefore fulfilling cosmic redemption and sanctification. Thus, the inseparable relation between the Spirit and the Son is basic not only to revelation but also to operation, and therefore essential to a doctrine of the knowledge of God and to a doctrine of creation.[133]

Torrance's work posits a much closer, and more dynamic, relationship between Christ, the Spirit, and the *telos* of the created order. That *telos* is not only revealed through the Son and in the Spirit, but can only be consummated upon that basis as well. His doctrine of creation is deeply trinitarian, and suggests in numerous ways that the reality we refer to as culture plays a vital role in Christ's atoning work, the Sprit's sanctifying work, and the agency of human persons in the world.

The work of the Spirit is not only intimately linked to the Person and work of the Son, but also the identity and agency of human persons as priests of creation. The identity and agency of these persons are deeply rooted in culture. Indeed, even as the creative activity of the Father is mediated through the Son and in the Spirit, so the work of the Spirit is often mediated through the agency of human persons as "mediators of order" and "priests of creation."[134] For Torrance human persons have been created in the image of God in order to serve as priests of the created order. Their unique identity is for the purpose of a unique task and vocation, having primarily to do with the stewardship of creation, and its transformation into a glorious hymn of praise

---

133. Torrance, *Theology in Reconstruction*, 217. We would also add that the inseparable relation between the Spirit and the Son is not only essential to a doctrine of revelation and creation, but for those reasons, a theology of culture as well.

134. These are phrases Torrance uses to describe the identity and vocation of human persons in relation to the created order. We will explore these descriptions in chapter 4.

to its Creator. This task cannot be fulfilled apart from the agency and empowerment of the Spirit.

This task also cannot be accomplished apart from the fact of human culture, for the human agents through whom the Spirit works are cultural beings—their identities and actions informed and guided by diverse cultural traditions. We will argue in chapter 4 that the source of this cultural diversity is rooted in the very constitution of the human person, and that cultural diversity is one of the goals intended when God created human persons in the divine image.

Perhaps more than any other Person of the Trinity, the Spirit has a very subtle and dynamic relationship with human agents and their cultural environments, working both in and through them while also for and against them. This is appropriate to the nature of the Spirit as transcendent, translucent, and free. The freedom and transcendence of the Spirit are tethered, as it were, to the person and work of the Son on the one hand, and the agency and cultural environments of human persons on the other. These are the boundaries within which the Spirit freely works to advance the purposes of God for the created order. Discerning the difference between the Spirit and the coordinates the Spirit works within is no easy task. It requires not only that an *intimate relation* between the Son and the Spirit be maintained, but also that a *critical difference* between the Spirit and human agency and creativity be preserved. The former is Torrance's most concrete means for maintaining the latter: "Apart from this indissoluble relation of the Spirit and the incarnate Son, we are unable to distinguish the objective reality of the Lord God, the Creator of the ends of the earth, from our own subjective states and conditions, or from our own creative spirituality."[135]

To be able to make this distinction is essential if the created order is to be moved toward God's *telos* and not our own *teloi*. If we are not able to do so then "the products of this consciousness [of the Church or the individual], in its collective or individual genius, are put forward as operations of the Holy Spirit."[136] It is only through the ministry of the *Spiritus Creator*, in his creativity and translucency, that we are delivered from being engrossed with ourselves in this fashion.

Here Torrance notes that the human person is capable of incredible creativity, however it falls to naught and turns against its Creator if

---

135. Torrance, *Theology in Reconstruction*, 227.
136. Ibid., 228.

not in accordance with the *telos* for which the created world has been brought into being. That *telos* is only discernible, and ultimately attainable, through the ministry of the Holy Spirit, and thus only through Jesus Christ, for God's eternal purpose for the created order was brought to its redemptive fulfillment in the incarnation. Jesus Christ is the central and pivotal reality of the universe since all things have been created in him and for him. This is why Torrance is adamant in asserting that the triune God of Jesus Christ is the Archimedean point for all social coefficients of truth, a point we will consider in detail in chapter 5. The teleological work of the Spirit orients us ultimately toward this Archimedean point, thus placing human identity and agency within its proper coordinates.

The Spirit Transforms and Consummates the Created Order: The Sanctifying Work of the Spirit

As noted above, Athanasius emphasized the "creative work of the Spirit in *renewing or sanctifying* the creature and consummating the relation of the creature to the Godhead."[137] The sanctifying, renewing, and perfecting ministry of the Spirit occurs in constant conversation with God's *telos* for the created order. It is that *telos* that serves as the goal and criterion for the Sprit's sanctifying work. That *telos* is revealed in the Person and work of Jesus Christ and it is through Christ's work that the *telos* of the created order is not only embodied and revealed, but also ontologically secured. It is the distinctive work of the Spirit to sanctify the created order by actualizing in the created order the future that Christ has secured for it.

With the incarnation, crucifixion, and resurrection of Jesus Christ, and the sending of the Spirit in his name, a tension between the "already" and "not yet" of God's rule is introduced into the fabric of the created order.[138] Torrance notes that the resurrection in particular involves "a profound interrelation between redemption and creation," in such a way that "the created order is set upon a wholly new basis."[139] The result, in Torrance's language, is an "eschatological pause" or

137. Ibid., 216. Italics original.

138. Elsewhere Torrance refers to this as the tension that results when "the Trinitarian order immanent in God" is brought to bear upon "the contingent order immanent in our world" (Torrance, *Christian Doctrine of God*, 221).

139. Torrance, *Space, Time, and Resurrection*, 175.

"reserve."¹⁴⁰ With this language Torrance notes that the created order is a single order existing under two overlapping conditions.¹⁴¹ As such, the created order is both fallen and redeemed. The "tension" or "pause" created by these conflicting conditions has been ontologically and objectively resolved through the Person and work of Jesus Christ. However, it is a "pause" that will not be fully resolved until the *parousia* of Christ at the end of time.

Until that time, and in anticipation of it, the Spirit is at work in the created order in a distinctive fashion, as the *Holy* Spirit, or the one who perfects and consummates what the Father has willed and promised and the Son has both revealed and secured. The distinctive and specific work of the Spirit is the resolution of this "pause" in a concrete and subjective sense. The Spirit does this by transforming the ambiguous state of the created order into the "order that ought to be."¹⁴² This particular aspect of the Spirit's work is mediated through human agents and thus the historical and cultural process.¹⁴³ The creative agency of the Spirit, where the fallen order is brought into ever-greater levels of congruence with the redeemed order, is the sanctifying or perfecting work of the Spirit.

---

140. Torrance speaks of this eschatological reserve with regard to the life and mission of the Church in the following way: "Although it is already one Body with Christ through the Spirit, it is yet to become One Body with him, but meantime in the world and history of the Church is a mixed body, with good and evil, true and false, wheat and tares in its midst. It is still characterized by sin and evil and partakes of the decay and corruption of the world of which it is part, so that it is not yet what it shall be, and not yet wholly in itself what it is already in Christ. In this eschatological reserve and deep teleological ambiguity the Church lives and works under judgment as well as grace" (ibid., 156). This simply means that "Christ holds back the physical transformation of the creation to the day when he will return to make *all things new*, and that meantime he sends the Church to live and work in the form of a servant within the measures and limits of the on-going world of space and time" (Torrance, *Space, Time and Resurrection*, 149).

141. See Torrance, *Christian Frame of Mind*, 17–34, for the language of "the order that is" and "the order that ought to be." We will discuss the nature of these conditions and Torrance's concept of order in the following two chapters.

142. This is language used by Torrance to refer to God's *telos* for various aspects of the created order. See ibid., 17ff.

143. John Douglas Hall and William Dyrness note the importance of human agency in the fulfillment of God's purposes for creation. See Hall, *Imaging God*, 21–60; and Dyrness, *The Earth Is God's*, 38–41.

The sanctifying or perfecting work of the Spirit in transforming the created order involves both judgment and grace, both a divine "Yes" and a divine "No." Torrance, citing St. Basil, notes that "if the creative work of the Spirit is essentially holy, then the fulfillment of that creative work, that is, the bringing of it to its proper *telos*, must involve judgment and salvation for the sinner, while in the original creation itself, it involves the conferring of grace."[144]

The judgment and salvation experienced by the sinner, and the grace conferred upon the created order, are due to the agency of the Holy Spirit. The Spirit perfects and sanctifies the created order, not simply by giving it life, or sustaining it in its being, but by actively working in it to actualize God's purposes for it.[145] As Torrance notes: "The Holy Spirit is God in his freedom not only to give being to the creation but through his presence in it to bring its relations with himself to their end and perfection."[146]

The sanctification and transformation of the created order towards its true end involves judgment and conversion, the outpouring of God's grace and patient working toward justice. It is a violent and anguishing task, even as it is carried out in hope. That is due to the fact that both divine and human power are being brought to bear upon the created order to shift its very momentum from a reality oriented away from God to one oriented toward God. That the transformation and sanctification of creation is an anguishing task seems clear from the crucifixion and resurrection of Jesus Christ.

God's "No" of judgment is delivered in such a way as to assert God's resounding "Yes" that the created order is good and has an abiding role to play in God's eternal purpose. However, this "good" created order exists in a precarious state due to its fallen condition. Though "good" in an

---

144. Torrance, *Theology in Reconstruction*, 221. See also Torrance, *Christian Doctrine of God*, 152ff.

145. Torrance would be quick to note that God's purposes for the created order are not latent in the created order itself. They cannot be discovered solely through an investigation of its contingent order, they must be revealed from without. It is these purposes that the Spirit actualizes through his sanctifying work, not some *telos* immanent to the created order itself. This is why Torrance, when affirming that there is indeed a correspondence between the created order and the divine order, clarifies that this correspondence is "a differentiated analogical correspondence." Torrance, *Christian Doctrine of God*, 220.

146. Torrance, *Theology in Reconstruction*, 248.

objective sense, it must also be properly directed and oriented if it is to realize its *telos*. Goodness is not simply a matter of substance, essence, or nature, it is also a matter of, what Al Wolters, in his brief book *Creation Regained*, refers to as "direction." We will quote Wolters at length, not only because this will be an important concept for this project, but because many aspects of Torrance's doctrine of the Spirit are implicit in his understanding of the details and dynamics of creation's "direction":

> Direction ... designates the order of sin and redemption, the distortion or perversion of creation through the fall on the one hand and the redemption and restoration of creation in Christ on the other. Anything in creation can be directed either toward or away from God—that is, directed either in obedience or disobedience to his law. This double direction applies not only to individual human beings, but also to such cultural phenomena as technology, art, and scholarship, such social institutions as labor unions, schools, and corporations, and to such human functions as emotionality, sexuality and rationality. To the degree that these realities fail to live up to God's creational design for them, they are misdirected, abnormal, distorted. To the degree that they still conform to God's design, they are in the grip of a countervailing force that curbs or counteracts the distortion. Direction therefore always involves two tendencies moving either for or against God.[147]

What Wolters refers to as "God's law" or "creational design," Torrance would refer to as God's purpose or *telos* for that thing. Where Wolters uses the language of "direction" to refer to aspects of the fallen and redeemed creation, Torrance uses the language of a single created order under the conditions of both the fall and redemption.[148] Wolters refers to a "countervailing force" created by the tension between distorted and properly oriented aspects of creation. This would seem to be the same dynamic referred to by Torrance as the "eschatological pause."

The language of "direction" and "orientation" fits well within the imagery and models employed by Torrance for understanding the

---

147. Wolters, *Creation Regained*, 49.

148. Wolters' language may be preferred at this point, since it leaves room to clearly assert that there is one created order and that order is fundamentally good. Torrance believes the same thing; however, the language of order as both fallen and redeemed as well as created leaves room for confusion, not only about how many "orders" there are, but about whether the created order itself is fundamentally good.

created order and its *telos*.[149] The sanctifying work of the Spirit can certainly be understood as bringing order to creation by aligning its various "coordinates" with God's will and purposes revealed in Christ as the "Archimedean point." However, the language of music might better capture the dynamics Torrance is discussing here, for it seems that the sanctifying work of the Spirit he is attempting to describe is akin to what a musician seeks to do when tuning his or her instrument. It also seems akin to the efforts exerted by a musical group when attempting to play a composition in a specific key, time signature, or tempo.

Nothing is being said about the structure of the music *per se*, only how it is played by the musician(s). So too, Torrance and Wolters are saying nothing about the nature, structure, or purpose of the created order. It is as God has declared: good. It is as God has embraced it: redeemed (in an objective sense). But, it is how we interact with the created order that makes our agency "in tune" or "out of tune" with the creative purposes of God. The standard by which this judgment is made is revealed in the person of Jesus Christ—the revelation of the purposes of God for creation. If this is so, to carry our analogy through, Christ would be the tuning fork and the agency of the Spirit would be the pressure placed, through human agents, on the various means used to bring an instrument into tune—whether that is tuning a string, adjusting a reed, etc. The creative agency of the Spirit directs God's power toward bringing the created order "in tune" with God's purposes for it. The process of "tuning" the created order involves the sanctifying work of the Spirit.

The language of "tuning" also captures the very subtle way in which the power of God through the Spirit works in and through the created order. Not to crush or set it aside, but to work with what is there, stretching and adjusting it to bring it in line with God's purposes, and by so doing to say a profound "Yes" to what is there. This seems precisely how

---

149. This project will terminate with a consideration of Torrance's concept of "the social coefficient of truth" as an approximation of his theology of culture. For Torrance, every social coefficient has a number of coordinates peculiar to it. These coordinates are located in the created order and are used to understand a given reality more deeply. However, these coordinates alone cannot provide the ultimate purpose for a given reality. To discover the *telos* of a thing an overarching "Archimedean point," located outside the boundaries of the created order, is necessary. When the created coordinates are properly aligned with the Archimedean point, the true *telos* of a thing is discovered, which in turn informs how that reality is expressed and socially embodied.

God works in the midst of human culture and through human agency. This comes through wonderfully in many of Torrance's writings, in particular when referring to the work of the Spirit:

> Far from suppressing, crushing or extinguishing the frail forms of contingent rationality with which we are endowed as human beings created after the image of God, the presence of the Holy Spirit empowers, integrates and establishes them while overcoming the alienating deficiencies and contradictions which we have introduced into them, so that they may be made to realize their true end in the Love and Wisdom of God the Father, the Maker of heaven and earth and of all things invisible and visible.[150]

That is a beautiful description of the Spirit's sanctifying work. Torrance sees evidence of the work of the Spirit in this fashion with regard to the incarnate humanity of Christ, where the divinity of the Son does not overcome or displace the humanity of the Son.[151] The nature of God's power, again, is defined with reference to the power of God as revealed in the Son, and it is an intensely personal form of power with very concrete salvific goals.

Whatever language one may choose to employ, the transformation and sanctification of the created order involves a deep and profound shift in the orientation of the created order and the human agents in it. Indeed, the language of conversion and judgment, grace and justice, seems quite appropriate. However, though the almighty power of God is brought to bear on the created order through the agency of the Spirit to transform creation, that power is not exercised in a way that subverts the integrity of the created order or human agency, but rather affirms, heals, and transforms even as it judges and converts.

The creative and translucent Spirit not only brings the holiness of Christ to bear upon the created order, but brings the created order to bear upon the holiness of Christ, in that the created order, in all its diverse forms, are employed in the glorification of God and the fulfillment of God's purposes. The Spirit shines through Jesus Christ, but also, through the creative agency of the Spirit, Jesus Christ shines through the cultural media of human life.

---

150. Torrance, *Christian Doctrine of God*, 220.
151. Torrance, *Trinitarian Faith*, 230.

The Spirit accomplishes this dual task by enabling human creatures as cultural and social beings to participate in, and respond to, God in such a way that God's purposes for the created order are embodied within the coordinates of space and time. Indeed, for Torrance there can be no relation with God apart from the Spirit's work in initiating and sustaining such a relation: "The doctrine of the lordly freedom of the Spirit to be present to creation and bring its creaturely relations to their proper *telos* in the Creator, means that the creature does not have continuity in relation to God that belongs to the creature in itself, for this is continuously given and sustained by the Spirit."[152]

Christ's prayer, that things may be on earth as they are in heaven, is a prayer for the sanctification of the created order. Towards this end, human agents are allowed, through the Spirit, to participate in the fulfillment of the purposes of God. It is towards this end that the gifts of the Spirit are given.

The Spirit not only mediates the work of God, but also the work of human agents as that work is directed toward the glorification of God, and as it is offered to God in the Spirit. The Spirit accomplishes this sustaining and perfecting work through the "gifts of the Spirit,"[153] and does so both "from the side of the creature"[154] and in the context of community. In other words, human forms are not crushed, but integrated, into God's perfecting work; human agents are not set aside, but employed and empowered, for the fulfillment of this work. This is the sanctifying work of the Spirit as God's creative power. This is God's *modus operandi*

---

152. Torrance, *Theology in Reconstruction*, 223. See also Torrance, *Christian Doctrine of God*, 152ff.

153. Torrance, commenting upon the work of St. Basil, notes that one of the distinctive aspects of the Spirit's work in sustaining and perfecting creation is that the Spirit gifts human agents for this work and by so doing confers grace upon the created order. Citing St. Basil: "There is indeed not one single gift which reaches creation without the Holy Spirit." These gifts are given, not in order to confer upon human agents ecstatic experiences, but to equip them to participate in the sanctifying work of the Spirit. See Torrance, *Theology in Reconstruction*, 222.

154. The Spirit, though "exalted infinitely above and beyond all creatures and all the powers of heaven is yet free to be present to the creature and to fulfill from the side of the creature the perfecting work which binds the creature in relationship to the Creator, and so to realize its life ... It is through him that the economies of God are carried out from beginning to end, creation, old covenant, the Incarnation itself, the ministry of the Church, and the future Advent of Christ" (ibid., 223).

with regard to the created order because God is a personal being and we are, as created in God's image, personal beings as well:

"Within [a] trinitarian perspective, the power or almightiness of God is revealed to be essentially *personal*, defined by God's triune Nature and Being as Father, Son, and Holy Spirit. This personal power of God is not power that overrules the creature but sustains the creature, not power that negates the freedom of the creature, but the power of the love that God is, power therefore that sustains the relation and freedom of the creature before God, for it is always creative, and in relation to his human creatures always personalizing and humanizing power."[155]

Again, emphasizing the sanctifying and perfecting work of the Spirit as essentially personal, Torrance asserts that "God does not exercise his sovereign Power upon us from above and beyond us like some impersonal *force majeure*, but in an intensely personal patient way from below, by penetrating into the dark disordered depths of our alienated creaturely existence in order to work savingly, healingly and preservingly within it."[156]

God does not crush what is personal, but heals and establishes it, and part of that work is the healing and establishing of the social relations and cultural products that make personal life possible, for personal life is life in relation, life in community. There is no culture without community and no community without culture. We should not be surprised to find Torrance making this connection, and he does so through his understanding of the Spirit's work. This comes out in his emphasis upon the Church and God's agency through it, but also in less "religious" forms of human community, such as Torrance's references to "social coefficients," a concept we shall develop at length later on. The Spirit accomplishes God's perfecting work through both of these forms of community and they refer to the particular and universal work of God in creation respectively. Speaking of the work of the Spirit in the formation of that human community called the Church, Torrance notes: "The personalizing incorporating activity of the Spirit creates, not only reciprocity between Christ and ourselves, but a community of reciprocity among ourselves, which through the Spirit is rooted in and reflects the Trinitarian relations in God himself. It is thus that the Church comes into being ... This is the Church of the triune God, embodying under

---

155. Torrance, *Christian Doctrine of God*, 206.
156. Ibid., 222.

the power of the Spirit the Lord and Giver of life, the divine *koinonia* within the conditions of human and temporal existence."[157]

For Torrance, the perfecting and sanctifying work of the Spirit is mediated through two primary forms:

- Through a particular human community, specifically the community of the Church, whose task is to "embody, [through] the power of the Spirit the Lord and Giver of life, the divine *koinonia*."
- Through human agency in general, rooted in a particular community or "social coefficient" and thus a specific historical context. It is here where God's will and purposes are actualized as the Spirit mediates our response to God "within the conditions of human and temporal existence."

There can be no doubt that the Spirit is the primary agent involved in the transformation and sanctification of the created order. That has been clearly highlighted above. However, just as the Son and the Spirit are the "two hands" through which God accomplishes his work in creation, so too, the Christian community responding to the Spirit from within the conditions of history, society and culture are the hands through which the Spirit works to "sanctify" the created order and actualize in it the future Christ has secured for it.

At the outset of this section on the Spirit's perfecting work as the *Holy* Spirit, we cited the following material: "If the creative work of the Spirit is essentially holy, then the fulfillment of that creative work, that is, the bringing of it to its proper *telos*, must involve judgment and salvation for the sinner, while in the original creation itself, it involves the conferring of grace."[158]

We then noted that the judgment, salvation, and conferral of grace attributed to the work of the Spirit did not entail a setting aside of "contingent rationality," but rather its incorporation into the work of God:

> Far from suppressing, crushing or extinguishing the frail forms of contingent rationality with which we are endowed as human beings created after the image of God, the presence of the Holy Spirit empowers, integrates and establishes them while overcoming the alienating deficiencies and contradictions which we have introduced into them, so that they may be

---

157. Torrance, *Trinitarian Faith*, 250–51.
158. Torrance, *Theology in Reconstruction*, 221.

made to realize their true end in the Love and Wisdom of God the Father, the Maker of heaven and earth and of all things invisible and visible.[159]

Could it be that "conferring grace" upon the created order might involve not only the agency of the Spirit through the Son, but also the agency of human stewards working in the power of the Spirit? Could it be that human agents are involved in the task of "empowering, integrating, and establishing … frail forms of contingent rationality" through their socio-cultural activity guided by the Spirit? Could it be that "overcoming the alienating deficiencies and contradictions" of this contingent rationality is a cultural task and that by engaging in this task faithfully we play a part in transforming the created order into a "hymn of praise" to is Creator? Finally, could it be that human persons have been created by God in such a way that the fulfillment of this very task is essential to the realization of their created *telos*, and that the particular environment they have been placed within (contingent creation) facilitates this task?

We can answer the above questions with a resounding "Yes" based solely upon Torrance's doctrine of God as triune. However, Torrance's understanding of creation as contingent and human agents as "priests of creation" must also be considered. These areas of Torrance's thought point to the pivotal role human agency plays in the transformation of the created order. However, that agency must first be placed in its proper context. This is the primary concern, not only of this chapter, but also of chapters 2–4 of this project, to which we now turn.

---

159. Torrance, *Christian Doctrine of God*, 220.

2

Torrance's Doctrine of Creation I
Order as Contingent

THE CONCEPT OF ORDER IS A DOMINANT THEME IN EVERY ASPECT OF Torrance's thought and serves as an integrating motif for much of his work. Torrance draws upon the concept to develop his understanding of God ("divine" or "trinitarian order"), creation ("contingent order") and humanity ("mediators of order") and the goal toward which human activity in history is to be oriented ("the order that ought to be"). We will use it later in this project to understand the nature of culture as a reality that arises from the ordering activity of human persons as stewards of creation. For these reasons it deserves careful definition and development.

The idea of order, because it is a fundamental assumption of rational inquiry and interaction with the world, is a difficult one to circumscribe. In fact, the very examination of it presupposes it. In an essay entitled "The Concept of Order in Theology and Science,"[1] Torrance notes that "order is not something that we can ever prove, for we have to assume order in any attempt at proof or disproof." Consequently, order "constitutes one of the ultimate controlling factors in all rational and scientific activity."[2]

This is certainly true of Torrance's theological work, not only because he describes his work as "rational and scientific," but also because the concept of order has played a fundamental and regulative role in his published work from its initial appearances[3] and throughout the

---

1. This essay may be found in Torrance, *Christian Frame of Mind*, 17–34.

2. Ibid., 18.

3. One of his earliest essays exploring the significance of order for the Church and its ministry is "The Meaning of Order," in Torrance, *Conflict and Agreement in the Church*, 2:13–30. The publication of this essay took place at the same time Torrance was

entire range of his thought on matters biblical, theological, scientific, ecumenical, ethical, cultural, and aesthetic.[4]

Richard S. Kirby, in his doctoral research on the concept of cosmic disorder in Torrance's thought, notes that the twin concepts of order and ontology are central in determining the underlying "grammar" or "syntax" of Torrance's thought irrespective of the subject.[5] Though Kirby thinks that Torrance has not taken proper account of the reality of sin in relation to the created order and the scientific enterprise, the importance of the concept for Torrance's thought remains.

---

delivering his 1959 Hewitt Lectures at Andover Newton Theological School under the title *The Nature of Theology and Scientific Method*. These lectures were then substantially expanded and published ten years later as *Theological Science*. It would appear that the origins of Torrance's interest in the significance of order for the church arose in tandem with his interest in the concept of order as a presupposition of scientific methodology. Therefore it serves as an important integrative concept for the entirety of his thought. Another essay considering the implications of the biblical term *oikonomia* for a concept of order, and in particular its implications for our knowledge of God, is Torrance, "The Implications of *Oikonomia*." The idea of *oikonomia* serves as a springboard for Torrance's earliest reflections on the concept of order.

4. Other developments and applications of the concept in the various fields just mentioned may be found in Torrance, *Conflict and Agreement in the Church*, vol. 1. This entire volume draws upon the concept of order to address ecclesiological and missiological issues. Torrance begins to develop his theological anthropology around the concept with his March 1978 acceptance speech, for the Templeton Prize, titled "Man, The Priest of Creation" published in *Ground and Grammar of Theology*. His most extended treatment of the theme, directed primarily to scientists, but laden with implications for theologians, appears in *Divine and Contingent Order*. The concept of order remains just as prominent, but less technically discussed, in *Christian Frame of Mind*. Of particular interest are the essays "The Concept of Order in Theology and Science," and "Man, Mediator of Order," where the conceptuality of priesthood and creation in his 1978 address are exchanged for the conceptuality of mediation and order. The concept of order is drawn into nearly all of Torrance's ethical discussions. See in particular Torrance, "The Atonement: The Singularity of Christ and the Finality of the Cross"; and "The Ought and the Is." In terms of aesthetics and order one might consider the final pages of "The Transfinite Significance of Beauty in Science and Theology," where Torrance reflects upon Barth's appreciation of Mozart, and "The Social Coefficient of Knowledge," in Torrance, *Reality and Scientific Theology*, 98–130 where the reflections include other facets of contemporary culture. On the relation of order and law see in particular *Juridical Law and Physical Law*.

5. Kirby, "Theological Definition of Cosmic Disorder," 96: "[Torrance's] method emphasizes the ordered nature of the contingent creation, and his ontology emphasizes the relational nature of being. . . . Thus, to do justice to the 'grammar' or theological 'syntax' of Torrance's thought on any subject, it is reasonable to give a thorough account of these essential elements of his theology." See in particular chapter 3: "Christ and the Cosmos: Order and Ontology."

In the light of Torrance's publishing career and Kirby's observations it would not be reckless to conclude that the concept of order not only functions as a central integrating motif in Torrance's work, alongside that of the *homoousion*, but surpasses it in many ways, as it is a concept used to explicate the very significance of the incarnation itself. For Torrance, the incarnation is an event that binds together the created order with the divine order, redeeming the fallen order and inaugurating an eschatological order whereby the actual (fallen) order of the world is driven towards the "order that ought to be," realized partially in this world and consummated in the *eschaton*.[6] Indeed, the concept has received a breadth and depth of treatment[7] not extended to the concept Torrance is known best for advocating—the *homoousion*.

However, it should be added that Torrance's concept of order, or the way in which he has nuanced and transformed it, arises from theological forces that are grounded in the assumption of the *homoousion*. Torrance's particular concept of order has been formed through a thinking together of the doctrines of creation and incarnation—the main fruit of this being his development of the idea of contingence.[8] It is this thinking together that has given Torrance's concept of order a distinct identity and differentiates it from more generic and stereotypical conceptions that see the concept as inherently static, closed, and inflexible and, as such, one that suggests a homogenizing impact upon the diversity and particularity of the created order.

Presently, we will examine what the concept of order refers to and what differentiates one order from another in Torrance's thought. As we will discover, Torrance talks of what appears to be several kinds of order: created, contingent, divine, redeemed, fallen, eschatological,

---

6. See the essay "The Concept of Order in Theology and Science," in Torrance, *Christian Frame of Mind*, 17–34.

7. We refer here to the extended treatment given to the concept in Torrance's *Divine and Contingent Order*.

8. With reference to the fundamental role of a doctrine of creation, "Contingence and order are assumptions of that [unprovable] kind, yet we do not derive them from natural science but from a fundamental outlook upon the nature of the universe that is the correlative of a distinctive doctrine of God as the Creator of the universe" (Torrance, *Divine and Contingent Order*, 27). See also Torrance, *Christian Frame of Mind*, 20: "This is the concept of order in which Christian theology seeks to think out by relating the Incarnation of the Word of God in Jesus Christ to the creation which was brought into being from nothing through the creative power of that Word."

and moral. But what is the nature of the order that all these adjectives describe?

Approaching Torrance's doctrine of creation through the concept of order as a noun, as opposed to that of contingence as an adjective, will grant us a better understanding of the various "stages" or "conditions" that qualify the created order[9] and the personal and historical relations that are significant to these transitions/conditions. The concept of order becomes an important entry point for asking the following questions:

- What distinctive qualities, or what kinds of change, require the concept of order to be qualified in these different ways?
- What distinctive kinds of agency characterize these differing forms of order, and in what way are they involved in the move from one quality of order to another?
- What kind of continuities and discontinuities are there between these different forms of order?

The Inner-Logic of Order

As mentioned earlier, the concept of order is a difficult one to circumscribe, let alone concisely define. Torrance himself refrains from any concise definitions or treatments of the concept, preferring to let the significance and boundaries of the idea unfold through his use of it in various contexts. Consequently, the most appropriate way in which to unfold the contours of the concept is to draw upon material from throughout Torrance's work where the concept is actually put to use. By so doing we will be able to develop a comprehensive account of the term's meaning and the dynamics that underlie it.

As a first step toward this comprehensive account, we will have to lay down the basic grammar of the concept by reading between the lines of Torrance's work. In doing so we are looking for what Torrance has elsewhere described as the "inner-logic" of the concept. We here inquire after the essential components of meaning inherent in the term

---

9. Even if the transition from stage to stage, or condition to condition, has much to do with how the contingent relation between God and the world is defined and its dynamics effected by sin and redemption. But, our point here may not be valid as contingency is a characteristic of the created order even in its fallen, redeemed, and eschatological states. It is the character of the created order that changes, not its essential nature as contingent.

as Torrance uses it by asking what order is *prior* to it being characterized as fallen, redeemed, eschatological, moral, etc.

Perhaps the closest one will get to capturing the many themes and overtones of meaning inherent in Torrance's use of the concept in one citation is in the opening paragraphs of his essay "The Meaning of Order."[10] The citation is a long one, and many further points of expansion and clarification are made subsequent to it, but it will serve as a helpful point of entry to the broad contours of the concept in Torrance's thought. It will also provide a necessary foundation upon which to further develop and integrate Torrance's other uses of the term.

> Apart from the ordering activity of God's creative Word the world is without form or void, but into the ordered cosmos there has broken the disorder of sin. It belongs to the very nature of sin to divide, to disrupt, to be anarchic—sin is lawlessness, *anomia*. The opposite of all that is order, harmony, communion. When God made the world He made it in order and everything was set in its due proportion. But through the lawlessness of sin the world fell out of proportion, out of order, and was threatened with sheer chaos. Were it not for the persistent fact of God's purpose of love the world would destroy itself; but in His covenant mercy God holds the world together in spite of its chaos, and to that end He has promulgated His law which restrains and contains disorder (as long as it is obeyed) and chaos, and reduces it to a measure of proportion, even while it is in the grip of *anomia*, or lawlessness. But God's Covenant contains the promise of a new order, of a new creation when all things will be restored to their obedience and perfection in the divine Will. Meantime wherever there is *anomia* it is met by the divine *nomos*, and there is conflict between disorder and order.[11]

We will condense this statement by making five general points about Torrance's specifically Christian concept of order:[12]

---

10. This essay can be found in Torrance, *Conflict and Agreement in the Church* 2:13–30. As further testament to the centrality and flexibility of the concept in Torrance's thought he here uses it as an integrative motif to clarify and relate the ideas of creation, fall, covenant, redemption, church, economy, and *eschaton*.

11. Ibid., 13.

12. For an even more generic concept of order one could replace God with any agent and still retain the basic dynamic described here: order presupposes an ultimate agent, and any given order reflects the character of that ultimate agent and his/her presuppositions about the world. The Christian understanding of the concept adds that our cultural ordering of the world should be congruent, not only with the particular

- Order is a *theological* concept in that it arises through the agency of God's creative Word and derives its essential character from that Word.

- Order is a *relational* concept in that it has to do with the establishment of unique relations between things based upon the nature and purpose of those things.

- Order is a *teleological* concept in that the nature and purpose of those things are ultimately grounded in God's loving purpose and design for them and for the created order in general.

- Order is a *cultural* concept in that God's loving purpose for the created order is to be embodied in, and reflected through, the socio-cultural structures of human life.

- In light of the four points above a fifth follows: Order is a *multi-leveled and integrative concept* in that lower levels of order refer beyond themselves to higher levels of order and higher levels of order, while implicitly present in the lower levels, cannot be reduced to them.[13]

Using these five points as a guide, a tentative theological understanding of the concept of order in Torrance's thought might run something like this: Order refers to a particular way of organizing created reality by establishing flexible relationships between different aspects of that reality in accordance with their particularity and purpose and with reference to a transcendent design so that those interrelated spheres of reality reflect in a creaturely way the divine intent for the world.

These statements and definition will serve as an adequate starting point for the further development of the idea in Torrance's work as they

---

agent/s and their particular purposes for the world, but ultimately with God's. Human orders are not ultimate but penultimate reflections of an ultimate order established by God and revealed in the divine economy.

13. There is no explicit mention of this point in the citation we have just noted; however, it becomes an important factor in the overall dynamic (inner-logic) of the term as Torrance develops it later through his engagements with natural science and his interaction with the work of Michael Polyani. We include it here at the outset of our discussion due to its centrality in Torrance's later expositions. Torrance refers to this elsewhere as "ontological stratification" where "the universe in its immanent structure comprises a hierarchy of levels of reality which are open upward but not reducible downward" (Torrance, *Divine and Contingent Order*, 20). This is an inherent implication of Torrance's understanding of "contingency" that we will explore later.

capture the inner-logic of the concept in such a way that little alteration of it will be necessary as we proceed. With the essential and identifying structure of the concept in place we may now embellish it; teasing out the implications inherent in the inner-logic of the concept and by drawing in complementary concepts Torrance has developed elsewhere. It is hoped that by so doing we will further clarify the essential structure Torrance has put in place, even while it is tailored in such a way as to be useful for the development of a theology of culture.[14]

As we move through an explication of Torrance's concept of order we will also be considering the many stages, forms, or qualities of order that Torrance refers to, specifically, created, fallen, redeemed, eschatological, and socio-ethical/cultural. We will consider the continuities and discontinuities between these stages and the personal and historical relations important to each. In closing, a number of inter-connected statements will be made so that the many strands of the concept may be woven together and its central dynamic exposed.

Order as a Theological Concept: The Ground and Purpose of Order in God the Father

When we speak of order in Christian terms we speak of something that arises fundamentally from God's creative initiative and is sustained due to God's ongoing providential activity. To reiterate the words of Torrance: "Apart from the ordering activity of God's creative Word the world is without form or void."[15] Order is a concept that carries with it an ultimate reference of some kind, and for Torrance that ultimate reference is the triune God. It is not enough that order refers generically to some ultimate ground of order, for Torrance this ultimate reference must have concrete content—it must be *theological* and therefore trinitarian. Any other ultimate reference will have significant consequences upon how we conceive of order, how we investigate and manipulate it, and how our ordering of the world subsequently forms and manipulates

---

14. This process is not much different from the way the jazz improviser works, for such a person does not pick notes out of thin air, but expands upon the essential structure of a piece of music—drawing out its inherent potential while adding nuances of his/her own that are context specific. See the work of Berliner, *Thinking in Jazz*; and Monson, *Saying Something*.

15. Torrance, *Conflict and Agreement in the Church* 2:13.

us.[16] For Torrance order arises from the agency of the Word of God and "has its ground in the love of God, for it is ultimately God's love which is the power of order in created existence."[17]

For order to be understood theologically, it must be properly qualified and thus differentiated from ways of conceptualizing order that are not theological. It is for this reason that Torrance introduces and develops the idea of "contingence" in the way that he does and rarely discusses order apart from it being explicitly qualified as contingent.[18] For that reason a brief introduction to the concept is in order. We will then go on to develop two particular aspects of contingence that make it a distinctive qualifier of Torrance's overall understanding of "order."

Contingence: Introducing and Defining the Concept

As with the concept of order so with the concept of contingence—it is another fundamental assumption of all rational inquiry that cannot be proved but must be assumed if scientific inquiry is to proceed.[19]

For Torrance, contingence "is to be regarded as a basic and essential feature of the universe, a constituting condition of its reality and actuality."[20] With this statement, the importance of the concept in Torrance's thought seems self-evident. However, as a "basic and essential feature of the universe" it does need some development and clarification in order to find its appropriate place in our project.

---

16. See in particular Torrance's critique of determinism in Torrance, *Divine and Contingent Order*, 1–25, where he notes that "deism and determinism go together" (10). The way the ultimate ground of order is construed holds significant consequences for how human beings understand themselves and their relations to one another, God, and the world. Torrance uses the history and philosophy of science to exemplify the theological, social, and scientific consequences of our misconstruals of "God" as the ultimate ground of order. While Torrance's emphasis has certainly been upon the scientific consequences, the dynamics of his thought are readily applicable to other spheres of human culture as well.

17. Torrance, *Christian Frame of Mind*, 19.

18. In fact, for Torrance order cannot be anything other than contingent, for it arises solely through the agency and creativity of the divine Word.

19. "Contingence must take its place among the ultimate normative beliefs with which science operates, along with order, rationality, simplicity, etc." (Torrance, *Divine and Contingent Order*, 28).

20. Ibid., 37.

The irreducible kernel of the concept is provided by W. Jim Niedhardt in his "Introduction" to the second edition of Torrance's 1985 book *The Christian Frame of Mind*. Very simply, "contingency refers to the fact that a physical entity is never haphazardly formed but *exists as one of many possibilities*."[21] Consequently, that which is contingent is "neither necessary not eternal"[22] and therefore, contains no intrinsic reason why it should exist or why it should be what it actually is.[23] This kernel of meaning may be faintly detected in two descriptions of the term offered by Torrance himself—one for "contingence" and the other for "contingent order":

- "By contingence is meant that as created out of nothing the universe has no self-subsistence and no ultimate stability of its own, but that it is nevertheless endowed with an authentic reality and integrity of its own which must be respected."[24]

- "By contingent order is meant that the orderly universe is not self-sufficient or ultimately self-explaining but is given a rationality and reliability in its orderliness, which depend on and reflect God's own eternal rationality and reliability."[25]

For Torrance, contingency carries with it many of the same components of meaning found in his use and understanding of "order"—perhaps this is why the terms are so often found complementing and even standing in for one another. Contingency implies purpose, design, dependence, and relation even if that which is contingent is the actualization of only one of many possible choices, and in fact need not have been actualized at all. As a result, that which is contingent is neither necessary nor eternal, but neither is it random or chaotic.[26]

---

21. Torrance, *Christian Frame of Mind*, xxi. Italics mine.

22. Torrance, *Ground and Grammar*, 53.

23. Torrance, *Divine and Contingent Order*, 36. This has important implications for Torrance's response to natural theology.

24. Torrance, *Christian Doctrine of God*, 217.

25. Torrance, *Divine and Contingent Order*, viii.

26. Some, such as Roland Spjuth, in his excellent treatment of Torrance's thought, contend that Torrance has so circumscribed the idea of contingency that it has been expunged of the elements of chance and chaos that are meant to characterize it. See Spjuth, *Creation, Contingency and Divine Presence*, 105–16.

As with the concept of order so with the concept of contingence—the content of the term is filled with meaning through the thinking together of the doctrines of creation and incarnation. Of particular importance is the doctrine of *creatio ex nihilo*, which Torrance refers to in order to outline the central implications of the concept of contingency for Christian thought about the created order.[27]

In its creation out of nothing the created order has had freely conferred upon it:

- A *contingent rationality/intelligibility* of its own derived from (not participating in) the uncreated rationality of God, yet transcendentally (not ontologistically) grounded in it.

An implication of this facet of contingency is that the created order is a rational unity of form and being and a singularity of an open structured nature. "The universe constitutes an essentially *open* system with an ontological and intelligible reference beyond its own limits."[28]

- A *contingent freedom* of its own derived from (but not as an extension of) the self-sufficient freedom of God, yet transcendentally (mediately, not immediately) grounded in it.

An implication of this facet of contingency is that the created order is characterized by flexibility and multi-variability that is due in large part to its open structured nature in allowing God's interaction with it and our manipulation of it.

- A *contingent stability* of its own derived from the eternal faithfulness of God. The stability of the created world is therefore maintained through God's loving interaction with it, not through immutable laws immanent within it.

An implication of this facet of contingency is that the created order, while being open structured and flexible is nevertheless bounded, directed, and upheld by God toward a determinate end.

Torrance has elsewhere referred to these as the "three masterful ideas" of the Early Church[29] and it is the combination of these qualities

---

27. See Torrance, *Divine and Contingent Order*, 21.
28. Ibid., 36.
29. See Torrance, *Ground and Grammar*, 52ff.

in the created order that give it its "remarkable character."[30] Much of the responsibility for the "remarkable character" of the universe must be firmly laid upon the shoulders of Torrance's conception of contingence. There are two features in particular that must be developed further as they are central to the meaning and function of the concept in Torrance's thought: 1) the interlocking nature of contingency and 2) the reflective purpose of contingency.

Contingence: Its Interlocking Nature and Dynamic

We noted above that the kernel of the concept of contingency has to do with that which is neither necessary nor eternal. However, that does not render contingent realities inherently random or chaotic, as products arising from God's arbitrary willing or out of coincidental processes in nature. By discussing contingence in relation to a doctrine of *creatio ex nihilo* Torrance affirms both truths and singles out the idea of dependence as being central to his understanding of contingence. Contingent realities are dependent upon the God that brought them into being out of nothing and in accordance with his free pleasure and will.

Yet in the two descriptions Torrance gives of his understanding of contingence he notes that while contingent realities are *dependent* upon God for their being, intelligibility, and freedom they nevertheless have a reality in utter distinction and *independence* from him. Contingence therefore carries within it an inner-logic of its own that centers around the interplay between the dependence and independence of the created order in relation to God. Torrance describes this as the "two-fronted character" of contingence or "its orientation toward God and away from him, its radical dependence and independence."[31] This *dynamic* is absolutely central to Torrance's conception of contingence and makes the concept a difficult one to understand and draw boundaries around. As Torrance himself notes: "What makes contingence so baffling is the peculiar interlocking of dependence and independence that it involves. The independence of the world depends entirely upon the free creative act of God to give it being and form wholly differentiated from himself,

---

30. Torrance, *Divine and Contingent Order*, 21.
31. Ibid., 40.

but that is then an independence that is delimited by the dependence that anchors the world beyond itself in the freedom of the Creator."[32]

In short, "the independence of the universe is both grounded in and limited by its radical dependence."[33] The interlocking of dependence and independence that characterizes the created order gives the created world its unique *form* and enables it to fulfill its distinct *purpose*. However, it is this same interlocking that is the most difficult facet of contingence to understand and keep in balance.[34]

The constitutive relation thus established between God and the world needs careful articulation if the elements of dependence and independence are to remain properly balanced in such a way that the integrity and character of each is not compromised, or the purpose of their relation subverted. Torrance makes three points of clarification in this regard. The constitutive/contingent relation between God and the world may be described as:[35]

- *Asymmetrical*, in that "the world needs God to be what it is but God does not need the world to be what he is." Creation is an act of pure liberality and grace on God's part and was not motivated by any necessity whatsoever.

- *Irreversible*, in that "there is no statically continuous and logically compelling relation between the being of the creature and the being of the self-existent Creator." The existence of any form of *analogia entis* is ruled out and conceptions of natural theology are radically questioned. Knowledge of God cannot be necessarily derived from reflection on the created order.[36]

---

32. Ibid., 35.

33. Ibid., 36.

34. When an overemphasis is placed upon, either the dependence of the created order *on* God, or the independence of the created order *from* God, a Christian doctrine of creation is lost, and a deterministic relation takes the place of a free and contingent one. For a fine statement of the proper balances necessary in order to maintain the integrity of contingence as a description of the world's relation to God, see ibid., 21.

35. See ibid., 34–35 for the following points.

36. See Torrance's reflections on the proper role of natural theology within the bounds provided by revealed theology in "The Transformation of Natural Theology," in Torrance, *Ground and Grammar*, 75–109; "The Status of Natural Theology," in Torrance, *Reality and Scientific Theology*, 32–63; and, with particular reference to Karl Barth, "Natural Theology in the Thought of Karl Barth," in Torrance, *Karl Barth: Biblical and Evangelical Theologian*, 136–59; and Anderson, "Barth and a New Direction for Natural Theology," in *Theology beyond Christendom*.

- *Personal*, in that the world is "correlate[d] so closely with himself [God] that it is made to reflect and shadow forth on its contingent level his own inner rationality and order" even while being upheld in its creaturely otherness and particularity. This intimate and sustaining ontological relation may be "theologically traced back to the free, ungrudging will of God's love" which creatively imparts to the created order a rationality of its own "which is not incongruous with God's rationality."

This final point leads us to a consideration of the second central feature of the concept of contingence: its reflective purpose.

Contingence: Its Reflective Purpose

The *inner-logic* of contingence, though difficult to pin down and balance, is appropriate to the *purpose* of contingence. Contingency enables a given order distinctively and faithfully to fulfill its *telos* by reflecting the will/design of its Creator through its own creaturely particularity. It can only do this within the dynamics of its own dependence and independence in relation to God.

Though it has been created to reflect the will and purposes of its Creator it does not contain within itself divine principles, nor is it the home of immanent divine forces.[37] In the words of Robert Jenson "that God creates means there is other reality than God and that it is really other than he."[38] However, more must be said, and for that reason we introduce two additional concepts that will be useful in developing the implications of Torrance's thought for a theology of culture without blurring the qualitative distinction between Creator and creation that he has been so careful to develop. The first will be Torrance's understanding of "the legislative activity of the transcendent God"[39] and along with it a Christian conception of natural law, which is for Torrance equiva-

---

37. The order that characterizes the world is not the embodiment of divine principles, but rather the place for the working out of the divine purpose. It is not the body of God, but the sphere of his loving activity. It is not an organic part of God's being, but cannot be divorced from him. We might say that the micro-ordering of our socio-cultural worlds takes place within the boundaries of God's macro-ordering presence in and to the world.

38. Jenson, *Systematic Theology* 2:5.

39. Torrance, *Divine and Contingent Order*, 37.

lent to his understanding of contingent order.⁴⁰ The second will be what Torrance has variously referred to as a "temporal analogue," "social coefficient," "created correspondence" or "empirical correlate."⁴¹

The Creation of the Powers: The Legislative Activity of God

An extended quote is in order here as means of both introduction and orientation:

> The Christian conception of law relates to the legislative activity of the transcendent God, who does not embody his own eternal Logos in nature as its universal law, but who through the unifying power of his Logos creatively imparts to the world as he creates it a pervasive rational order on its own level subordinate to himself on his transcendent level, as its determinate ground. The creation of the universe as an autonomous reality distinct from God while dependent upon him *also involves the endowment of the universe with autonomous structures of its own*. Natural law, thus understood, refers to the God given normative patterns in the universe and has to do with the intrinsic truth or objective intelligibility of contingent being.⁴²

This is a helpful passage as it directly connects Torrance's conception of law and natural law with his understanding of contingence, thus making law a contingent reality with a dual reference and orientation both towards God and away from him. The connotations of law as something that is rigid, inflexible, necessary, and eternal is replaced with a conception that is dynamic and multivariable—open towards completion and intelligibility beyond itself, but with a rationality and integrity of its own that must be respected.⁴³

---

40. Torrance, *Juridical Law and Physical Law*, 34ff.

41. The most recent label for the concept can be found in Torrance, *Christian Doctrine of God*, 220, where it is described as "a differentiated analogical correspondence."

42. Torrance, *Divine and Contingent Order*, 37. Italics mine.

43. Two authors seeking to address the stereotypes of the past in order to rehabilitate the concept of natural law for the present are Braaten, "Natural Law in Theology and Ethics"; and Porter, *Natural and Divine Law*. I believe they would be in general agreement with the way Torrance has modified the concept, and the broader framework he places it within. See also Torrance's treatment of natural theology in Torrance, *Ground and Grammar*, 75–109.

While Torrance uses this understanding of natural law in his conversations with natural science, and develops it further in that context, our interest is not in natural science *per se* but in the socio-cultural ramifications of Torrance's trinitarian thought. We want the dynamic that Torrance ascribes to natural law as contingent and the trinitarian framework within which it is developed. In other words, Torrance has given us the appropriate theological tools but it is our purpose to utilize them, not in engagement with natural science, but in the development of a theology of culture.

For that reason we will have to "transplant"[44] Torrance's trinitarian framework and with it his conceptions of order, contingency, and law into a tradition of thought concerned with addressing social-scientific issues as opposed to natural-scientific ones.[45] Torrance is no stranger to this type of inter-disciplinary conversation and mutual modification. It has been a hallmark of his theological work.[46] However, his interactions with disciplines outside the realm of the physical sciences have been brief and few.[47]

For that reason we require a similar term that will be more congenial for translation into the concepts of contemporary social science. Such a term will open up to us a wealth of reflection upon concerns

---

44. Torrance engages in such activity by proposing "scientific transplants" into the field of juridical law. This simply refers to inter-disciplinary research and conversation. See Torrance, *Juridical Law and Physical Law*, 22ff.

45. Torrance is no stranger to interdisciplinary discussion, and he could accurately be described as a contextual theologian *par excellence*. As such, however, one becomes necessarily absorbed in the context and concerns of the audience one is addressing. This does not subvert Torrance's theological framework, but it does limit the scope of its influence. It is our hope that "transplanting" Torrance's theological paradigm into a different sphere of concerns will enrich his theological project by concretely expanding its realm of relevance and applicability.

46. See in particular the series of essays in Torrance, *Transformation & Convergence*. Torrance notes in the preface that the ultimate motivation behind his interdisciplinary conversations is that "the Christian Faith be brought to bear transformingly upon the whole frame of human culture, science and philosophy in every age" (vii). He sees this goal as congruent with the work of the Early Christian Church "which set itself not only to communicate the Gospel to the Graeco-Roman world but to transform the prevailing frame of thought and culture so that the Gospel could take deep root and develop within it" (vii).

47. Torrance's most extended treatment of a subject matter not falling within the realm of the physical sciences is *Juridical Law and Physical Law*. It provides suggestive guidance that illuminates how Torrance understood the socio-political implications of many facets of his thought.

flowing out of contexts alien to those of the physical sciences, but without subverting the meticulous trinitarian theological paradigm Torrance has developed in conversation with those sciences. It is our belief that Torrance's reference to natural law as a consequence of the "legislative activity of God" and as signifying "the God given normative patterns in the universe" that have to do with the "intrinsic truth or objective intelligibility of contingent being" is fully congruent with the Pauline language of "principalities and powers" and the way this language has been developed and employed by missiologists and social ethicists in their concerns to describe, engage, and transform human culture. In fact, John Howard Yoder has noted in the second edition of *The Politics of Jesus* that: "It would not be too much to claim that the Pauline cosmology of the powers represents an alternative to the dominant ("Thomist") vision of 'natural law' as a more biblical way systematically to relate Christ and creation."[48]

We do not see it as an alternative vision, but a complementary one. By bringing Torrance's conceptions of natural law and contingent order into conversation with that of the Pauline "principalities and powers" we not only have an appropriate entry point to a whole new field of reflection but also a way to interact with that field from within Torrance's trinitarian perspective. It also serves as a way of drawing these two fields together around a trinitarian grammar—something Torrance would no doubt applaud. This "drawing together" is present in the thought of Lesslie Newbigin: "What I have called the structural elements in the world as we know it, from the basic structures of the physical world to the social and political structures of the nations, to the customs and traditions by which human beings are normally guided, to what the sociologists call the 'plausibility structures' by which all human thinking is guided: all of these are part of God's good ordering of his creation."[49]

Newbigin agrees with Torrance that "the basic structures of the physical world" are a consequence of God's creative ordering of the cosmos. But God's good ordering of the world does not end with the structures of space and time. Rather, the structures of the physical world and the structures of the social world are complementary forms of order that come together under the heading of "the powers." Social order and physical order share the same ultimate origin and purpose

48. Yoder, *Politics of Jesus*, 159.
49. Newbigin, *Gospel in a Pluralist Society*, 208.

even though different in nature and design. They are the fundamental structures within which human life is lived out and God's purposes are worked out.

At this point we find ourselves introducing the idea of "structures" in order to define the content and dynamic of Torrance's "natural law" and Newbigin's "powers." Both terms refer to structures that are created and contingent and share all the characteristics of Torrance's conception of order. This is why there is so much potential for Torrance's thought to stand at the basis of a theology of culture, while in turn being critiqued by the social realities it supports and explains. Such a conversation has been thwarted due to an unnecessary division between the natural and social sciences and to a proliferation of confusing but inherently complementary concepts.[50] Torrance's concept of order presented alongside that of the powers as structures promises to cut through this impasse and facilitate the inter-disciplinary conversation that is necessary to develop a theology of culture that is trinitarian in nature.

We will here briefly expand upon the concept of the powers by drawing upon the thought of John Howard Yoder and Lesslie Newbigin, two contemporary thinkers who have defended and developed the concept in the fields of social ethics and missiology respectively.[51]

The Language of the Powers: Structures and Patterns

There is a great variety of language associated with the concept of the powers. Yoder provides an adequate summary: "[Paul] speaks of 'principalities and powers,' and of 'thrones and dominions,' thus using lan-

---

50. It seems that both disciplines are coming to a greater realization that the flourishing of the natural world is intimately intertwined with the activities of the social world while the human world is increasingly realizing that social life is not possible apart from the physical environments that determine it. The knowledge and integration of both are essential to any theology of culture, for culture is not the domain or product solely of the social world, nor is it possible to come to a knowledge or unfolding of the natural world apart from the social networks of those who investigate it. A theology of culture must be based upon a social paradigm that construes the relations between humanity, nature, and God in a trinitarian fashion. Torrance's thought offers us just such a paradigm.

51. See in particular Yoder, *Politics of Jesus*, 134–61; and Newbigin, *Gospel in a Pluralist Society*, 198–210. More extensive treatments of the theme may be found in Berkhof, *Christ and the Powers*; and Dawn, "Biblical Concept of 'the Principalities and Powers.'"

guage of a political color. But he can also use cosmological language like 'angels and archangels,' 'elements,' 'heights and depths.' Or the language can be religious, such as 'law,' or 'knowledge.' Sometimes the reader perceives a parallelism in all these concepts, sometimes not."[52]

Lesslie Newbigin expands Yoder's selection of terms somewhat by noting that "with these [authorities, rulers, etc.] we must also look at what the Gospels have to say about hostile spiritual powers, about Satan, and about what the Fourth Gospel calls 'the ruler of this world.'"[53]

Both authors criticize the West in its dismissal of this language as mythological and fanciful, part of a world view we have grown out of and therefore having no concrete reference. Such reductionism is combated by Yoder and Newbigin as they demonstrate the validity of Paul's language for referring to fundamental features of our social and physical worlds. Colin Gunton, in his brief study, points to the importance of the language in relation to the nature and breadth of the atonement and understands the concepts referred to as having a metaphorical function, not a mythological one.[54] All three writers share the same conclusions: the powers are objective realities referred to with metaphorical language due to their complex and ambiguous nature. What results from the Pauline language is a "general trend of meaning" but also a "stimulating confusion" that can have a great deal of heuristic power.[55] The powers "symbolize a phenomena that is no less real for being difficult to localize with exactitude."[56]

Yoder notes that this same complexity and ambiguity attaches to our use and understanding of the concept of structures. Structures "point to the patterns or regularities that transcend or precede or condition the individual phenomena we can immediately perceive . . . It is

---

52. Yoder, *Politics of Jesus*, 137.

53. Newbigin, *Gospel in a Pluralist Society*, 200.

54. Gunton, *Actuality of Atonement*, 53–82.

55. These phrases are from Yoder, *Politics of Jesus*, 137.

56. Ibid., 138. Newbigin notes this as well: "these powers do not exist apart from the human agencies in which they are embodied . . . yet they are not identical with these particular individuals. They refer to that which is behind them, to the power which they represent and exercise but which is not identical with them . . . Clearly this 'something' has reality. But we cannot locate it spatially within, behind, or above its visible embodiment" (Newbigin, *Gospel in a Pluralist Society*, 202).

this patternedness that the world 'structure' tries to enable us to perceive within all the varieties of its appearance."[57]

The powers are therefore the structures of the contingent world and a consequence of God's creative ordering of it. It seems apparent that when Torrance speaks of such things as "order" or "natural law" he is referring to the same reality Paul refers to as the "principalities and powers" and as Yoder and Newbigin refer to as the structures, patterns and elements of the created world. As all of these things are created, they are also contingent and share in Torrance's trinitarian construal of the term.

THE FUNCTION OF THE POWERS: MEDIATING AND MAINTAINING ORDER

God's creative action flows freely from his triune nature. This was the point asserted in chapter 1. That creative action not only brings the world into being out of nothing but also imparts to it a form and order with a concrete purpose and design—to reflect the glory of its Creator. The powers are meant to serve God by facilitating the ordering of the world after this design and towards this purpose. Yoder notes that "society and history, even nature, would be impossible without regularity, system, order—and God has provided for this need. The universe is not sustained arbitrarily, immediately, and erratically by an unbroken succession of new divine interventions. It was made in an ordered form and 'it was good.' The creative power worked in a mediated form, by means of the Powers that regularized all visible reality."[58]

Newbigin observes that "these structural elements are necessary to guide and protect human life."[59] This is the chief function of the powers

---

57. Yoder, *Politics of Jesus*, 138. We are here reminded of Torrance's concept of order once again and its similarities to the concept of powers being developed by Yoder and Newbigin. Of particular interest at this point is Torrance's understanding of order as a multi-leveled and integrative concept. The intelligibility or reality of a thing cannot be reduced to its appearance but refers beyond itself for its ultimate rationality or the ground of its "patternedness."

58. Ibid., 141. Perhaps some clarification should follow Yoder's capitalization of "Powers" at this point in order to differentiate his understanding from an understanding of divine, immanent principles in the created world—something Torrance would repudiate. However, no further clarification is given.

59. Newbigin, *Gospel in a Pluralist Society*, 205.

in the creative purposes of God. However, in guiding and protecting human life the created order is formed in such a way that the glory of the Creator might be reflected in the process. This is the purpose of the powers, a purpose that is not always fulfilled in their functioning, for the order that the powers often times produce is not the order that is in accordance with the design and purpose of God for his creation. This deviance from God's design is something we will treat shortly, but one final facet of Torrance's concept of order as contingent and reflective needs to be described—his conception of the world as a "temporal analogue" and the appearance of "empirical correlates" and "social coefficients" as consequences of divine and human agency in history.

The Purpose of the Powers: Temporal Analogues, Empirical Correlates, and Social Coefficients

When we place together the ideas that human life is lived out within the boundaries of God's ordering of the contingent world, and that God's purposes are worked out within these same boundaries, we approach something akin to what Torrance refers to as the essential ingredients of a "temporal analogue" or the basis of an "empirical correlate."[60] A temporal analogue is the reflection of the divine purpose or design within the structures of the contingent world. Since these structures refer to normative patterns in both the physical and social worlds, we can expect temporal analogues to be found in both of these spheres. Though Torrance is fond of pointing out analogies between the physical world and the divine order, he is sensitive to the fact that social analogies can and must be made.[61]

As a rule, temporal analogues are given in the structure of the created order and stand as mute witnesses or "creaturely correlates" to the reality and rationality of God in a *passive* way. This seems to be the thrust of Torrance's thought when he notes that "the startling patterns disclosed by scientific research in the space-time universe [constitute] in [their] contingent rational order a 'created correspondence' . . . to the

---

60. The phrases "temporal analogue" and "created correspondence" are borrowed from Karl Barth. They can be found in Barth, *Dogmatics in Outline*, 52.

61. See, for example, Torrance's use of the idea of *analogia relationis* to refer to the image of God in humanity and his drawing of parallels between physical law and juridical law.

uncreated rationality of God himself."[62] "Empirical correlates" and "social coefficients" on the other hand are *actively* formed. Although they arise within and are determined by the created structures of the world they are the direct result of divine and human agency in history where that agency is directed toward concrete purposes that are based upon, or at least congruent with, God's design. This emphasis can be noted in Torrance's doctrine of the church, where he notes that the clauses in the Nicene Creed in regard to the church "do not constitute an independent set of beliefs, but follow from belief in the Holy Spirit, for *holy* Church is the fruit of the *Holy* Spirit, the result of his sanctifying activity in mankind, and as such is, as it were, the empirical correlate of the *parousia* of the Spirit in our midst."[63]

For this reason, Torrance's concept of a "temporal analogue" refers to the created structures within which cultural activity occurs. Therefore all cultural activity will bear some resemblance to the divine intent or design for human life even if at a very generic level. This however, does not mean that a natural theology is appropriate or possible, as we will shortly see when we consider the effects of evil upon the created order. "Empirical correlates" on the other hand, while based upon the same structures refer to those structures which have been collected together, empowered, transformed, and directed to serve as concrete and active witnesses to the reality of God and his purposes for the world (i.e., the Church). With temporal analogues we have to do with the stuff of culture, in empirical correlates we have to do with the formation and transformation of culture toward a particular end. This happens when God binds himself to particular cultural forms and uses them to ac-

---

62. Torrance, *Christian Frame of Mind*, 28. Torrance expands upon this: "The created order reflects to a certain extent the God who has brought it into being, since its intent and purpose for being is the glorification of the Creator. The universe has been brought into being by the Triune Creator 'from the Father, through the Son and in the Holy Spirit.' As a result, there must be the possibility of a created correspondence to the Holy Trinity" (Torrance, *Trinitarian Faith*, 93). Understood in this way the created order may be "regarded as a manifestation of divine grace—not that it is itself that grace but the result of it which bears the imprint of divine grace in its contingent character" (Torrance, *Divine and Contingent Order*, 109). This imprint, however, can only be discerned through the medium of divine revelation. See Torrance's essay "The Transformation of Natural Theology," in *Ground and Grammar*.

63. Torrance, *Trinitarian Faith*, 252.

complish his purposes. In so doing God transforms and sanctifies them (for example, Israel and the Church) for a particular use.[64]

The contrast between "temporal analogue" and "empirical correlate" having been made we will now focus a bit further upon what Torrance has in mind when he refers to the created order as an analogy of the divine (temporal analogue).

Torrance's understanding of analogy is as developed and nuanced as his conception of contingence, primarily because he wants to draw close and intimate parallels between God and the world, yet without violating the ontological difference or contingent relation between them. This is a difficult balancing act. For Torrance an analogy is:

- A correspondence in difference: a similarity within dissimilarity created by the grace of God, apprehended by faith (not imposed by humanity) and based upon the utter transcendence of God in relation to the world.

- A disclosure model that is heuristic in character—signifying neither a pictorial representation, formal correspondence, nor logical relation between God and the world. Rather it discloses the truth of one level of reality within the structures and dynamics of another level (i.e., as the contingent order discloses truths about the divine order).

- Helpful to humanity as opposed to being descriptive of God. It is a reflection that is true without being pictorial, signitive without being descriptive, suggestive without being exhaustive.[65]

For Torrance, the character of the divine order is somehow reflected in the created order without violating the ontological distinction between them: "Perceived through the 'ears and eyes of faith' *the creation is not God but has imprinted on it the trace of his nature.*"[66] This imprint is real but the nature and dynamics of it must be understood analogically according to the above criteria. Consequently, recognition of the grace of God and the necessity of faith are essential. This is why "the ears and eyes of faith" are required if the analogy is to be perceived. However, our

64. See Torrance's work on "The Social Coefficient of Truth," in *Reality and Scientific Theology*.

65. These points have been developed from Torrance, *Karl Barth: Biblical and Evangelical Theologian*, 187; and Niedhardt, "Key Themes," xxvii.

66. Niedhardt, "Key Themes," xxxi. Italics original.

perceiving does not make the imprint any more real than it objectively is. The correspondence is after all created by the grace of God not the creativity of humanity. It has been placed there by God for us to discover and benefit from, not to create and manipulate.

The created order as a temporal analogue is therefore meant to serve the purpose and design of the Creator for the creation. This is clearly evident in the following citation: "The created order reflects to a certain extent the God who has brought it into being, since its intent and purpose for being is the glorification of the Creator. The universe has been brought into being by the triune Creator 'from the Father, through the Son and in the Holy Spirit.' As a result, there must be the possibility of 'a created correspondence to the Holy Trinity.'"[67]

Torrance is simply asserting here that a composition not only requires a composer but also reflects the character and purposes of that composer *in a contingent way*. Though Torrance does not use the terminology of *analogia relationis* very frequently, it does seem to be equivalent in meaning to how he understands the concept of analogy as it relates to the created order. Also important to note is Torrance's continued emphasis upon this correspondence being one that obtains between the *triune* Creator and the *contingent* creation. For Torrance a generic or deistic God could not create such a world as we discover through our scientific research. Nor could a mechanical cosmos even mutely refer beyond itself to the triune God. For Torrance, the terms and conditions for positing a correspondence are clear, even if they can only be truly discovered upon the basis of a loving disclosure on God's part and an act of faith on our own.

In closing, contingence and order belong inseparably together in Torrance's thought.[68] In particular, "contingence" qualifies "order" as a distinctly theological concept by specifying that contingent realities:

---

67. Torrance, *Trinitarian Faith*, 93.

68. "The contingency of the creation as it derives from God is inseparably bound up with its orderliness, for it is the product not merely of his will but of his eternal reason. It is not only the matter of the universe, therefore, but its form that comes into being out of nothing, for under the rational creativity of God matter and form are fused indivisibly together from the very beginning. There is no contingence without order and no order without contingence, for contingence is inherently orderly and order is essentially contingent" (Torrance, *Divine and Contingent Order*, 109).

- Are neither necessary nor eternal, nor merely random or chaotic.
- Exist as both dependent and independent realities in relation to God and, as such, are inherently flexible and multivariable as well as unitary and stable.
- Exist for a purpose that is grounded in the will and design of God, but reflected through their particularity and in accordance with their created *telos* in the purpose of God.

3

Torrance's Doctrine of Creation II
Order as Redeemed

Order as a Relational Concept: The Revelation and Reconciliation of Order in God the Son

FOR TORRANCE, THE BIBLICAL REVELATION IS A WITNESS TO THE FACT that "the whole concept of order is [to be] viewed over against disorder and chaos,"[1] and so we will treat the latter subject now.[2]

We also include our discussion of the fallen order under the heading of the redeemed order, as Torrance considers any discussion of sin or disorder in isolation from God's gracious redemptive activity inappropriate. Sin and disorder should always be approached from within the "framework of grace" and cannot be fully understood apart from such a context. On this point Torrance follows Calvin's leadership[3] and we shall as well.

---

1. Torrance, *Conflict and Agreement in the Church*, 2:13. This perspective is maintained in Torrance, *Divine and Contingent Order*, 114, where he notes that "evil would present no problem to us at all—we would not even be aware of it—if there were no objective and coherent rational order, for what 'constitutes' evil [as] 'evil' is its contradiction of objective order on the one hand and its negation by that objective order on the other hand." This has implications for how Torrance understands the nature of sin and evil, and also why he chooses, as Calvin did, to discuss sin and evil only in the context of grace and redemption.

2. For a thorough examination of Torrance's understanding of "cosmic disorder" and its implications for his formulation of theology as a "science," see Kirby, "Cosmic Disorder." Kirby also notes its implications for Torrance's theological project as a whole.

3. See his comments in Torrance, *Calvin's Doctrine of Man*, 83. It is only from the perspective of resurrection and redemption that the full magnitude of evil and disorder can be comprehended without ourselves being drawn into its "abysmal" depths and fall-

We begin our discussion of disorder by referring to some of Torrance's earliest thoughts on the subject, and with a citation from the same essay we used to introduce Torrance's concept of order: "Into the ordered cosmos there has broken the disorder of sin. It belongs to the very nature of sin to divide, to disrupt, to be anarchic—sin is lawlessness, *anomia*."[4]

As order is the consequence of the creative activity of the triune God, so disorder is the consequence of human agency.[5] The disorder of the world is a result of humanity's disobedience and sin. This is the overwhelming implication of the biblical witness, even if, as Robert Jenson has noted, the serpent was ominously present prior to the human pair's first act of "freedom."[6] We will not venture a detailed discussion of the

---

ing prey to "misanthropy, pessimism, and despair," for only this vantage point will allow us to "reflect on the radical nature of evil without suffering morbid mesmerization or pathological distortion" (Torrance, *Divine and Contingent Order,* 115–16). Torrance appreciates the power of evil and the depths to which disorder infects humanity. However, this appreciation flows from the magnitude of God's gracious and saving action in the cross and resurrection, not from any consideration of evil as a reality in itself. Torrance notes, "It is because the ontological and epistemological situation has been altered in that way, that Christian theology ventures to say something definite about evil which could not be said from any other ground" (ibid.).

4. Torrance, *Conflict and Agreement in the Church,* 2:13; italics original. Torrance treats the concept of disorder at length in two places. The earliest and least developed we have just cited. The latest and most extensive is *Divine and Contingent Order,* 85–142.

5. This holds true not only for the moral order of the universe but its physical order as well since evil infects more than just "human hearts and minds." As Torrance notes, "Since it is through man's interaction with the physical universe that its empirical and contingent order comes to rational expression, it is not unlikely that, man being the kind of being he is, any physical evil or disorder that may emerge will also have to do with his interaction with the physical universe." Moral evil and physical evil become intertwined in the fall through human agency just as the redemption of the *entire* created order is a consequence of the agency of Christ. Again, "the incarnation, passion, and resurrection conjointly tell us that far from evil having to do only with human hearts and minds, it has become entrenched in the ontological depths of created existence and that it is only from within those ontological depths that God could get at the heart of evil in order to destroy it, and set about rebuilding what he had made to be good." Torrance sees this as the broader significance of the "nature miracles." See Torrance, *Divine and Contingent Order,* 116. A further exploration of the relationship between moral and natural law may be found in Torrance, "Ought and the Is," 49–59.

6. Torrance seems more interested in the role of humanity as a carrier and transmitter of disorder than as an original initiator of it. The origins of evil are inexplicable to Torrance, but the transmission of evil *via* human agency seems more conducive to explanation. Torrance does not discuss the matter of original sin, and at times his explanations seem quite congruent with sin as socially originated (through a breach of contingent relations) and transmitted.

idea of sin or what it entails.[7] It is not a pervasive category in Torrance's thought[8] and he seems more interested in the consequences of sin as disorder than the conditions that made the first sin a possibility and reality. Perhaps this focus of interest is a direct result of Torrance's own emphasis upon *a posteriori* thinking and his conclusion that sin is by its very nature inexplicable and irrational, if not in its transmission then certainly in its origins.

As noted in chapter 1, the creation of the world out of nothing was mediated through the Son and the Spirit. They are the mediating agents of God's creative ordering of the world. Humanity is a product of that creative ordering. However, though humanity was created to mediate God's creative activity by acting as stewards over and within creation, exercising their creative gifts within the boundaries of the created order and according to God's purpose and design, they have in fact become idolaters, usurping to themselves the authority to order the world in whatever way they see fit according to designs of their own making. They have become, in the words of Colin Gunton, "the world's most problematic inhabitant."[9] Needless to say, disorder and conflict come forth as the fruit of their misdirected stewardship. Order is mediated through the Son, disorder through those created in his image.

We have chosen to discuss disorder at this point not only because Torrance will only consider disorder, sin, and evil through the spectacles of redemption but because disorder is the opposite of order and is therefore intimately related to it, even if the opposite of it. Disorder is the perversion of order and is parasitic upon it.

Order as Fallen: Human Agency and the Subversion of Order

As noted earlier, Torrance's conception of order has five central components. Order is theological, relational, teleological, cultural, and multi-

---

7. Robert Jenson offers a very matter-of-fact definition of his own: "The only possible *definition* of sin is that it is what God does not want done." See Jenson, *Systematic Theology*, 2:133; italics original. He later develops this by understanding sin as idolatry (134ff.).

8. Although he does concentrate on the subject in Torrance, *Calvin's Doctrine of Man*, 83–116, in relation to the topic of total depravity; and in Torrance, *Divine and Contingent Order*, 113ff., in relation to the fact and nature of evil; all his conversations on the theme occur in clear view of the atonement and Christ's vicarious humanity.

9. Gunton, *Triune Creator*, 166.

leveled. Of particular interest to us in this section on the redeemed order will be the relational component—even as the theological component received the most development in the previous section. However, the emergence and transmission of disorder, as well as its redemption and sanctification, involve all of these components, as they together comprise a multi-leveled and integrated whole.

In chapter 4 of *Divine and Contingent Order* Torrance discusses the concept of disorder and the emergence of evil. His entire discussion revolves around his understanding of contingence, its definition in relation to Christ, and its place in the cosmos as "a distinctive property of its creaturely perfection."[10] This is in marked contrast to Greek perceptions, which understood contingence to be a feature of all that was transient and defective in being. Torrance believes that *evil and disorder are parasitic in nature,* and comes to the following conclusions:

- Evil and disorder are not properties of contingent being as such "for that would be tantamount to denying that what God has made he has made to be good, as well as charging him with defective handiwork."[11]

- Evil and disorder are not the inevitable consequences of the negative aspect of contingence (the autonomy of the created order in relation to God) "for that would split apart the negative (autonomy from) and positive (dependence upon) aspects of contingence, making nonsense of it as well as implying that contingent reality is not inherently orderly."[12]

- Evil and disorder do not arise through the privation of good or a defection from being "for evil can have no independent existence of its own."[13] In Torrance's view there needs to be discontinuity

---

10. Torrance, *Divine and Contingent Order,* 117.

11. Ibid.

12. Ibid. Parentheses mine. For Torrance this makes the concept of contingence nonsensical since the very independence of the contingent order is dependent upon the reality of God, and since the character of the created order is correlated to the character of the Creator. Thus any disruption to the contingent relation subverts the very existence and character of the created order. This in fact is how evil and disorder work and spread, as we will explore further below.

13. Ibid. Though Torrance does grant some limited justification for this view, he ultimately rules it out. The Augustinian-Thomist approach that characterizes this view contains "an inadequate notion of contingence," an "absence of any real notion of contingent order," and "an inadequate appreciation for the gravity of evil."

between goodness and evil but without granting evil an independent existence of its own. Torrance believes that the discontinuity proposed here may be eventually rationalized away and does not adequately account for the gravity of evil revealed in the crucifixion of Christ.

This leads us into a consideration of Torrance's own proposal.

Torrance's fundamental working assumption is that evil is "an utterly inexplicable 'mystery'... but a fearful actuality" that cannot "be explained, even in part, either by reference to the Creator or by reference to the creature as its author." It must be "totally and consistently opposed by man as it is by God."[14] Evil is to be regarded as "something like 'anti-being' that has unexplainably irrupted into created existence... as a direct negation of being rather than as a mere defection of being."[15]

For Torrance, evil as defection of being or privation of goodness is not radical enough, but evil as having an autonomous reality of its own is excessive. Torrance is aware that even a proposal as qualified as his own "runs the risk of a kind of dualism," however, "it would appear to be truer to what evil is actually found to be in our experience."[16] Evil "introduces disorder" and brings about "ontological collapse" by 1) "breaking into creaturely being," and 2) by becoming inexplicably intertwined "with the act and being of the creature." Evil "becomes rooted in the creature in such a way that the creature becomes evil and does evil of itself."[17]

At this point it would seem that evil and disorder become parasitic, relying upon the act and being of the creature to perpetuate, complicate, and magnify the disorder evil initiates, spreading it through the essential framework of human life (in particular the *relations* that obtain between human persons and God, human persons with one another, and human persons and the environment). This has enormous cultural implications for the role of human persons in the world as agents who are not only responsible for initiating and perpetuating disorder but

---

14. Ibid., 118.

15. Ibid.

16. Ibid., 119.

17. Ibid., 118. Evil is ultimately inexplicable, and whatever grasp we may have upon it can only be obtained from the vantage point of God's response to it in Christ. See Torrance, *Divine and Contingent Order*, 114–17.

counteracting and defeating it.[18] Torrance hints at this when he says: "Since it is through man's interaction with the physical universe that its empirical and contingent order comes to rational expression, it is not unlikely that, man being the kind of being he is, any physical evil or disorder that may emerge will also have to do with his interaction with the physical universe."[19]

For Torrance the *modus operandi* of evil, since it has no reality of its own, or any "natural counterpoise within [man's] being," is to subvert the contingent relation between Creator and creation via the act and being of the creature as the "priest of creation" and "mediator of order." This is how evil becomes rooted and intertwined in the act and being of the creature. How it does so remains "inexplicable."[20] However, Torrance does push for more detail by focusing upon a particular aspect of contingence that he believes evil "latches on to": "Evil should be regarded ... as latching on to the negative aspect in contingent existence or its natural independence, thus getting a hold within it and functioning in such a way as to alienate the negative from the positive aspect of contingence; that is, contingence *from* God is wrenched away from contingence *toward* God. In bringing about this break between the creature and the Creator *evil disrupts the inner equilibrium of contingent order* and causes the collapse of contingent existence toward nothingness."[21]

We noted in the previous section that order was a theological concept and that the idea of contingence qualified order in such a way as to make it inescapably so. Here we continue with the idea of contingence and order as *theological* concepts, but add to them a further component

---

18. That Torrance is aware of these implications can be seen in the fact that his discussion of disorder is followed directly by a section on "Man's Priestly and Redemptive Role in the World," in Torrance, *Divine and Contingent Order*, 128–42. We note also Torrance's speculation when he wonders whether evil and disorder are realities that "he [man] experiences as independent of himself but which he intensifies in his interaction with [them]" (Torrance, *Divine and Contingent Order*, 117). Humanity has a role in both mediating order and defeating disorder.

19. Ibid., 116. We note here that for Torrance much depends upon "man being the kind of being he is." We will develop this aspect of his thought, and how his anthropology fits into his theology of culture, in chapters 4 and 5.

20. We will rely later in this project upon the work of Peter Berger to offer an explanation of our own that follows Berger's proposal for relating the subjective and objective aspects of culture or the reciprocal relation between personal agency and social structure.

21. Torrance, *Divine and Contingent Order*, 119; italics mine.

in that they are also *relational* concepts. This is the second component of the concept of order we discussed under the "inner-logic" of order, and it becomes particularly important at this point as a means of exploring how the created order has become a fallen one and how it may be redeemed.

The transition of the created order to one that is fallen and redeemed revolves around the *relation* that obtains between the Creator and the creature. This transition also involves the agency of humanity and that of the divine economy, particularly the Son. For these reasons the association of the Son with the revelation and redemption of order (as in the chapter title) seems appropriate. This relation always obtains as it is a fundamental and irreducible aspect of Torrance's concept of order, but the *character* of the relation undergoes a transformation due to the agency of humanity and the agency of the triune God. This is what Torrance describes as he unfolds his understanding of evil, disorder, and redemption: the "transfer" from one form of the contingent order to another (from created, to fallen, to redeemed) is a consequence of the dynamics of this relation. In particular, the contingent relation that obtains between humanity and God. Human agency brings about the subversion of the relation, with disorder as a consequence. Divine agency, in particular the agency of the Son, is responsible for the revelation and reconciliation of this fallen relation. This makes a trinitarian conception of creation and culture not only possible but also necessary. When we speak of order as a relational concept we refer in particular to the contingent relation between Creator and creature and how the agency of the creature has subverted this relation (fallen order) while the agency of the Son not only reveals its true nature but also redeems it (redeemed order) and enables its original purpose to be realized through the work of the Spirit (eschatological order).

According to Torrance, evil inexplicably latches on to the contingent relation between humanity and God and introduces into it disequilibrium. In other words, it has focused upon one aspect of the notion of contingence that we highlighted in our discussion under point one: its interlocking nature. But in attacking the interlocking nature of contingence it also undermines the second aspect of contingence we highlighted: its reflective purpose. When evil "disrupts the inner equilibrium of contingent order and causes the collapse of contingent existence toward nothingness" the consequence is that "the semantic reference of its contingent order would be refracted and bent, and the Creator would be obscured from his creation."[22]

This loss of "semantic reference" is an attack upon the *contingent intelligibility* of the creation and thus its ability to fulfill its purpose in reflecting the glory of its Creator through its contingent structures and powers. However, the *contingent being* of the creation does not dissolve into nothingness for it is held in being by the gracious will and providence of God; although the direction in which the created order is now oriented (and its semantic reference along with it) is toward meaninglessness, death, and nothingness.[23] In addition, with the contingent intelligibility of the created order subverted and refracted and its contingent being threatened, its *contingent freedom* is also undermined. With these three spheres of contingency threatened (contingent intelligibility, being, and freedom) those other characteristics of the created order that work in cooperation with them (multi-variability, rational unity, etc.) are also threatened and their semantic reference, theological functions, and creative dynamics lost. As opposed to enriching the created order they undermine it by providing the conditions in which determinism, fragmentation, homogeneity, and meaninglessness may flourish and become embodied in the world's structures.[24] Colin Gunton has pointed

---

22. Ibid., 119. Additional components could be added here. See *Divine and Contingent Order*, 128–34.

23. See Becker, *Denial of Death* for the psychological dynamics of such an orientation, especially as exemplified in Western culture. For a pastoral approach to the issues that integrates the insights of Becker with the theological framework of Torrance, see Anderson, *Theology, Death and Dying*.

24. We note at this point striking similarities between Torrance's thought and that of sociologist Peter Berger, similarities we will draw out at a later point. Suffice it to say here, both of them see human persons as irreducibly social and relational, and contend that a major function of human activity revolves around the quest for meaning. For Torrance and Berger the quest for meaning centers on the creation of order. For both, order always has a semantic reference, and what that order refers to will determine its character and how it is "objectified" in social and physical structures. We note this common ground here but will develop it at a later point when we discuss the vocation of human persons as "mediators of order." Though they work in different fields and address vastly different questions and contexts, the proposals of Torrance and Berger appear to share a good deal of common ground (in spite of Torrance's often dismissive attitude toward sociology as a "positivist" science). We only note here that all sociologists are not created equal and Berger is quite aware of the problems associated with positivist science. See Wuthnow et al., *Cultural Analysis*.

out the strange and paradoxical mix of attributes that characterize the modern world as it develops under these conditions.[25]

How are these conditions to be reversed, or at the very least opposed? How are we to make the transition from the fallen order to the redeemed one? What conditions will be necessary and what forms of agency, both human and divine, will be required so that we may claim that the created order is not only fallen, but also redeemed?

Order as Redeemed: The Divine Economy and the Redemption of Order

We have already discussed the role of human agents in relation to disorder. Their role in relation to the redemption of the fallen order will concern us in chapter 4. At present, further consideration of the agency of the triune God in relation to the redemption and sanctification of the created order is necessary if our proposal is to remain a trinitarian one.

We touch base yet again with some of Torrance's earliest reflections on the subject of order by introducing the role of the law and the covenant as, not only the basis upon which God orders the world, but also the means by which he judges its disorder, restrains its chaotic elements, and promises an entirely new order to come.

The Ultimate and Penultimate Function of the Law

The ultimate and penultimate functions of the law and the covenant are grounded in God's purpose of love. What they ultimately refer to is God's love for the created order. This is entirely consistent with the inner-logic of Torrance's conception of order. Torrance notes: "Were it not for the persistent fact of God's purpose of love the world would destroy itself; but in His Covenant mercy God holds the world together in spite of its chaos, and to that end He has promulgated His law which restrains and contains disorder and chaos, and reduces it to a measure of proportion, even while it is in the grip of *anomia*, or lawlessness. But God's Covenant contains the promise of a new order."[26]

---

25. See Gunton, *Enlightenment and Alienation*; and Gunton, *The One, the Three and the Many*, 11–123.

26. Torrance, *Conflict and Agreement in the Church*, 2:13.

The function of the law as a judgment upon disorder, restrainer of chaos, and witness to a yet-to-be new order is an important feature of this early essay. Many of these functions are transferred to Christ and reoriented in recognition of his Person and work. However, the functionality of the law as a socio-cultural approximation of the divine intent and design appears to be lost in Torrance's emphasis upon a new universal order revealed and established in Christ. We are not implying that the two are mutually exclusive, but rather that the functionality of the law seems diminished by appearing to be not only fulfilled in Christ but also set aside by him. This seems to be a matter of emphasis in Torrance and not necessarily a matter of substance, however a closer relation of the two in the context of the new creation would be helpful. Does the law have a continuing role to play in the judgment and restraint of disorder, as well as the orientation of the new order? If so, this function would be served, not so much in terms of its specific regulations, but in its general functionality as a socio-cultural approximation of the divine intent, only now subservient to Christ and in service to the sanctifying and perfecting work of the Spirit.

For now let us note the penultimate role of the law in Torrance's understanding. The law serves two primary and penultimate functions that are negative in nature.

Firstly, it is the means by which God, in his mercy and love, "holds the world together in spite of its chaos" by *restraining and containing disorder*. This restraining and containing purpose is fulfilled through the law as it serves to realign and reorient the human social framework in relation to God's purpose and design for it. By so doing the disorder and chaos that characterizes and threatens the world is reduced "to a measure of proportion, even while it is in the grip of *anomia*, or lawlessness."[27] In this sense the law serves a providential function, not a redemptive one.

Secondly, the law is the means by which God passes judgment upon the world in its idolatry, fallenness, and rebellion, unmasking it for what it is by bringing to bear upon it intimations of what it was created to be. This is accomplished by forcing the stewards of the created order to consider the imprints of divine grace present in its created structures, but also by cultivating an anticipation of a new order that is to come. In this sense the law serves as *a criterion by which the world is*

27. Ibid., 13.

judged and God's purposes and design revealed and anticipated. In this sense the law serves a critical function, not a revelatory one. This leads us to consider the ultimate function and purpose of the law.

The positive function of the law, and its ultimate purpose, is to serve as a carrier of "the promise of a new order, of a new creation when all things will be restored to their obedience and perfection in the divine Will."[28] The institution of the law is not equivalent to this restoration, nor does precise obedience to its precepts result in the revelation or embodiment of the divine will. For the law to function in this way would be for it to draw too much attention to itself and by so doing only participate further in the disorder it was meant to judge, reveal, and restrain. The ultimate function of the law is "*to point beyond itself to the new law, the new order of the Covenant.*"[29] The law is a form of order and as such refers beyond itself for its ultimate ground, purpose, and design. In this way it is not unlike any other form of order in the contingent world. The particularity and uniqueness of the law is in the specificity of its transcendent reference—it "points ahead to the new Covenant when the Covenant Will of God will bring and manifest a new form of administration or economy."[30]

The Divine Economy and the New Covenant

This new form of administration will carry with it the same negative functions of the law, as it will pass judgment upon the disorder of the world by revealing it for what it really is. It will also reaffirm the restraining and containing function of the law in bringing proportion to creaturely relations. However, both the critical and providential functions of the law will be set upon a new basis and relativized so that they might be set free to serve a redemptive function. What we see here in Torrance's understanding is not an essential antithesis between law and gospel, but rather a complementary relationship, with the gospel fulfilling the law and then validating its function within the redemptive purposes of God.

An additional differentiating factor between the old covenant and the new is that the new will perform its redemptive ordering of the

28. Ibid.
29. Ibid., 14.
30. Ibid.

world from within its contingent structures, as opposed to the external restraint and containment of disorder represented by the old covenant. In addition, while the very *telos* of the old covenant lay in its transcendent reference to a new order to come, this feature drops away in the new covenant as the Creator comes to dwell with the creature and within the created structures of the world. By so doing the divine will is creatively revealed and constructively operative within the deep structures of the contingent order. The consequence of this divine redemptive activity is that the created order is set upon an entirely new basis and oriented toward an entirely new goal. This is "a new order that comes from without and is planted within."[31] The concrete establishment of this new order takes us to our final point in this section.

Restoration and New Creation in Christ

The new order is "the order of redemption." It is the confrontation, reorientation and transformation of the powers of the world by the power of God in Christ and the Spirit. This order is not simply the reestablishment or propping up of the original order of creation, rather it "reaches back to the original order of creation and far transcends it. Order in the new creation is to be regarded as a third dimension."[32] The recapitulation and transcendence of the original order of creation is focused upon the ministry of Jesus Christ, for through his life and ministry the structures of the world have been re-ordered and the relations necessary to it redeemed. This is why the focus of the redeemed order is upon the person and work of the Son. It is the Son who reveals and reconciles the relations that give the created order its shape and dynamic, even as the Father grounds and sustains these relations in his love and the Spirit orients and perfects them based upon the work of the Son in congruence with the will of the Father. Christ's ministry of revelation and reconciliation is focused upon three events that highlight the nature and purpose of God's redemptive power and are congruent with his eternal being-in-communion:[33]

---

31. Ibid.

32. Ibid., 15. This same expression is used in Torrance, *Divine and Contingent Order*, 114, where it is referred to as a "fuller dimension."

33. The exercising of God's redemptive power is no different from the creative power exercised in the creation of the world. As pointed out in chapter 1, the power

The Incarnation and the Power of Identification

The incarnation signals the entry of the Creator into the world of the creature, where the divine Logos *through whom* God created the world, *from whom* it received its order, and *in whom* its structures hold together, enters the fallen order of the world to redeem, reorient, and reorder it. For Torrance the purpose of the incarnation was "to penetrate into the innermost center of our contingent existence, in its finite, fragile, and disrupted condition, in order to deliver it from the evil to which it had become subjected, healing and re-ordering it from its ontological roots and entirely renewing its relation to the Creator."[34]

Torrance envisions here a great deal of continuity between the created order and the redeemed order. He is not willing to divorce the two, but neither is he willing simply to say that the redeemed order is an enhanced version of the created order. In the incarnation something unprecedented has taken place, "God has made himself present within his creation in an entirely new way,"[35] and this has forever altered the contingent world in which we live. The created order is enabled to be itself through the redemptive activity of Christ in a way that would not have been possible were it left to itself. For Torrance "the incarnation is to be interpreted as the alliance of the Creator with his creation in actualization of his will to make himself responsible for its preservation and salvation."[36]

For this reason Torrance can claim that "the whole universe pivots upon Jesus Christ,"[37] and that creation must be thought of "as proleptically conditioned by redemption."[38] Indeed, the incarnation and the sequence of events that follow it, must be thought of as "completing the work of creation" while revealing and initiating "a fuller dimension of order than might have been possible otherwise."[39] It is a "new creation

---

of God is conditioned by the personhood of God as triune—a communion of three persons in love and freedom. God's power in creation and redemption works in the same way to create and redeem a created order that is meant to be a temporal reflection of his divine being as triune.

34. Torrance, *Divine and Contingent Order*, 134.
35. Ibid.
36. Ibid., 135.
37. Torrance, *School of Faith*, ciii.
38. Torrance, *Trinitarian Faith*, 102.
39. Torrance, *Divine and Contingent Order*, 114.

out of the old order."⁴⁰ Torrance elsewhere refers to this "fuller dimension" as a "third dimension" where "a divinely provided fulfillment of the divine Law" brings about a new creation.⁴¹

This new creation is grounded in the hypostatic union between Christ's divine and human natures, where the divine and human are indivisibly united in the single person of Christ "through whom the created order is preserved and secured in such a way that it can no more disintegrate and disappear than the incarnation, passion, and resurrection of Jesus Christ can be undone."⁴² The contingent being, intelligibility, stability, and freedom of the created order are focused upon the person and work of Christ. For this reason he becomes the pivot of the whole universe, the tuning fork by which and to whom the universe is tuned.

The Resurrection and the Power of Love and Grace

For Torrance the incarnation, crucifixion, and resurrection of Christ binds the created and redeemed orders completely together under one covenant of grace "in such a way that they gather up all the past and proleptically include the consummation of all things at the end."⁴³

The resurrection and incarnation are not to be understood as "direct act[s] of sheer almighty power" but rather movements of "God's holy love into the heart of the world's evil and agony."⁴⁴ Based upon this understanding of God's power as revealed in Christ, Torrance makes an important differentiation between "the agents and embodiments of evil in the world" and "the innermost center of evil power." We cite him in full:

> It is not God's purpose to shatter and annihilate the agents and embodiments of evil in the world, but rather to pierce into the innermost center of evil power where it is entrenched in the piled-up and self-compounding guilt of humanity in order to

---

40. Torrance, *Space, Time and Resurrection*, 78.

41. Torrance, *Conflict and Agreement in the Church*, 2:15. For a discussion of many facets of Torrance's work, see the excellent treatment provided by Roland Spjuth in *Creation, Contingency and Divine Presence*. The interrelation between redemption and creation in Torrance's thought is treated on pages 68–93.

42. Torrance, *Divine and Contingent Order*, 135.

43. Torrance, *Space, Time and Resurrection*, 58.

44. Torrance, *Divine and Contingent Order*, 136.

> vanquish it from within and below, by depriving it of the lying structures of half-truth on which it thrives and of the twisted forms of legality behind which it embattles itself and from which it fraudulently gains its power. Here we have an entirely different kind and quality of power ... the power which the Bible calls *grace*.[45]

Torrance shows himself to be acutely sensitive to the frailty and goodness of the created order in all its various forms and agencies. Such sensitivity is important to note, as Torrance's Christocentricity, realist epistemology, and emphasis upon theology as a science have led many to criticize his work as downplaying plurality, diversity, and the goodness of human agency.[46] And yet, it is Torrance's Christocentricity that is here the source of this sensitivity, as God's means of eradicating and vanquishing evil takes place without destroying the contingent agents and forms it embodies itself in. This is the power of the incarnation and resurrection and the scope of God's affirmation of the goodness of his creation in all its multi-variability, fragility, and diversity. Upon a single ground in Christ the created order is redeemed and freed to flourish. Unity of origin and goal is not exclusive of plurality in expression and fulfillment.

Perhaps this is due to the fact that Torrance does not understand Christ's work to be the imposition of order *from without* but rather the penetration of the created structures of the world that enables their transformation *from within*. This is the "third dimension" Torrance describes and it is this dimension that makes the redeemed order discontinuous with the created order, even while being the fulfillment of it. Once again, all hinges upon the Person and work of the Mediator and the hypostatic union of the two natures in him: "While it is irreducibly the work of God in his saving penetration into the ontological depths of human being, it is nevertheless the work of God *as man*, translated into and rising out of human being as genuinely the work of man."[47]

---

45. Ibid., 136.

46. This is a common stereotype of Barth's work, and in particular of his doctrine of creation. However, it is also a mistaken one—and no less mistaken when applied to the thought of Torrance. See Mangina, "Mediating Theologies."

47. Torrance, *Divine and Contingent Order*, 137.

This hypostatic union enables Torrance to pass divine judgment upon the evil and disorder of the world while celebrating its frailty, particularity, and goodness for the purposes and glory of the Creator.

The redemption of space and time through the hypostatic constitution of the Mediator carries with it three significant points:[48]

- It reinforces the unique place of humanity in the universe.
- It signifies that physical and material reality fall within the range of the divine purpose.
- It means that the ontological relation between the contingent universe and the Creator is securely anchored in God himself.

These three points will become increasingly important as we move forward in our project for all three sustain and guide human cultural activity in the world. Human persons as mediators of order and priests of creation will be the theme of chapter 4. For now we conclude with some final thoughts from Torrance on the ultimate significance of the resurrection: "the resurrection means *the redemption of space and time,* for space and time are not abrogated or transcended. Rather, they are healed and restored, just as our being is healed and restored through the resurrection."[49]

The healing and restoration of space and time secured in Christ are carried forward by the work of the Holy Spirit in the midst of the world through the mission of the Church. However, one final aspect of Christ's ministry must be noted in order to make this transition from the redeemed order to an eschatological one. It is the ascension of Christ to his present role as Priest and King and his sending of the Spirit into the world.

The Ascension and the Power of Pentecost

The ascension of Christ is an important theme in Torrance's thought. It plays a central role in his understanding of the identity and mission of the Church in the world as the Church is empowered by the Holy Spirit.[50] The ascension is also fundamental to the establishment of Christ

---

48. See ibid., 138–40.
49. Torrance, *Space, Time and Resurrection,* 90; italics original.
50. See in particular ibid., 106–59; and Torrance, *Kingdom and Church.*

in his High Priestly office, a role central to Torrance's Christology and Ecclesiology.[51] Through the Holy Spirit God's power is operative from within the conditions and structures of the created order (through the Church) just as it was through the incarnate Son (through his vicarious humanity). For Torrance "Pentecost means that God's own eternal and supernatural life overflowed upon the Church, and that God himself, in his own divine being and power, was present in its midst."[52]

In fact, for Torrance the ascension is not meant to draw our attention away from the historical Jesus or the created structures of the world to the ascended Christ but rather the opposite. The ascension and "disappearance" of the glorified Christ is meant to focus our attention all the more upon the historical Jesus as the place in space and time where God and humanity may meet and where God is normatively active in the world.[53]

This is because Torrance understands the ascension to be correlated to the incarnation "as the *anabasis* (ascent) of the Son of God corresponding to his *katabasis* (descent)."[54] Consequently, it is not an event that can be isolated from the incarnation, crucifixion, or resurrection. Rather, it is continuous with them as the penultimate episode in the single *parousia* of Christ.[55] For Torrance "the ascension of Christ in this sense is his exaltation to power and glory but *through the Cross*, certainly an exaltation from humiliation to royal majesty, but through crucifixion and sacrifice, for the power and glory of the Royal Priest are bound up with his self-offering in death and resurrection."[56]

Understanding the *parousia* of Christ as a single reality with four movements, (descent in the incarnation, ascent in the *parousia*, descent in judgment and glory, ascent as consummating King), forces the church

---

51. See Torrance *Mediation of Christ*; and Torrance, *Royal Priesthood*.

52. Torrance, "The Mission of the Church," 132. The power of Pentecost is the distinctive power of the triune God and not any other. The paradigmatic display of that power is in the person and work of Christ.

53. Torrance, *Space, Time and Resurrection*, 129–34.

54. Ibid., 123; italics original.

55. "It is plain that *the Parousia*, whatever it may signify in its eternal dimension, is not to be understood in separation from the Incarnation and from Calvary. It is not discontinuous with the latter but is their consummation." Ibid., 145; italics original. Torrance's view here echoes his view of the relation between creation and redemption, law and gospel.

56. Ibid., 111; italics original.

to recognize the non-triumphalist nature of Christ's identification with us and the corresponding nature of her work in the world as a witness to Christ. The power of the Spirit is exercised in congruence with the nature and witness of Christ and so the witness of the church in the world will take a similar form. Revelation and reconciliation entail suffering and sacrifice. The power of Pentecost forms a people for witness and the witness of this people, if it is to be a witness to Christ, will take the form of Christ's witness and thus a witness characterized by humiliation and abasement as well as glorification: "All contact with the majesty of God as of the glorified Lord is in and through the crucified One."[57]

At this point however we tread a bit too far into the subject of our next section. Let us note briefly some of the more salient features of Torrance's understanding of the ascension.

- Jesus Christ has ascended from humanity's place to God's place, and yet he is in himself the one place in our human and created reality, and therefore, in the immanent order of time and space, where God and humanity fully meet.

For Torrance, this has two implications: First, the ascension *reveals a gap* between the time of the new man and the time of the old man, the gap between the resurrection reality of our humanity in Jesus Christ and the corruptible existence which we still wear, and in which we are fully implicated. Second, the ascension is "*the exaltation of the new man*, with his full and truly human nature, and therefore of man with his 'place' as man, with the 'room' which he is given for his human life, to his participation in the divine 'place.'"[58] Torrance notes that "the exaltation of human nature into the life of God does not mean the disappearance of man or the swallowing up of human and creaturely being in the infinite ocean of the divine Being, but rather that human nature, remaining creaturely and human, is yet exalted in Christ to share in God's life and glory."[59]

The ascension thus signals an important and abiding role for human life, for what Christ has assumed he has not only healed but also exalted. In that exaltation, God through Christ has conferred upon creaturely life a doxological function, for now creaturely life has been

57. Ibid., 134.
58. Ibid., 133.
59. Ibid., 135.

bound to the life and witness of Christ in such a way that its true *telos* is only realizable in him.

- By his ascension Jesus Christ establishes man in man's place in space and time.

The "disappearance" of the glorified Christ in the ascension is an affirmation of and witness to the historical Jesus as "the covenanted place on earth and in time which God has appointed for meeting between man and himself."[60] Consequently, "the ascension is the opposite of all demythologizing" for it affirms concretely that God may be encountered and obeyed within the created structures of the world. For Torrance, the ascension of Christ is as much an affirmation of the reality, goodness, and redemption of the created order as the incarnation, for "the ascension means that we cannot know God by transcending space and time, by leaping beyond the limits of our place on earth, but only by encountering God and his saving work within space and time, within our actual physical existence."[61]

Consequently, Torrance affirms the uniqueness and normativity of the historical Jesus Christ as *the* meeting point between God and humanity, as well as the adequacy of physical reality and human culture in the mediation and embodiment of this relationship.

These two affirmations coalesce in "the establishment of a Church in history, within space and time on the historical foundation of the Apostles and Prophets. The ascension finalizes the grounding of the Church on the historical Jesus Christ, and its confirmation on that foundation through the Baptism of the Spirit at Pentecost."[62] Through the withdrawal of Jesus in the ascension and the sending of the Spirit at Pentecost the meeting point between God and humanity in Christ is placed within the sphere of the Church and the Church is founded as an institution which bears witness to the historical Jesus through the particularity of its communal life.

We have touched upon Torrance's understanding of the ascension as an event that validates the goodness and integrity of the created order as an instrument for the worship of God and the context for our relation to God: God both meets humanity in the created world ("man's place")

60. Ibid., 133.
61. Ibid., 134.
62. Ibid., 136.

and exalts the created world by drawing it up into himself through the ascension of Christ ("God's place"). Through the gift of the Spirit, God's place and man's place are brought together in the formation of the Church as a reality that shares in both the already and the not yet of the Kingdom of God. This leads us to our third point, noted briefly above:

- The ascension *reveals a gap* between the time of the new man and the time of the old man, the gap between the resurrection reality of our humanity in Jesus Christ and the corruptible existence that we still wear and in which we are fully implicated.[63]

This gap is what Torrance refers to as an "eschatological pause"[64] and it is within this pause where the life and mission of the Church, empowered by the Spirit, is carried out. This eschatological pause is the space between the first and second advents of Christ but is a part of the single *parousia* of Christ where the church exists under "the two conditions of the Kingdom." This leads us to a consideration of the final aspect of Torrance's concept of order: order as a teleological concept, or the eschatological order.

Order as an Eschatological Concept: The Orientation and Sanctification of Order in God the Spirit

We open this section with a citation from Torrance's most recent work *The Christian Doctrine of God*: "Far from suppressing, crushing or extinguishing the frail forms of contingent rationality with which we are endowed as human beings created after the image of God, the presence of the Holy Spirit empowers, integrates and establishes them while overcoming the alienating deficiencies and contradictions which we have introduced into them, so that they may be made to realize their *true end* in the Love and Wisdom of God the Father, the Maker of heaven and earth and of all things invisible and visible."[65]

More need not be said to demonstrate the validity of our heading for this section. For Torrance the work of the Spirit has to do with the perfecting of the created order so that it may realize its true end in the love and wisdom of God. That is what eschatology is all about—the

---

63. Ibid., 132–33; italics mine.
64. Ibid., 145.
65. Torrance, *Christian Doctrine of God*, 220; italics mine.

realization of that true end, or what Torrance has elsewhere referred to as "the order that ought to be." As such there is a teleological drive and focus to the work of the Spirit through the Church. The eschatological order is not yet the "order that ought to be" but rather is the overlapping of that order with the fallen and redeemed order. The "order that ought to be" is realized and experienced in a provisional manner in the eschatological order, but will not be finally revealed until the second advent of Christ— the *Eschatos*. Though fallen, the created order has been redeemed through the work of Christ and with the gift of the Holy Spirit and the formation of the Church an "eschatological pause" is inserted into the very structure of the created order so that its completion and perfection, though foreshadowed in the present, will have to await the future. As Colin Gunton notes: "Creation is a project. As created, it is perfect, because it is God's project: what he purposes for that which is not God but creation, and therefore intrinsically finite and temporal. But it is not perfect in the sense that it is complete. It has somewhere to go."[66]

That the created order "has somewhere to go" means that the redeemed order has introduced an eschatological order or tension and that this eschatological order, based as it is upon the work of the incarnate and ascended Christ, has everything to do with the present "ambiguous order" of our created world as simultaneously fallen, redeemed, and destined for perfection. Torrance will have nothing to do with an eschatology that is "other-worldly."

We noted earlier that an attempt would be made to point out how the created order moves through the various "stages" it does: created, fallen, redeemed, and eschatological. We have seen that there is a great deal of continuity and discontinuity between the stages, much of this having to do with the character of the agents involved, while the inner-logic of Torrance's concept of order remains intact. The *redeemed order* was dominated by the agency of Christ: his incarnate nature and redemptive work. The *fallen order* was dominated by the agency of human persons: their social nature and contingent relation to God as being the locus for the parasitic work of evil and disorder. With the *eschatological order* we are confronted with two agents: the agency of the Spirit and the agency of the Church. Perhaps this would be better described as the agency of the Spirit though the Church, however, while the Spirit is

---

66. Gunton, *Triune Creator*, 202.

to be closely identified with the Church we do not want to equate the Spirit with the Church, so some distinction is appropriate.[67] As we approach the idea of order as a cultural project in chapter 4, we will again focus upon the agency of human persons, but only within this broader picture of order as created, fallen, redeemed, and eschatological.

For Torrance the eschatological order is characterized by the following characteristics:

- The absence of Christ in body, but his presence through the work of *the Holy Spirit* which establishes an *eschatological relation* between Creator and creature and in particular with Christ as the *Protos* and the *Eschatos*.[68]
- The nature, identity, and mission of *the Church* in the world as the "social coefficient of the knowledge of God" and the "earthly-historical form of Christ's body."
- The already-but-not-yet nature of *the Kingdom of God,* and its embodiment in the ambiguous and overlapping "time-forms" of this world. The *eschatological relation* established by the Spirit introduces an *eschatological tension* in the created order.
- *The sacraments* as concrete symbols of our present participation in the life of the ascended and glorified Christ and his continuing high priestly ministry on our behalf.[69]
- *The New Heavens and the New Earth* as the consummation of history and the unveiling of Christ's completed work.

Each of these characteristics fit together to form a coherent "eschatological logic" in Torrance's thought, a logic that revolves around the nature and mission of the Church.[70] It is the eschatological logic that we are

---

67. Torrance, *Conflict and Agreement in the Church*, 2:17.

68. Torrance, *Space, Time and Resurrection,* 151.

69. Many of Torrance's treatments of the sacraments discuss them only in relation to eschatology. See in particular "Eschatology and the Eucharist," in Torrance, *Conflict and Agreement in the Church*, vol. 2.

70. Torrance's predominant images for understanding the nature and mission of the Church are a communion of the Spirit, a community of the New Covenant, the Kingdom of Christ and the one body of Christ. All these images are based upon the work of the Spirit who enables the *participation* of the Church in Christ, for it is only through union with Christ that these things may be said of the Church. See Torrance, "Mission of the Church." A recent work developing the themes of union and participation as central to Torrance's theological vision is Lee, *Living in Union with Christ*.

primarily interested in at this point, and not so much the development of Torrance's thought on each aspect of it. Consequently, 1) an attempt will be made to highlight this logic by adding brief statements at the end of each heading considered below and, 2) our treatments of each heading will be necessarily brief, as Torrance has produced a wealth of material on each of these themes. Where appropriate we will refer the reader to these sources, as well as to those who have interacted with Torrance on these subjects.

We begin with the Holy Spirit, since the eschatological order and its inner-logic revolves around the Person and consummating work of the Spirit as the Spirit of Christ.

A Pneumatological Order: The Participatory and Sanctifying Work of the Spirit

The Eschaton as Based upon a Relation with the Eschatos

For Torrance, the eschatological order is based upon a relation with Christ the *Eschatos*, and this relation is established and maintained by the Holy Spirit on the basis of Christ's Person and work. This relation is of a two-fold nature:

- It is "*a relation here and now between the old and the new*, as through the Spirit we partake already of the new creation in the risen Christ."

- It is "*a relation between the present (including the past) and the future*, as through the Spirit we are united to the ascended Christ who is still to come again."[71]

The Spirit establishes and maintains this eschatological relation to Christ in the following three spheres, and through these relations these different aspects of reality are made to participate in the redemptive purpose of God revealed and sealed in Christ.

---

71. Both citations from Torrance, *Space, Time and Resurrection*, 152; italics and parentheses original.

The Cosmic Sphere

In this sphere the cosmos participates in the work of Christ due to his assumption of fallen humanity and with that assumption the entire created order along with it. As Torrance notes: "when he became incarnate, and divine and human natures were united in his one Person, his humanity was brought into an ontological relation with all creation."[72] Consequently, "the resurrection of Christ in *body* becomes the pledge that the whole physical universe will be renewed."[73] One might understand this as participation *in* Christ through the incarnation *of* Christ and the role of the Spirit in maintaining this relation as *providential*.

The Corporate Sphere

In this sphere the relation to Christ is determined by the *koinonia* of the Spirit, where this *koinonia* stands as the basis for the formation of the Church as the Body of Christ.

The Individual Sphere

In this sphere the relation to Christ is determined by the indwelling of the Spirit as we are united to Christ as individual believers in a corporate body.

THE ESCHATON AS THE SPHERE OF THE SPIRIT'S SANCTIFYING WORK

This sanctifying work of the Spirit is carried out in all three of the spheres mentioned above. In each sphere "the special work of the Holy Spirit is to be discerned in that he brings the life-giving power of God to bear upon the creature in such a way that through his immediate presence to the creature and in spite of its creaturely difference from God he sustains it in its being and brings its relation to the Creator to its true end in him. This is what St Basil called 'the perfecting cause' of the Spirit, or the *sovereign freedom of the Spirit*."[74]

---

72. Ibid., 154.
73. Ibid., 155; italics original.
74. Torrance, *Christian Doctrine of God*, 218.

Colin Gunton provides a more concise description of this aspect of the Spirit's perfecting work: "The Spirit is God present to the world at particular times and places, giving to it the liberty to move into the future prepared for it."[75] This is quite congruent with understanding the work of the Spirit to consist in the freedom of the Spirit since the work of the Spirit is to confer upon the created order the freedom to be what it is in Christ. This is an eschatological work and this is essentially what sanctification and perfection in the Spirit are all about.

An Ecclesiological Order: Through the Agency and Mission of the Church[76]

However, this work of the Spirit does not take place in a vacuum. Just as the Father works through his two hands (the Son and the Spirit) so too the Spirit works through the Church as the Body of Christ in conferring freedom upon the created order to be what it is in Christ and by so doing, serving as an agent in the sanctification and transformation of the world *in each of the spheres mentioned above*. This is the mission of the Church in the world. For Torrance "it is through union and communion with Him actualized in the Spirit that the Church is quickened into life as His living body on earth and is empowered in its apostolic mission to be His representative among men."[77]

The Church as the body of Christ is thrust forward in its work and mission as an agent in the mediation of order by an eschatological impulse and goal. As the earthly-historical form of Christ in the world and as the body of not only the crucified and risen Christ but also the ascended and advent Christ, the Church, through union with him, "is necessarily thrust urgently forward through history to meet its coming Lord."[78] The Spirit is the one who unites the Church to its ascended and coming Lord and as such provides the impetus and guidance for its mission in the world.

This emphasis is present in the following description of the Church by Torrance: "It is through this earthly historical Church that the Lamb of God gains a purchase upon history and exerts His redeeming power

75. Gunton, "Triune God and the Freedom of the Creature," 64.
76. See Torrance, *Royal Priesthood*, 23–42 for further development of this theme.
77. Torrance, "Mission of the Church," 130.
78. Torrance, *Space, Time and Resurrection*, 156.

among the nations ... the Church is the body of Christ, the *instrument and medium* on earth through which God Almighty is at work. It is around this Church, transfixed by the infinite axis of the Love of God, that the whole of history now revolves."[79] The Church is eschatologically oriented but concretely, and culturally, engaged.

The instrumentality of the Church and its mediatorial function will feature in our development of Torrance's anthropology and his understanding of human persons as "priests of creation" and "mediators of order." This will concern us at length in chapter 4, but leads nicely into our next point.

An Ambiguous Order: Relating Actual Order to the Order that Ought to Be

In each of the spheres mentioned above the primary work of the Church in mission is relating the actual order of the fallen world to the "order that ought to be" as it has been revealed and redeemed by Christ. The eschatological order in which the work of the church is carried out is an ambiguous one for two reasons: First, as an eschatological order the created order is characterized by an overlap of "two ages." Second, the freedom of the Church in this eschatological order creates its own ambiguity, since the Church "lives and fulfills its mission within the ambiguities of history, society, politics, world events, etc."[80] Consequently, the Church by necessity takes upon itself the ambiguity of the world in which it is formed and to which it is called in mission. It is "a mixed body, with good and evil, true and false, wheat and tares in its midst."[81] As such "the Church lives and works under judgment as well as grace, so that it may constantly put off the 'image of the old man' that passes away and put on the 'image of the new man' who is renewed in the likeness of Christ."[82]

Torrance's comments regarding the ambiguity of the present order of the world and the participation of the Church in that ambiguity lead

---

79. Torrance, *Apocalypse Today*, 22; italics mine.
80. Torrance, *Space, Time and Resurrection*, 156.
81. Ibid.
82. Ibid. This same imagery is repeated on the next page in reference to "the individual aspect of eschatology." The "putting off of the old man" and the "putting on of the new man" are activities that are done on an individual and corporate level.

him to make a disturbing comparison between "the nomistic structures and patterns of creaturely and historical being"[83] and "the scaffolding of a building ... which is cast away when the building stands complete."[84] This is particularly troubling for our project, concerned as it is with placing Torrance's trinitarian thought at the basis of a theology of culture! Is Torrance saying that the powers that enable and form our social life and personal identities, both in the Church and without, will be cast away when the "new creation" is unveiled at Christ's second advent? This would appear to be the obvious conclusion, but even Torrance's critics are not willing to make such a bold charge.[85] They do, however, wonder aloud whether at this point a fragment of dualism might still be present in Torrance's thought.[86]

For Roland Spjuth and John D. Morrison[87] the source of the problem lies in Torrance's emphasis upon the immediacy of our communion with the humanity of Christ through the Spirit.[88] For Spjuth this emphasis has the effect of rendering the social and historical institutions that mediate that communion as insignificant in the eternal scheme of things.[89] For further evidence pointing to a dualism that renders the contingent order practically useful but inherently insignificant, he cites Torrance as noting that in worship "we are lifted up above our peculiarities and cultural and national divisions."[90] Spjuth makes the following conclusion: "When Torrance speaks about a vertical spiritual communion that is direct and which lifts us up above the level of particularities and cultures, it seems that he rather unproblematically asserts a direct relationship with God that can be distinguished from the plurality of

---

83. Essentially a description of the powers we have developed above.

84. Torrance, *Space, Time and Resurrection*, 137.

85. See in particular Spjuth, *Creation, Contingency and Divine Presence*; and Morrison, *Knowledge of the Self-Revealing God*.

86. Spjuth, *Creation, Contingency and Divine Presence*, 161–65.

87. Morrison, *Knowledge of the Self-Revealing God*, chapter 7. See in particular pages 316–20.

88. The emphasis in Torrance's thought that is suspect is discussed in Richardson, "Revelation, Scripture, and Mystical Apprehension of Divine Knowledge." Torrance's response to Richardson may be found on pages 324–29.

89. Spjuth, *Creation, Contingency and Divine Presence*, 161.

90. Ibid., 161. Quoted from Torrance, "Relevance of Orthodoxy," in *Relevance of Orthodoxy*, 13.

institutional and communal mediation."[91] Spjuth not only asserts that Torrance makes a distinction between the horizontal and the vertical, but concludes that this distinction also results in a prioritization of the vertical over the horizontal: "[For Torrance] the purpose of the historical plane is very much defined as that which makes the vertical relation possible, but with this move Torrance also makes the historical relation secondary to the immediate and vertical relationship that it serves."[92]

Spjuth's critique, as well as those of John Morrison and Ray S. Anderson, has pointed out a weakness in Torrance's thought that revolves around the relationship between the horizontal and vertical aspects of our communion with God. Is the horizontal plane merely "scaffolding"? Is it to be transcended? Will it be left behind at the second advent of Christ with no purpose to serve once our communion is grounded in sight as opposed to faith?

At this point we can only offer a provisional "No" as our response, and that for reasons we cannot develop as yet. And even if Torrance does prioritize the vertical over the horizontal, as Spjuth asserts, he certainly does not do so "unproblematically." Our rejoinder to Torrance's critics on this point will require us to develop other aspects of his thought a bit more thoroughly before providing a detailed critique. Suffice it to say at this point that what we perceive Torrance as doing is relativizing the historical plane to the vertical relationship and by so doing placing the horizontal plane in a relationship where it may serve the purpose for which it exists and by so doing arrive at its true *telos*. To distinguish between the historical and vertical relation is neither to separate the one from the other nor to prioritize one over the other but to seek a proper parity and complementarity between them with the goal of placing them in proper relation to one another and by so doing to bring the created order with all its particularities under the Lordship of Christ. This is the mission of the Church in the ambiguous order of the world and these are the implications of the contingent relation between God and that world. Torrance's purpose for construing the relationship between vertical and horizontal in this way is properly to orient and direct the horizontal plane toward its *telos*. This is the best way to affirm its reality and inherent significance—by placing it firmly within the purpose and design of God. Without this teleological dimension, or the ability

91. Spjuth, *Creation, Contingency and Divine Presence*, 161.
92. Ibid., 162.

to point to a *distinction* between the vertical and horizontal planes, we would have no way to interact critically with the created order nor to sanctify it by relating the actual order of the world to the "order that ought to be" under the empowerment of the Holy Spirit.[93] Just because the horizontal plane is relativized in relation to the vertical does not mean it has no role or place in the eternal purpose of God. Spjuth correctly notes that for Torrance "the Chalcedonian Pattern must govern our understanding of the relationship between God and humanity." Consequently, "'all of grace' does not mean 'nothing of man,' but the very reverse, the restoration of full and authentic human being."[94] We would assert that the same dynamic pattern applies here: allowing the vertical relation to orient, condition, and guide the horizontal towards its true end does not mean the insignificance of the horizontal, but the restoration and affirmation of it. This seems to have been Torrance's thrust from the beginning:

> In that presence of the new time [of the Kingdom] all the historical time-forms of the Church are relativized and given new orientation—they are taken under the command of the risen and ascended Lord, are made obedient to his real presence, so that instead of being mere limitations to the Church's life and ministry they are the signs pointing beyond to the reality of the new time of the new creation. In so doing they are themselves transcended and made subordinate to communion with Christ in the time of his new humanity.[95]

The significance of the time-forms of the Church is rooted in their ability to draw attention to themselves in order to refer beyond themselves. They are what Torrance has elsewhere referred to as aspects of the Spirit's "translucent witness." Their translucency depends wholly upon

---

93. Many arguments that seek to provide a theological response to ecological issues either dissolve God into the world by making the created order sacred, or propose that human involvement in the world be reduced to an absolute minimum, as the created order does not need our help to praise its creator. Both solutions fail theologically, practically, and existentially. The *character* of human mediation, not the absence of it, is central. Torrance provides a firm footing for a more creative solution. See also Rae, "To Render Praise: Humanity in God's World."

94. Torrance cited in Spjuth, *Creation, Contingency and Divine Presence*, 130. The citation is from Torrance, *Mediation of Christ*, 105. See also Torrance's development of the couplet *anhypostasis* and *enhypostasis* in Torrance, *Conflict and Agreement in the Church*, 1:243; and Torrance, *Karl Barth: Biblical and Evangelical Theologian*, 199–201.

95. Torrance, *Conflict and Agreement in the Church*, 2:27.

their adequacy in referring beyond themselves while nevertheless retaining their particularity. Simply because something in its particularity is designed to refer beyond itself does not mean that it is insignificant, but that it's significance is grounded in its translucency or its ability to fulfill its created purpose or *telos*.

A Sacramental Order: A Doxological Response to the Lord of Space and Time

Just as the Church spans the two ages that characterize the eschatological order so do the sacraments. In addition, as the sacraments are concerned with the nature of God's presence in the world it is only appropriate that they be treated in a theology of culture for they bring one "directly into the center of an analysis of God's presence in creation."[96] This is an issue touched upon in our previous discussion but whose full analysis will have to be delayed for a later time. Needless to say, here again we approach an issue that has a long tradition in formulating the precise nature of the relationship between the vertical sphere and the horizontal.

A Heavenly and Earthly Order: In Anticipation of His Final Act

Torrance does not develop this particular aspect of his thought much beyond mention of it, and the assertion that there will not be the radical discontinuity between heaven and earth as some might imagine. In keeping with his views on the relation between creation and redemption, as well as law and gospel, Torrance sees the new heaven and the new earth as the final unveiling of Christ's completed work. It will not be the replacement of the old with the new but the revelation of the new that is presently bursting the wineskins of the old. As Torrance himself notes: "The whole of creation falls within the range of his Lordship, as he works out his purpose by bringing redemption together with creation, and actualizing the holy will of the Father in everything. Eschatology

---

96. Spjuth, *Creation, Contingency and Divine Presence*, 123. Spjuth provides an excellent treatment of Torrance's thought on the sacraments. See also Hunsinger, "Dimension of Depth."

has here a teleological relation to the whole realm of created existence, and leads into the doctrine of 'the new heaven and the new earth.'"[97]

Miroslav Volf stresses the continuity even further, noting that "the eschatological consummation is not simply about the creation of a new future. It is rather about the future of yesterday, today, and tomorrow, about the future of all lived times."[98]

Our present reality will not be set aside for the sake of creating another *ex nihilo*, rather it will be transformed under "the Lord of space and time." In closing, we remind ourselves again of the words of Colin Gunton: "Creation is a project. As created, it is perfect, because it is God's project: what he purposes for that which is not God but creation, and therefore intrinsically finite and temporal. But it is not perfect in the sense that it is complete. It has somewhere to go."[99]

This leads us nicely into the next section of our project dealing with human persons as mediators of order and priests of creation. It is through their agency based upon the work of Christ, the will of God, and the empowerment of the Holy Spirit that the created and redeemed order continues on its way to its final destination, a destination that is realized partially in the present and fully upon the second advent of Christ. Human persons as stewards have a unique role to play in the redemption and perfection of the created order.

Consequently, if human persons are to be understood as mediators of order then it is appropriate to understand order as a cultural project as it flows from the hands of human persons in their response to God and their ordering activity in the world. Human persons as stewards are involved in what Torrance refers to as "the creative re-ordering of existence" under the guidance and empowerment of God. This by its very nature is a socio-cultural activity.

In chapters 4 and 5 we will deal specifically with the idea that order is a cultural as well as a multi-leveled concept in addition to being a theological, relational, and teleological one. For this reason we will continue to view human persons and their cultural activity as bounded by and understood within Torrance's conception of order just described. This means that the work of humanity as stewards of the created order is to serve an integrative role in the created order. Indeed, Torrance sees

97. Torrance, *Space, Time and Resurrection*, 155.
98. Volf, "Final Reconciliation," 101.
99. Gunton, *Triune Creator*, 202.

the roles of steward and scientist to be roughly equivalent, so that we may gather what he understands the role of human stewards to be from his understanding of the role of the scientist.

The role of the scientist is to allow the mute creation to bring forth the praises of the Creator by integrating the various forms of order in the world and directing them toward his praise, allowing them to refer beyond themselves to their origin and end. Human persons as scientists accomplish this task through the development of cultural tools. Through these tools the various levels of the created order may be coordinated into an integrated whole. This will require a multitude of cultural constructs. The only restraint upon these constructs is that they be congruent with the fundamental order of the world as well as the nature and purpose for which that world was brought into being. Torrance has noted that the unique character of the world (its contingency) makes it possible for multiple interpretations of its nature and purpose. The creative ambiguity implied in contingency leaves room for diversity in relating the multi-leveled world, but also acknowledges that there is an interpretive standard that our cultural constructs are meant to approximate. For these reasons it is sensible to assume that Torrance's thought is not obsessed with uniformity and homogeneity over plurality and diversity as long as that plurality has an accurate transcendent reference in the nature, purposes, and character of the triune God.

4

Torrance's Doctrine of Humanity
Priests of Creation, Mediators of Order

THIS CHAPTER SEEKS TO ACCOMPLISH TWO GOALS, THE FIRST OF WHICH is to present the salient features of Thomas F. Torrance's theological anthropology. As such, it will be descriptive in nature. Secondly, an interpretive proposal will be made upon the basis of this exposition which suggests that Torrance understands the human person as a cultural being, and that this feature of his anthropological thought may be usefully applied in order to understand more fully the goals and objectives of his theological and scientific work.

Torrance's published material in this area is small and spans a long period.[1] It consists primarily of a book,[2] two booklets, and essays in festschrifts[3] and anthologies.[4] While additional material may be gleaned

---

1. The first essay on the subject appeared as "The Word of God and the Nature of Man," and was included in a 1947 Festschrift for Karl Barth titled *Reformation Old and New*. It appears to be a condensed version of his *Calvin's Doctrine of Man*. Torrance's next writing on the subject does not appear until 1979 with the publication of his Richard Lectures under the title *Ground and Grammar of Theology*, which included as chapter 1 his acceptance speech for the 1978 Templeton Prize, titled "Man, the Priest of Creation." The remainder of Torrance's work occurred in the 1980s, with the exception of his latest booklets *The Soul and Person of the Unborn Child* and *The Being and Nature of the Unborn Child*.

2. The book is *Calvin's Doctrine of Man*, which is more a compendium of Calvin's thought on the subject than a presentation of Torrance's views. Torrance states as much in his preface to the work (7).

3. Torrance, "Goodness and Dignity of Man," and "Soul and Person, in Theological Perspective."

4. "The Word of God and the Nature of Man," in Torrance, *Theology in Reconstruction*, 99–116. This essay is essentially a compressed version of his book *Calvin's Doctrine of Man*. The other essays are "Man, The Priest of Creation," in Torrance, *Ground and Grammar*, and "Immortality and Light," in *Transformation & Convergence*.

from his writing on the person and work of Christ, this material does not add substantially to his specifically anthropological work.

This is because Torrance's creative powers were never turned fully upon the subject matter as a whole. His more focused attention upon the doctrine of creation and the dynamics of human knowing certainly contain an implicit anthropology, but his development of the topics of the *imago Dei*, human depravity, and the body/soul relation, to mention a few, lack the breadth and depth of engagement found in other more systematic treatments of this theme. However, Torrance does address, in adequate detail, many areas of a theological anthropology that will be useful to us for the purpose stated above.

In the process of accomplishing this purpose, and as a creative device, we will utilize musical imagery to illumine this particular area of Torrance's thought and how the various aspects of it cohere together.[5] Our development of Torrance's theological anthropology will take place in two stages. In part 1 we will consider the human person as a multi-stringed instrument, defined by, and sustained within, its relations to God, the created order, and fellow human beings. This will be accomplished by considering the components in Torrance's understanding of the image of God. In part 2 we will consider the human person from a Christological perspective, as an eschatological being determined by Christ and oriented toward the future. At this point we will introduce the idea that Torrance sees the human person as a cultural being that has been created in a particular way in order to fulfill a particular task, with both identity and task analogically rooted in the triune being of God.

Part 1: Humanity as a Multi-Stringed Instrument

The human person in the hands of God is an instrument, just as the created order under the agency of the human person is meant to be the same. They are objects that require the agency of another to fulfill their purpose—their created and redeemed *telos*.

---

5. Torrance uses the terms "midwife" and "instrument" at times to describe the role of humanity in relation to the created order. Though many of his discussions in this area are couched in scientific terminology, the imagery we employ here is not foreign to his thought. See Torrance, *Reality and Evangelical Theology*, 26.

However, human persons are more than simply instruments; they are a particular kind of instrument. Specifically, they are multi-stringed instruments. Stringed instruments require the resonance of more than one string in order to create their distinctive sounds. In addition, those strings, if the instrument as a whole is to function according to design, must be properly balanced and tuned to each other.

We may liken the various strings of an instrument to the three fundamental relations that sustain and define human life. These are the relations that exist between God, humanity, and the world. We will understand this cluster of relations, and the dynamic that exists between them, as a "core social paradigm"[6] and to be implied, for Torrance, in the affirmation that human beings have been created in the image of the triune God.[7]

In this chapter, string #1 will refer to the image of God as a *creaturely reflection* because human beings are *embodied beings*. String #2 will refer to the image of God as a *spiritual reflection* because human beings are *personal beings* and constituted as such through a relation to God. String #3 will refer to the image of God as a *social reflection* because human beings are created as male and female and as such are *relational/sexual beings*.

We will consider each of these relations and how they might be defined and interrelated in engagement with Torrance's work.

String #1: Humanity as Embodied Being

The majority of Torrance's reflections on matters anthropological open with a consideration of the human person as an embodied being, and

---

6. See Anderson, "Socio-Cultural Implications."

7. That human persons have been created in the image of God is the clear, if sparse, witness of Scripture. What is less clear is what this phrase refers to and how it is meant to distinguish human creatures from the remainder of the created order. We will only enter into this debate so far as to offer a view of our own based upon a reading of Torrance's published material. In short, what the image of God is, or how it is meant to function, cannot be summed up under a single capacity, function, phenomenon or relation that is uniquely human. Rather, the image of God is a reality that must be understood within the entire ecology of human personhood. Subsequently, it should be understood to refer to a cluster of relations or relational capacities that are mutually constitutive and ontologically integrated and that are unique to the human person. These relations are the "strings" that make the human person a creature in the image of God and an instrument in the hands of God.

specifically the soul/body relation.[8] Fundamentally, Torrance's understanding of the relation of body and soul flows from his distaste for dualisms of any kind[9] and his interest in grounding his doctrine of humanity in a trinitarian doctrine of God. This he does by "thinking together" the doctrines of creation, incarnation, and resurrection.[10] What follows will be a summary of this "thinking together."

For Torrance, humanity as an embodied being is, in its totality, a created and contingent being, consisting of body and soul, material and immaterial aspects. In particular, the soul, like the body, is a created reality, and whatever quality of immortality is to be ascribed to it, comes "through the grace of a relation with God who only has immortality."[11] This is a direct implication of the doctrine of *creatio ex nihilo*.

The body itself is to be understood as neither a prison nor even container for the soul but a created reality that has been declared "good" by the Creator. The assumption and redemption of the body by Christ, and the entirety of the created order with it, is the fullest affirmation of

---

8. See "Man, Mediator of Order," in Torrance, *Christian Frame of Mind*, 35–36; as well as Torrance, "Soul and Person, in Theological Perspective," 105–10; Torrance, "Goodness and Dignity," 370–71; and "Immortality and Light," in Torrance, *Transformation & Convergence*. Wolfhart Pannenberg provides an excellent discussion of this subject and points out its relevance not only for how one understands the relation of humanity to the created order but also its importance for the relation of humanity to God and to other persons. See Pannenberg, *Systematic Theology*, 2:181–202. We find many of the same points made in Jenson, *Systematic Theology*, 2:53–112. Torrance spends little time discussing this subject in *Calvin's Doctrine of Man* as compared with in his later anthropological essays, which generally begin with this very subject.

9. Torrance's work as a whole may be understood as a long-running polemic against dualisms of any kind and the destruction such dualisms introduce into our relations with God, other persons, and the created order.

10. See in particular Torrance, "Soul and Person, in Theological Perspective"; Torrance, "Man: Mediator of Order," in Torrance, *Christian Frame of Mind*; and "Immortality and Light," in Torrance, *Transformation & Convergence*. From the latter essay, 337: "The doctrine of the incarnation, together with the doctrine of creation out of nothing, implied a radical distinction between God and the creature . . . but it also had the effect of unifying the sensible and intelligible, or material and rational elements, in created realities, which changed the understanding of human nature." The thinking together of these doctrines challenged Greek notions about the separability of form and matter, and specifically the immortality of the soul, making it impossible to separate and prioritize one facet over the other. Form and matter were understood as two facets of a single rational and contingent order created out of nothing by the address of God.

11. Torrance, "Soul and Person, in Theological Perspective," 105.

human corporeality that may be sought. That this body was included in the resurrection and glorification of Jesus is the final and ultimate verdict upon its value and place in the consummation of the kingdom of God.[12]

Both the material and immaterial aspects of human being are "essentially complementary and ontologically integrated."[13] The equal value placed upon both the material and immaterial facets of human life translate into an understanding of human persons as embodied souls and ensouled bodies. Such a description recognizes that there is a distinctive integration between soul and body, where they are neither collapsed into one another, nor are they antithetical to one another. Wolfhart Pannenberg puts it well when he notes that "the soul and consciousness are deeply rooted in our corporeality."[14] This has important implications for the continuation of life after death that cannot be pursued here.[15]

This ontological integration of body and soul is grounded in the doctrines of creation, incarnation, and resurrection. In creation "God did not give being and life either to the soul by itself or to the body by itself, but to man in whom body and soul form a single living entity."[16] That Christ became this "single living entity" in the incarnation and redeemed it from corruption and disorder in the resurrection must be understood as the "affirmation and finalizing of man's creation [as a 'unitary being']."[17]

That body and soul should be related in a complementary and integrated fashion is based not only upon God's created determination of humanity but upon a continuing gracious relation to God that exists beyond the capacities of body and soul, individually or together,

---

12. That Torrance understands the soul/body relation to be central in properly understanding the relation between humanity and the world is clear in his writings, where he shows how the very idea of scientific investigation could never have arisen apart from the Hebraic understanding of this relation. See Torrance, "Man, Mediator of Order," 35–64, in Torrance, *Christian Frame of Mind*.

13. Torrance, "Soul and Person, in Theological Perspective," 105.

14. Pannenberg, *Systematic Theology*, 2:182. See also Anderson, "Spiritual Saga."

15. Torrance notes that, contra the Greek view, "a continuing personal life after death has to include the body as a basic equation of existence" (Torrance, "Soul and Person, in Theological Perspective," 105).

16. Ibid., 106.

17. Ibid., 107.

to initiate or sustain. This continuing relation is Christologically and Pneumatologically determined[18] and integrates body and soul by enabling the human person to be addressed as a unitary whole and to respond as such.

However, it seems clear from both the biblical witness and personal experience that complementarity and integration are far from what we experience as embodied souls and ensouled bodies. This is due to the reality of sin and disorder. Torrance cites George Florovsky in this regard: "In separation from God human nature becomes unsettled, goes out of tune, as it were. The very structure of man becomes unstable ... the body and the soul are no longer ... secured or adjusted to each other."[19]

This situation is objectively resolved through the incarnation and atonement, where Christ has taken upon himself the fallen status of our human nature, particularly the dissonant relation between body and soul, and created a harmonious relation between the two, to be realized partially in this life and perfectly in the consummation of the kingdom.[20]

Although this complementarity and integration have as their objective basis the work of Christ, the ongoing work of keeping these two aspects "in tune" based upon this work is a function of the Spirit. The body/soul relation is held together and integrated by a transcendent reality beyond the potencies of the soul, the body, or both of them combined. That transcendent reality is the Spirit of God. Torrance understands the Spirit of God to be "the freedom of God to be present to the creature, sustaining it in its creaturely being and realizing the relation

---

18. More detailed discussion of the role of the Spirit in relation to the human person as a body/soul duality may be found in Torrance, "Goodness and Dignity," 370–71, 382–83; and Torrance, "Soul and Person, in Theological Perspective," 110–13. Excellent discussions may also be found in the work of Ray S. Anderson: "Spiritual Saga"; and *On Being Human*, 207–14.

19. Quoted in the essay "Immortality and Light," in Torrance, *Transformation & Convergence*, 339.

20. Harmony and dissonance are not created either by exaggerating or minimizing the difference between two things, or by prioritizing one over the other, but rather by the proper proportioning and balancing of two things in relation to each other. This is accomplished through the process of "tuning" or "adapting" the relation, a process not expanded upon by either Torrance or Florovsky, but implied in their discussions.

of the creature to himself, so that the creature may reach its true end beyond itself in God."[21]

What differentiates human creatures from other creatures is that the "spirit" that "enlivens" the soul/body duality is called forth, sustained by, and identified only in relation to, the Spirit of God. The "spirit" of humanity therefore is not some third entity in the constitution of human persons but rather "a dynamic correlate to the Spirit of God."[22] This phrase, at the very least, emphasizes that human creatures are determined from beyond their natures by God, whereas other creatures are determined by their natures. Therefore, what differentiates the human from the non-human is that the human person is addressed and constituted by the Word of God as a unitary whole and enabled by that same Word to respond as such. This receiving from God and responding to God is mediated though cultural forms and structures.

To be addressed and constituted by God is to be called into some form of relation with God. This brings us to the second string or relation that we would like to discuss: human being as personal being and the image of God as referring to a spiritual reflection.

String #2: Humanity as Personal Being

To be addressed as a unitary whole and to respond as such entails both vertical and horizontal relations, the vertical relation (to the Father, through the Son and in the Spirit) grounding and orienting the horizontal relations (between other human persons and the created world) and the horizontal relations imaging and reflecting the vertical relation. These relations, and the dynamic that obtains between them, form the basis of what Torrance calls "the personal or inter-personal structure of humanity,"[23] or what we have referred to above as a "core

---

21. Torrance, "Goodness and Dignity," 370.

22. Ibid., 382. Torrance notes further that the human spirit refers "not to a third thing in man beside soul and body, but to a transcendental determination of his existence in soul and body, constituting him as a human being before God in relation to other human beings. The 'spirit' of man is . . . the ontological qualification of his soul, and indeed of his whole creaturely being, brought about and maintained by the Holy Spirit, in virtue of which he lives and moves and has his being in God, as man made in his image and likeness." Torrance, "Soul and Person, in Theological Perspective," 110.

23. See Torrance, "Soul and Person, in Theological Perspective," 109; Torrance, "Goodness and Dignity," 372; and Torrance, "Man, Mediator of Order," in Torrance,

social paradigm." In his 1989 essay "The Soul and Person, in Theological Perspective" Torrance states that "there is an inherent relatedness in human being which is a creaturely reflection of a transcendent relatedness in divine Being. This is the personal or inter-personal structure of humanity in which there is imaged the ineffable personal relations of the Holy Trinity."[24]

We will consider first the interpersonal structure as grounded in the vertical relation between God and humanity as *personal* beings. We will then consider the structure as reflected in our horizontal relations with other persons as *relational* beings, this horizontal relatedness being manifest most concretely in the form of human sexual differentiation.

The interpersonal structure of humanity has as its origin, ground, and orienting touchstone a spiritual relation established by the personal address of a triune God who has his being in communion. This interpersonal structure therefore, is a creaturely, contingent, and analogical reflection of the God who has called it into being. As such, its integrity, intelligibility, and functionality are dependent upon a *continuing relation with* and a *proper orientation towards* that same God. This continuing relation is defined and secured through the work of Christ.

The necessity of a continuing relation with, and orientation to, Christ is best captured in Torrance's understanding of Jesus as both "Personalizing Person" and "Humanizing Man."[25] With these phrases Torrance affirms that all that makes us human is contingent upon the person and work of Christ, whether the reality of Christ or the efficacy of Christ's work is acknowledged or not. However, although this continuing relation is defined and secured through the work of Christ it is also continually oriented and sustained through the work of the Spirit.

The Holy Spirit is a communion constituting Spirit who "coming from the inner communion of the Holy Trinity, creates communion between man and God."[26] The fellowship thus created is based not upon an ontological continuity between God and humanity, but upon the

---

Christian Frame of Mind, 38. This phrase plays a central role in all of Torrance's anthropological reflections. When these relations are properly tuned, the result is a "created correspondence" to the Holy Trinity.

24. Torrance, "Soul and Person, in Theological Perspective," 109–10.

25. See Torrance, *Mediation of Christ*, 67–72; and Torrance, "Goodness and Dignity," 380–81.

26. Torrance, "Soul and Person, in Theological Perspective," 112.

objective otherness of God in relation to humanity. Individuality and sociality flow from this objective otherness and are the consequence of the personalizing activity of the Spirit.

We have been speaking about the interpersonal structure of humanity and its constitution through a vertical relation to God based upon the work of Christ and the ministry of the Holy Spirit. Now we must turn to the way in which that vertical relation is reflected contingently and analogically through our horizontal relations with one another and the created world. That brings us to a consideration of the third and final string in our development of the idea that the human person is a multi-stringed instrument, namely, humanity as a relational being and the image of God as referring to a social reflection.

String #3: Humanity as Relational Being

The work of the Spirit as a "communion constituting Spirit" is more complex than simply the establishment of personal reciprocity between God and humanity, for the Spirit may also be described as the "community constituting Spirit" who in the very process of establishing our vertical relation with God constitutes and becomes the basis for our horizontal relations with one another.

Torrance points out the inter-relatedness of the vertical and horizontal spheres when he notes that "man is constituted a relational being basically through a 'vertical' relation to the Creator, but within his God-given existence as man and woman."[27] One's vertical relation with the triune God is established and sustained in the midst of horizontal human relations, specifically the community of the Church, which exists as a result of God's personalizing activity and as the "social-coefficient" of our knowledge of, and relation to, God.[28]

This is entirely congruent with the fact that the Spirit is the Spirit of the Father and of the Son and therefore, the Spirit whose being and

27. Torrance, "Goodness and Dignity," 372.

28. "Since it is God as a Communion of personal Being who communicates himself to us through Christ and in his Spirit, it is a community of persons in reciprocity both with God and with one another that is set up. In other words, the person-constituting interaction of God with us calls into being a church as the spatio-temporal correlate of his self-giving and self-revealing to mankind" (Torrance, *Reality and Evangelical Theology*, 46). Torrance's understanding of the "social coefficient of knowledge" will be developed at greater length in the next chapter.

personhood arise from the perichoretic and consubstantial relations that obtain between them. Human sociality is meant to be a "temporal correlate" to the communion that exists between the persons of the Holy Trinity and as such the medium through which the divine image is reflected within the coordinates of space and time. That the human person is created in the image of God simply means that human persons are placed within, and constituted by, a network of relationships. These relationships enable the human person and the created order, not only to exist, but to reflect the divine order in their reciprocal and complementary relationships to the glory of God and towards the fulfillment of God's will and purpose. The image of God is not an individual possession but a social reflection. Human persons as image bearers or "mirrors"[29] do not contain the image in a static sense, but reflect the image in a dynamic sense. The image therefore, is not only a creaturely reflection, nor simply a spiritual reflection, but also a social reflection. All three of these relations make up a composite mirror so to speak, that alone is suitable for humanity in the image of God to fulfill its calling and vocation as such a being.

In order to understand this social aspect of the image of God we will continue to think together the implications of the doctrines of creation, incarnation, and resurrection for this particular facet of the human person. We begin with the fact that the fundamental constitution of human life as social life is through the creation of humanity as co-humanity, or a polarity of personal being.

The interpersonal structure of humanity, which Torrance understands as fundamental to our understanding of the image of God, incorporates our relations with the created order, with God, and with other persons into a single ecology that is meant to reflect the purposes of the Creator for the created order and sustain the creatures fashioned after God's image. The structure of human sociality revolves around human sexuality, for sexuality conditions who we are as personal, social, and embodied beings. Barth said it best with these words: "This [sexual] distinction and relation is of all human distinctions . . . the decisive one . . . for only it is structural."[30]

---

29. This is imagery suggested by Calvin and developed by Torrance in *Calvin's Doctrine of Man,* 36ff. See also the discussion by Douglas John Hall in *Imaging God,* 104ff.

30. Cited in Jenson, *Systematic Theology,* 2:89.

For Torrance, human sexual differentiation is not simply an external convention, as with the rest of the created order, but also a qualification of the human person as a whole, since body and soul are integrated in an ontological and complementary way: "Sexuality ... determines the innermost being of people, making them either male or female in themselves."[31] The basic form of humanity is also characterized by this complementary otherness and ontological togetherness since humanity as such is neither male or female in isolation from one another but male and female in the form of "co-humanity."

Torrance understands "co-humanity" to refer to what he calls an "onto-personal relation," or "the kind of relation subsisting between things which is an essential constituent of their being, and without which they would not be what they are."[32] Consequently, sexuality becomes the basis for sociality and sociality becomes the context in which human individuality and uniqueness emerge. Sexuality, sociality, and individuality are complementarily related and ontologically integrated in both the constitution of humanity by God and the response of humanity to God, other persons, and the created order.

At this point we note an aspect of Torrance's anthropology that is underdeveloped. Where we might expect Torrance to draw out some of the socio-cultural implications of his anthropological and theological assumptions little is offered. Beyond assertions that human sexuality stands as a witness to the "interpersonal structure of man" that in turn is to be understood as a creaturely reflection of the triune nature of God, little explicit ethical guidance is offered. Yet Torrance understands the image of God to be a dynamic and relational reality that is not only given in the interpersonal *structure* of humanity but is reflected in humanity's *response to and activity with* God and other persons in the context of the created world. For Torrance the image of God is both a noun and a verb, it is both structure and reflection; it is both nature and calling.[33] Consequently, we would expect that there would be some

---

31. Torrance, "Soul and Person, in Theological Perspective," 109.

32. Torrance, *Reality and Evangelical Theology*, 42.

33. We do not wish to enter the debate brought to a head in the exchange of Barth and Brunner over this issue. To say that the image of God refers to both nature and calling, structure and reflection, does not necessitate the view that the image is an immanent or autonomous capacity of the human person. It is an endowment given and continuously sustained by God and is in no sense to be understood as a private possession. See Brunner and Barth, *Natural Theology*.

guidance regarding what kind of activity is both congruent with the structure of humanity, the structure of the world, and the will of the triune Creator for creation; not to mention what kind of activity might adequately reflect the image of the God after whom human persons have been created. Torrance has made an effort to address this problem in the areas of marriage, abortion, and donor insemination,[34] but the broader implications of his trinitarian thought for social ethics remain undeveloped.[35]

Does this mean that there is no room in Torrance's theology for the socio-ethical guidance we are interested in? Not in our opinion. It only means that the resources present in Torrance's thought need to be appropriated and engaged with particular concerns in mind. It will be our assumption that the lack of socio-ethical specificity in Torrance's work is due to the fact that he felt engagement with the epistemological and cultural dualism of the West was a more urgent and foundational task, a task that would no doubt bear fruit in the area of social ethics even if he could not produce that fruit himself.[36]

Let us now refer back to what we have just said about human sexuality and move forward from there. The particularity of male and female stands as the structural basis for the basic form of humanity as co-humanity. Co-humanity is a term that understands the male-female relation to be one of "complementary otherness and ontological togetherness"—a phrase we first encountered in Torrance's articulation of the relation between body and soul. Consequently, there exists a dialectic between particularity and universality that is the essence of

---

34. For these reflections see Torrance, "Soul and Person, in Theological Perspective," 108–9. Also of note are Torrance, "Donor Insemination," 37–38; and Torrance, *Juridical Law and Physical Law*.

35. If the mission of the church is to include cultural transformation as a direct, as opposed to an indirect, focus of its ministry, more concrete ethical guidance is required. We also note a tendency in Torrance to underestimate the structural problems of human sinfulness that are grounded, not only in the "inversion of the *imago Dei*," but also in the way we relate to one another and the world around us. This is reflected in Torrance's comments on pages 71–72 of the second edition of *The Mediation of Christ*, where he states, "there is no way through external organization to effect the personalizing or humanizing of people in society or therefore of transforming human social relationships." We fully agree with this, but not to the exclusion or neglect of social structures and their impact upon human personhood.

36. See Yu, *Being and Relation*. Yu makes a direct connection between the Western dualism Torrance critiques and a number of socio-ethical issues.

human being. Capturing the balance, or properly tuning this dialectic, is extremely difficult. Emphasis upon either pole leaves us with an isolating particularity or a smothering universality.

From Creation to Incarnation, Crucifixion, and Resurrection

We see the proper balance of particularity and universality in the person and ministry of Christ. The particularity of Christ's humanity as a male Palestinian Jew became the basis for the universality of his ministry as the person who was from, for, and with others and as such *the* person for others. His particular features, such as male, Palestinian, and Jewish, made the universal scope of his ministry possible, for in assuming these features of human life he effectively said both a yes to them as valuable aspects of human being, and a no to them as ultimate determinants of one's identity and destiny, that ultimate determination being reserved for God. Hence through their judgment *in* Christ they were set free to find fulfillment through their incorporation in our human response *to* Christ, having been destroyed as powers able to *subvert* human life and set free to be powers that can *sustain* human life in the context of its relations to the world, to others, and to God. The tuning of this dialectic requires a transcendent integrator and objective basis. Both functions are provided for in the Person and work of Christ and mediated to humanity through the ministry of the Holy Spirit.

From Resurrection to Ascension and Glorification

This particularity and universality, and the proper balance between them, ought to be embodied in the life of the church and is the work of the Holy Spirit. For the particular humanity of Christ that was both crucified and resurrected, judged and affirmed, also ascended and was glorified. This same ascended and glorified Jesus sent the Holy Spirit to dwell in the midst of humanity and to constitute a *peculiar* and *particular* community as his *universal* body and availability to all persons. In congruence with the Person and work of Christ, as a particular Person for all persons, the work of the Spirit constitutes the Church as a universal community of particular persons who are to function quite appropriately as "the earthly historical form of [Christ's] body"; a phrase coined by Barth and cited frequently by Torrance. Christ was *the* man for *others*, a particular Person for all persons, and it is appropriate that Christ's body should be the same, if not in actual embodiment, then in missional intent.

Consequently, the socio-cultural form our communal/social life takes is meant to be a reflection of the God who has created us as personal and social beings. However, social life may take on a variety of forms, as any text on cultural anthropology will attest. At the basis of this variety are differences between the various tools, conceptual and otherwise, that we inherit, transform, and use to structure our life together. Which of these tools are congruent with the nature of the Creator and the creatures designed to image God? This question needs to be asked, for these social tools or "powers" not only sustain our social life as persons, but also bear witness to the reality and character of God. These tools become the means by which our relations with one another, with God, and with the created order are transformed and adapted, or, in keeping with the overall imagery of this essay, "tuned," in such a way that they either facilitate or thwart the divine intention for human life.

However, in order for us to "tune" these relations, and to discern whether the conceptual tools we have inherited through our common life together will serve to facilitate or thwart the purpose for which we were created, we will have to consider two additional subjects:

- Firstly, that the image of God is a Christologically determined reality, for it is Christ alone who is described as both the image and reality of God.
- Secondly, that our existence in, and reflection of, the image of God is distorted and perverted in nature. The full degree of this latter assertion is realizable only when brought into relation to the first.

Part 2: Tuning Up and Knowing the Score

In part 1, we noted that the human person is uniquely situated in the context of three relations: with God, with the created order, and with other persons. These relations form a core social paradigm upon which all social activity is based and in the context of which all human life emerges and fades away. This cluster of relations, and the dynamic that exists between them, are at the basis of what it means for human persons to be created in the image of God.

However, that these relations form an ecology within which the human person is both a dependent and constituent member is not enough to offer a full understanding of what the image of God is, let alone how it is meant to function. As with any stringed instrument, it is not enough that all the strings are present; they must also be tuned so that the dynamic between them produces the distinctive sound the instrument was meant to generate.

The New Testament's portrayal of Christ as the image and reality of God provides us with a "tuning fork" that will allow us properly to orient and configure the relations we have just described.[37] At this point, we will consider the image of God as a *Christological vision*.[38] In order for an instrument to be tuned, a standard is required *towards* which the tuning may proceed and *against* which it may be judged. That human beings are created in the image of God means that they are Christologically determined and oriented toward the future, where the consummation of that determination lies. Human beings are therefore *eschatological beings*.[39] Consequently, the image of God functions as both a calling and promise of what we shall become and a judgment upon what we presently are.[40]

Humanity as an Eschatological Being

We open this subsection with two quotes: one from jazz drummer Tomy Flanagan and a second from bassist Chuck Israels. Flanagan, in explaining the art of improvisation, notes that improvisation is not the plucking of notes from thin air but rather the disciplined and spontaneous elaboration of a given musical structure: "Soloists elaborate upon what the structure of the piece has to say; what it tells them to do."[41]

---

37. Torrance speaks elsewhere of the need for an "Archimedean point far beyond us" for these same purposes. See Torrance, *Reality and Scientific Theology*, 117.

38. For an elaboration of this theme see Jennings, "Conformed to His Image."

39. This is a fundamental emphasis in the work of Eberhard Jüngel. See in particular Jüngel, "Humanity in Correspondence to God."

40. It is the discrepancy between this calling and judgment that gives rise to "conscience," a vague and sometimes twisted witness to the fact that we stand in violation of our destiny as creatures of God and as faithful neighbors to our fellow humans. In this manner the image of God may be said to function as a "sentinel" and as such "the divinely given law and truth of his [humanity's] human being, even in the face of everything that contradicts it" (Torrance, "Goodness and Dignity," 376).

41. Tomy Flanagan, cited in Berliner, *Thinking in Jazz*, 170.

Flanagan's account offers a useful analogy of the relation between the image of God as structure and the image of God as reflection, for it is the structure of a piece of music that confers freedom upon the soloist to improvise, create, or, in the words of Flanagan, to "elaborate." When that structure is violated, the freedom of the musician is diminished and the quality of the music/performance impaired, but when it is cooperated with, the improviser's freedom expands exponentially. This interplay between structure and freedom is embodied in the music of pianist Bill Evans, here commented upon by his bass player, Chuck Israels: "People never understood how arranged Bill Evans' music really was. Sure it was free and improvised. But the reason we could be so free is that we already knew the beginning, the middle, and the ending."[42] The simplicity and beauty of Bill Evans's music concealed the complex interplay between structure and free improvisation that was at its core.

Human persons have been created in the image of God. This is both a gift and a calling, but we have no basis upon which to understand what this gift is, or how it ought to be embodied, apart from a humanity that encompasses both the image and the reality of God in one Person. That humanity is the humanity of Christ and knowing Christ is akin to knowing the beginning, middle, and ending of who we are and what our mission and destiny is.

This knowledge is meant to set the Church in particular free to "improvise" as she carries out her mission under the guidance of the Holy Spirit. It is not a freedom to alter her mission or renegotiate its terms. To do so would alter her identity and transform her into a different reality altogether. Rather, it is a freedom to integrate into her mission elements that will give it a peculiar shape and sound without violating the integrity or universality of the mission itself.

The mission of the Church is not spiritual in any narrow or disembodied sense, but cultural, since it is her function to stand as an embodied witness to the glory and eternal purpose of God. All of the relations we have just spoken of are to be gathered up into this witness, since the integrity and goodness of the created order is grounded in God, and because God has chosen to include this order in his eternal purpose. However, the created order is fallen and various aspects of it will be excluded from sharing in the consummation of the kingdom upon Christ's return. In order to discern what is to be transformed and

---

42. Chuck Israels, cited in ibid., 289.

included and what is to be rejected and excluded, we need to know "the beginning, middle, and end"—we need to know God's plan for the created order and our relations within it. In order to discern this purpose, we shall have to understand the image of God as a Christological and eschatological reality as well as a creaturely, spiritual, and social one.

The ecology within which human persons are set has a particular function, orientation, and *telos*. That particular goal is beyond our discernment, no matter how intense our reflection upon the relations that make us who we are. Rather, this particular goal is made evident to us, and is secured for us, through the self-communication of God to us in Christ through the Spirit.

Jesus Christ is both the image and the reality of God and as such, the "Archetypal and Dominical Man" from whom all that is truly human is derived, and to whom all humanity must be referred. Torrance notes: "It is in Jesus himself that we discern what the basic structure of humanity is and ought to be."[43] From Christ we learn that the basic structure of humanity is constituted by, and subsists within, three relations: those between the human person and the created order, the human person and God, and the human person and other persons.

However, when we discern in Jesus what the basic structure of humanity is and ought to be, we discover that our humanity falls short of its reality and destiny as revealed in Christ. We are fallen beings and this depravity extends through the entire ecology of our being. Torrance notes the ramifications of this total depravity, having its origin in our spiritual relation to God, extending through our social relations with others, and impacting not only our *relations* with the physical world but the physical world itself: "The breach between man and God enters into the inner being of men and women, so that they are no longer the beings they ought to be either in relation to God or in relation to one another. Even their physical existence in the world has become dislocated. The fact that human beings ought to be what they are not, now qualifies their very existence as human beings."[44]

The work of Christ as the image and reality of God however is more than revelatory, it is also salvific, and no sooner does Christ reveal to us what the basic structure of humanity is than he secures, in his own

---

43. Torrance, "Soul and Person, in Theological Perspective," 115.

44. Torrance, "Goodness and Dignity," 373: "Their very existence as human beings" refers to the entire ecology of created life.

Person, what it is meant to be. Revelation in Christ and reconciliation in Christ are two poles of a single movement, a movement that, through the incarnation, "has thrust through the center of the creation in such a way that everything in heaven and earth, eternity and time, is made to revolve around it." Torrance continues by noting that "the ultimate foundations of our being are lodged in him, and all the eternal purposes of God are gathered up and consummated in his life and work."[45]

The placement of our human ecology upon a new objective basis in Christ, while securing an ontological relation to Christ, does not resolve the discrepancy between our life and Christ's own.[46] However, upon this ontological basis personal and social transformation may proceed with powerful resources and a concrete and transcendent goal. Here we are concerned primarily with the work of the Spirit.

The Spirit, as the freedom of the Creator to be present to the creature, has been "poured out upon all flesh" as the promise that the Creator's purposes for the creature and the created order will be realized and completed.

The Spirit transforms our personal being and social life by bringing to bear upon them the work of the Son. This the Spirit does, not only by coming to dwell intimately with us, but, as a consequence of that intimate relation, by transforming the conceptual and social tools that we use to order and sustain our fallen life into those that will order our common life after the fashion revealed and secured in the Son. The way we perceive and organize our social life needs to be brought into conformity with the way it has been ordered by the Father and redeemed by the Son.[47] We see this dynamic broadly at work in Torrance's understanding of how the concept of the *homoousion* was developed and its later impact upon conceptions of creation and science.[48] It is also exemplified in the way Torrance describes the mission and transforma-

---

45. Ibid., 386. As if the point needed further laboring we add this statement from the same page: "With the Incarnation the original relation between the covenant and the creation has been reaffirmed by God and fulfilled in such a way that the whole creation has been redeemed, sanctified and renewed in Christ."

46. Torrance understands this discrepancy as the basis for conscience and the image of God as a "sentinel." See ibid., 374–76.

47. Torrance develops the idea of "conceptual tools" in a number of places, but at length in *Mediation of Christ*, 5ff.

48. See Torrance, *Ground and Grammar*, 44–74.

tion of Israel as "the womb of Christ," this also being the transformation of an entire social ecology towards a particular purpose.[49]

That Torrance understands his thought to have concrete social implications seems clear, even if they are not concretely spelled out. He has always understood himself as a missionary to Western culture and understands his work to be aimed towards "the transformation and convergence of knowledge," which is to say, the transformation of the very foundations of thought and culture.[50]

This particular interest is captured in his understanding of humanity as a "mediator of order" or "priest of creation." While the majority of this essay has dealt with the *structure* of humanity as an embodied personal, social, and eschatological being, the *task and vocation* of humanity as a "mediator of order" and "priest of creation" is equally pivotal to Torrance's anthropology and, consequently, to his understanding of the mission of the church in the world. These terms describe an identity, task, and calling that is oriented and sustained by the relations we have discussed here. The fulfillment of that task and calling is also directly influenced by the quality of these relations.

We close with a brief preview of where the image of God as vocation and calling might take us in the development of Torrance's anthropology. It leads us into a consideration of the human person as an irreducibly social being entrusted with a cultural task; with both aspects grounded in the tri-unity of God.[51]

Humanity as a Cultural Being

Tuning the three relations developed above against this Christological vision, grounded in the work of Christ and oriented toward the *parousia* of Christ, sets up a transformational dynamic. This transformational dynamic is a product of the work of the Holy Spirit, for the Spirit is

---

49. See Torrance, *Mediation of Christ*, 1–23.

50. Torrance's central concern in this transformation and convergence has been the destructive nature of epistemological dualism. We would like to see his achievements here brought to bear in other areas of thought as well.

51. The "cultural mandate" is not simply rooted in the command our first parents received to tend and care for a garden, but in the very constitution of their humanity as image bearers of the triune God.

the initiator and sustainer of personal and social transformation just as Christ is the ground and goal of the same.

However, to move from one state of affairs, personally or socially, to another implies that an inadequate state of affairs already exists and is in need of transformation. This inadequate state of affairs is the product of disorder in the relations mentioned above. This disorder becomes embodied/objectified in our social life/culture. It can only be transformed through the work of the Spirit, which is mediated through human agents and based upon the objective work of Christ. This transformation must take place both socially and individually in order for the relations to stay "in tune." With this final point, we simply acknowledge the fact that human being as holistic being is also a *fallen being* and that the reflection and image we often embody is a *perverted* one. This perversion extends beyond the activity of any single embodied soul and ripples throughout the entire cultural framework, the cultural framework then taking a shape that will support and sustain the behaviors and motivations that create and mold it. There is a reciprocal relation between individual human agency and social structure and we are not sure whether one pole can be prioritized over the other. It seems clear that human agents generate and mold social structures and, once those social structures gain momentum and a certain level of objective autonomy, they in turn exert a great deal of power over the individuals that participate in them. That power can either oppress or liberate.[52]

How does this illumine how we might understand the nature of the image of God and the calling of humanity in Christ? When it is granted that Christ is the standard against which these relations are to be tuned, and the Spirit the agent who initiates and sustains that transformation, what is it that is actually transformed that allows the above relations to come into tune with one another so that the created order may fulfill its *telos*?

Here we encounter another aspect of the image of God, perhaps the one that integrates all the others. We speak of the image of God as a *cultural reflection* since the image of God is closely associated with the vocation of humanity as the "priest of creation" or "mediator of order." This priestly vocation of mediation is fulfilled through cultural activity,

---

52. This conceptuality is drawn from Peter Berger's theory of culture. See in particular Berger, *Sacred Canopy*; and James Davison Hunter's essay on Berger's thought in Wuthnow et al., *Cultural Analysis*.

understood in its broadest sense as the formation of conceptual and physical tools with which we order and orient our life together. As created in the image of God the human being is essentially a social being, and therefore an irreducibly *cultural being*.[53] Human relations are only possible within cultural frameworks, frameworks that God has not only provided for, but condescends to work within. God binds himself to these cultural frameworks in grace and love all the while remaining transcendent over them as Savior and Lord.

In the words of Robert Jenson, we are uniquely related to God as "his conversational counterpart,"[54] a conversation initiated by the Father, secured by the Son and sustained by the Spirit. The entire created order is implicated in this conversation, for it provides not only the environment in which the conversation takes place but also the physical and social tools that make its dialogical and embodied character possible. The response that Christ secures and the Spirit enables is fundamentally a cultural response since it incorporates the entirety of our being. Our cultural life is made possible through the agency of the triune God and is intended to reflect that God, and by so doing to sustain the creatures crafted after his image.

We close this chapter with two quotes. The first from an essay Torrance delivered in 1986 at the Lam Chi Fung Memorial Symposium on Christianity and Chinese Culture titled "The Goodness and Dignity of Man in the Christian Tradition":

> It is now the role of man in union with Christ to serve the purpose of God's love in the ongoing actualization of that redemption, sanctification and renewal within the universe ... Thus man has been called to be a kind of midwife to creation, in assisting nature out of its divinely given abundance constantly to give birth to new forms of life and richer patterns of order. Indeed, as the covenant-partner of Jesus Christ man may be regarded as the priest of creation, through whose service ... the marvelous rationality, symmetry, harmony and beauty of God's

---

53. Thanks to Ray S. Anderson for pointing out the important distinction between the human person as first an essentially social being, and subsequently a cultural being. Human sociality is nurtured within, and finds expression through, a plurality of cultural forms, even if it is more fundamental than those forms. To note that the human person is a cultural being alone does not go deep enough to touch upon the "interpersonal structure of humanity" that Torrance equates with the image of God or the "core social paradigm" suggested by Anderson.

54. Jenson, *Systematic Theology*, 2:95.

creation are being brought to light and given expression in such a way that the whole universe is found to be a glorious hymn to the Creator.[55]

And, in his latest work, *The Christian Doctrine of God,* Torrance again notes the centrality of the created order and the unique role of human persons within it as central to the fulfillment of God's purposes: "Nature itself is mute, but human being is the one constituent of the created universe through whom its rational structure and astonishing beauty may be brought to word in praise of the Creator."[56]

It would seem reasonable to suggest that if we are to follow a line through Torrance's work, that line originates and terminates in the triune God, but not before it has drawn into the picture a created order freely brought into being by the will of God and graciously entrusted to a creature crafted after the image of God. It is this creature, peculiarly constituted and uniquely called, that God "improvises" with,[57] as "scientist," "midwife," "priest," and "instrument," in order to draw the created order toward its *telos*. This is a cultural task and, it would seem, the very basis and motivation for Torrance's entire theological project.[58]

If this is an accurate conclusion to draw then it would appear that the following words of Torrance, used to describe his theological work and its trinitarian basis, are an example of gross understatement: "Let us now reflect a little on the way in which Christian understanding of God as the Holy Trinity bears upon our human culture, in philosophy and science and in our social developments."[59]

---

55. Torrance, "Goodness and Dignity," 387. Torrance's presentation in particular is critiqued in Yeung, *Being and Knowing*. Torrance's parents were missionaries in China, and his longstanding interest in the country and its people continued throughout his life. For a biographical account see McGrath, *Thomas F. Torrance*.

56. Torrance, *Christian Doctrine of God*, 213.

57. God "improvises" with humanity upon the basis of a covenant relation established through the Son and in the Holy Spirit.

58. Torrance often described himself as a "missionary to Western culture" and as being called to "evangelize culture." See Bauman, "Interview with Thomas F. Torrance," 114; and Hesselink, "Pilgrimage in the School of Christ," 49.

59. Torrance, *Reality and Scientific Theology*, 192. Torrance's work contains a wealth of material for the development of a trinitarian theology of culture, specifically in his conception of the nature and dynamics of "social coefficients of knowledge," which in turn are grounded in his understanding of God as triune, creation as contingent, and human persons as stewards created in the image of God.

That Thomas F. Torrance is a scientific theologian seems beyond dispute.[60] But that he may also be understood as a theologian of culture is a permission given us through a consideration of his understanding of God as triune, creation as a contingent order (both fallen and redeemed), and the human person as the image of God. Having examined these three areas of his thought in the previous chapters, we are now obligated to see his theological project in this light and to develop it toward this end. In the following chapter we attempt to do just that.

---

60. This was the consistent claim of Torrance himself, and he spent a great deal of time and energy developing a scientific theological methodology and a body of work congruent with that methodology. Others are developing this material. See in particular the three-volume work by Alister E. McGrath, *A Scientific Theology*. What is overlooked or underdeveloped is that Torrance's theological and scientific work flows from an implicit theology of culture that sustains, nourishes and guides the work he is so well known for. Elmer M. Colyer provides insightful reviews of the entire series, pointing out the strengths and inadequacies of McGrath's project and his interpretation of Torrance. See Colyer, "Review of Alister E. McGrath's *A Scientific Theology*."

5

Torrance's Theology of Culture
A Social Coefficient of Knowledge

WITH THIS CHAPTER WE NOW COME TO THE END OF THE LINE WE have been following through Torrance's thought, a line we suggested would terminate in a trinitarian theology of culture. We began with a consideration of Torrance's doctrine of God, specifically noting how God's activity as Creator is conditioned and determined by his being as triune. We followed the trinitarian line (or logic) further, into Torrance's doctrine of creation as contingent, and specifically his understanding of creation as an order that is both fallen and redeemed. Then we considered the creation of the human person in continuity with this order, but also in distinction from it, as a creature given a unique constitution and identity and entrusted with a cultural task that is doxologically motivated. Both of these qualities are captured in Torrance's understanding of the human person as a steward, priest, or scientist created in the image of God.

At this point we need to introduce one additional concept in Torrance's thought, a concept that is different from the components that have led us here, but also profoundly integrated with, and founded upon, them. We refer to "the social coefficient of knowledge." The argument of this chapter will be to suggest the following:

- This concept continues the trinitarian logic and line we have been following thorough Torrance's thought.

- This concept, and the dynamics it seeks to describe, are based upon and integrated with Torrance's doctrines of God, creation, and humanity as developed in the preceding chapters.

- This concept may thus serve as a heuristic basis for the development of a theology of culture that is trinitarian in nature and congruent with Torrance's overall theological project.

Torrance mentions the concept of a "social coefficient of knowledge" throughout his writings, and it is a prevalent theme in his thinking. However, Torrance has only explicitly developed that theme on a few occasions: in his 1970 Harris Lectures, delivered at the University of Dundee under the title "God and the World" and in his Didsbury Lectures delivered at The British Isles Nazarene College in 1982. The former lecture series was expanded and published as the book *Reality and Scientific Theology*, with chapter 4 entitled "The Social Coefficient of Knowledge."[1] The latter lecture series was expanded and published as *The Mediation of Christ*, with chapter 1 treating Israel as a social coefficient of knowledge under the heading "The Mediation of Revelation."[2] The two treatments are complementary, the latter being an illustrative case study of how the conceptuality of the former functions in terms of God's formation of Israel as "the womb of Christ" and the "conceptual tools" that are necessary in order to apprehend divine revelation. Another case study may be found in Torrance's 1992 essay "The Christian Apprehension of God the Father," in *Speaking the Christian God: The Holy Trinity and the Challenge of Feminism*.[3] An additional work worth mentioning, and perhaps Torrance's most extended engagement with a facet of contemporary culture other than Western science (even though in conversation with it), is *Juridical Law and Physical Law: Toward a Realist Foundation for Human Law*. This monograph also incorporates Torrance's thinking on the social coefficient of knowledge as a basis for transforming the nature and function of canon law and legal institutions, and consequently the role a specific social coefficient may have on broader cultural structures. Torrance's conception of the social coefficient of knowledge also plays a significant role in his conclusions regarding the significance of the term "Father" in referring to God,[4] which in turn is part of his larger methodological reflections concern-

---

1. See Torrance, *Reality and Scientific Theology*, 98–130.
2. See Torrance, *Mediation of Christ*, 1–23.
3. Torrance, "Christian Apprehension."
4. Ibid., 120–43.

ing the contours of a realist evangelical theology and the relation of language to reality.[5]

Engagement with this aspect of Torrance's thought has been sparse, although some important and invaluable studies have appeared demonstrating the broad applicability of this concept for understanding the nature of doctrine[6] and accounting for social and subjective factors in the epistemological process.[7]

It seems clear the direct intention of Torrance in the development of this concept is for epistemological and doctrinal matters, however, Torrance also seems to suggest throughout his writings that with this concept he is articulating far more than simply the parameters of a "research tradition."[8] He refers not only to the Church as a social coefficient but Israel as well,[9] which suggests that the concept may be expanded and used as a model for understanding the nature and dynamics of society and culture. We will seek to undertake that task here.

Our primary task is to draw together into a coherent and workable model what Torrance has said regarding the formation and function of "social coefficients of knowledge." As we do so, we will point out points of convergence and divergence between Torrance's social coefficient of knowledge and contemporary anthropological understandings of culture. Some illustrative examples will be offered to show how Torrance has put the concept to use in the way he understands the nature and mission of Israel and the Christian Church as embodiments of truth and matrices for the transformation of culture. Finally, we will point out how this concept is founded upon, and coheres around, Torrance's doctrines of God, creation, and humanity by explaining the title we have chosen for this project: *Persons, Powers and Pluralities: Toward a Trinitarian Theology of Culture*.

---

5. Torrance, *Reality and Evangelical Theology*, 61ff.
6. See Colyer, *Nature of Doctrine*, 93–127.
7. See Achtemeier, "Truth of Tradition."
8. This is the way the concept is explored by Achtemeier.
9. Torrance, *Mediation of Christ*, chapter 1. Torrance also points out the correlation between the university as a place of research into the nature of the created order and the existence of a free society. Healthy social coefficients mediate knowledge of the real world that transforms persons and communities and so enables a free society.

Torrance's Social Coefficient of Knowledge

Introducing the Term

Torrance utilizes a plethora of terms, concepts, and images in articulating his understanding of the social coefficient of knowledge.[10] In order for us to begin to unfold this important conceptual tool, we will have to form a conceptual tool of our own by attempting an early and intuitive definition of the concept.

For Torrance, a social coefficient of knowledge is *the social embodiment of a knowing relation*. In short, the social coefficient receives from, responds to, and reflects the character of the objective reality it stands in relation to. It serves as a subjective and social lens through which persons are enabled to participate in a knowing relation with realities that are external to them, and to be modified by those realities in an appropriate manner. The consequence is a dynamic social reality that enables, sustains, and reflects the knowing relation that is central to it.

This definition is concise and needs to be expanded, but it captures succinctly the essence of the concept for Torrance. It is a definition we can refer back to as our expansion of the concept unfolds and our application of it becomes more creative. In order to begin our expansion of the term we will first consider briefly the constituent components of the concept—how Torrance has labeled it.

Torrance has chosen an interesting expression to refer to this particular aspect of his thought. Why the phrase "social coefficient of knowledge"? A brief reading of his writing on the subject reveals that Torrance is essentially talking about the same kind of social reality that other disciplines refer to as "society," "culture," "community" or "tradition"[11] along with the various components that go into the construction of these realities and ideas. His selection of terminology has

---

10. In a single essay Torrance has referred to the social coefficient of knowledge as a nurse, a framework, an environment, a matrix, and a medium. He refers to one of its central components as "a predisposition lodged in our social consciousness." It would seem that the anthropological equivalent to these descriptions would be "world view" and perhaps the sociological equivalent would be Berger's "plausibility structure." See Torrance, *Reality and Scientific Theology*, 98–127.

11. See in particular Achtemeier, "Truth of Tradition," for a comparison of the thought of Torrance and Alasdair MacIntyre, where the author concludes that Torrance's "social coefficient of truth" shares a number of commonalities with MacIntyre's understanding of "tradition."

important things to say as to why this expression and not another, as also about his particular vantage point and goals in using this concept. The term "coefficient" for instance is most common in the fields of mathematics and physics. This makes it a natural choice for Torrance, over against terminology more prevalent in the social sciences (which Torrance often criticizes as "positivistic" in orientation) and popular culture. Torrance is interested in an aspect of these terms that cannot be found readily, or expressed as clearly, as they have been developed and used in other fields. Yet, he also wants to draw upon the fruits of sociological and anthropological thought since he is speaking not of a mathematical coefficient but a *social* one.[12] By wedding these two terms, he is establishing a relation between two fields of inquiry and creating enough dissonance in their interpenetration to fill them with unique nuances—nuances and content drawn from his own particular understanding of theological science.[13]

Methodologically, Torrance is following his own advice, and the example of the Patristic theologians that have profoundly influenced his thinking. He does so by taking terminology from the common stream of human thought and culture, bringing it under the influence of divine revelation, and developing a conceptual tool that will further deepen our understanding of the world and expand our ability to reflect and embody the purposes of God for it.

We will first get to the common meaning of the terms individually and collectively and then attempt to develop the unique sense in which Torrance understands and utilizes the social coefficient of knowledge.

Defining the Term

The term "coefficient" is used in a number of disciplines and contexts, but may generally be understood to refer to:

---

12. Elmer Colyer notes that in Torrance's development of the concept "he concedes not a little to sociology of knowledge, yet he consistently argues for a critical, epistemic realism." Colyer, *Nature of Doctrine*, 93–94. We see here a recognition of the two disciplines Torrance is drawing together, wanting to acknowledge the subjectivity of the social world and how it is formed without surrendering the objectivity of the external world and its demands upon us.

13. Drawing these two fields closer together is precisely the burden of this project, a project already initiated in Torrance's own thinking and perhaps most evident in his development and use of this concept.

- A *joint agent or factor* in producing an effect or result. That which acts together with another thing.
- A number that is *constant* for a given substance, body, or process and which serves as a measure of one of its properties.
- A *multiplier* that measures some property of a particular substance for which it is constant, while differing for different substances.

Aspects of these definitions seem particularly relevant to our discussion here and a brief statement of their import will help orient our minds as we develop the concept further.

The Social Coefficient as a Multiplier and Measure

Firstly, Torrance uses the terminology of coefficient to refer to something that is *a multiplier of another quantity*, whether that quantity is known or unknown. For Torrance, the coefficient is social, not numerical, and it serves as a multiplier of particular forms of knowledge gained through particular relations with a real and external world. The quality of those relations is not yet a factor; they can be poor and maladjusted or healthy and "apposite." What is important is that a coefficient is a multiplier or measurement of a known or unknown quantity, though *not* the quantity itself, and that measurement is made in social terms.

Every social community has as its center a body of shared knowledge that makes communication and joint action possible. This body of shared knowledge is embodied in the social life of the community—in its values, rituals, and institutional life. This embodiment is a way of measuring, multiplying, or quantifying in social terms the "invisible" qualities that make the community both possible and distinct.[14]

---

14. We think here of the opening pages of Torrance's essay "Man, Mediator of Order," where Torrance identifies and discusses the Greek, Roman, and Hebrew conceptions of humanity. The images of humanity central to Greek and Roman societies were dualistic in nature, and that dualism became embodied in the social life and structures of each of these societies, albeit in different ways. The image of humanity central to the Hebrew worldview was unitary in nature, because it was informed by a different intellectual tradition and practice. There is a common dynamic responsible for shaping social communities. It is how that dynamic is informed, the tradition and history that lies at its center, that define and frame one community as different from another. See Torrance, *Christian Frame of Mind*, 35–40. Consequently, Roman, Greek, and Hebrew "societies" may be understood as tangible expressions of the images of humanity that lie at the center of these communities. The invisible body of knowledge held dear by a community comes to visible expression through its rituals.

For example, the community of Israel is not God, but bears witness to the character and purposes of God through its communal life. In that sense, the community of Israel serves as a multiplier and measure, in social terms, of the being and character of God. While God's being *per se* can not be measured or multiplied, it is safe to say that our human experience of God's being can, in the sense that the conceptual tools we utilize to apprehend God can be refined to describe more accurately what is already there. This is accomplished through the social coefficient as a multiplier and measure. Israel quantifies in a social way the God of Abraham, Isaac, and Jacob and what that God desires for the created order. Identity and agency are thus profoundly integrated, with both being qualified by the object one identifies with and the object that guides ones actions. It is because the social coefficient (Israel) serves as a multiplier and measure of the reality it stands in relation to (Yahweh) that Yahweh prohibits idols in the midst of any community that is to be called by his name. Israel is a community of persons who are to serve as the tangible expression of his character and will, not an object made of wood or stone. To place another object at the center of this community is to initiate the transformation of this community's identity and the nature of its agency in the world. Human persons become what they worship, not in any ontological sense, but in the sense that they assume the character and values of those things that they hold as ultimate concerns. This principle is at the heart of the biblical injunctions prohibiting idolatry and Torrance's understanding of the social coefficient as a multiplier or measure.[15]

---

15. Yahweh's concern with the presence of idols in the midst of the community of Israel is twofold: firstly, this is a *covenant community*, chosen for the purpose of bearing witness to Yahweh's reality and purposes. This goal cannot be accomplished if the dynamic at the center of Israel's life revolves around another god. The second point follows from the first. This is also a *human community*, and deviance from the will and purposes of Yahweh not only make it impossible for this community to bear witness to Yahweh, but also slowly degrades the humanity of the persons who make up this community. Identity and agency are intimately integrated and Israel cannot fulfill its epistemic calling or its redemptive one unless the object at the center of its life is Yahweh. Yahweh's concern with idolatry is rooted in his purpose to redeem human life, not simply his desire to have a group of people serve as his representatives on earth.

The Social Coefficient as Signifying a Relation that is Constant

Secondly, the term "coefficient" reminds us of another aspect of the relation between coefficient and the reality it measures—the relationship between the coefficient and the reality it measures and multiplies is *constant*. The term "constant" used in this context can carry a number of meanings, and it is here where some small adjustments are necessary in order to bring it in line with Torrance's actual usage of the term. A "constant" can refer to something that is (1) continually occurring or persistent, (2) unchanging in nature, value, or extent and hence invariable, or (3) a relation that is steadfast in purpose, loyal, or faithful. All three senses of the term are applicable if by "invariant" or "constant" one does not conclude that Torrance understands social coefficients to be unchanging in form or appearance, or that they are static realities that, once having assumed a particular social form, will remain in that state indefinitely. Torrance instead would understand the relation between a coefficient and the reality it measures as a dynamic relation, not a static one, and thus the constancy of the relation refers to a *constancy of purpose*, namely, faithfully and socially to measure the reality it stands in relation to. If that relation reveals new knowledge that radically alters the social coefficient then, in order for the social coefficient to stand in a faithful and constant relationship to the quantity it seeks to measure, the nature of its social embodiment *must* change. Not to do so would be an act of infidelity and a violation of the constancy of the relation. It is a relation where invariance requires flexibility, where the coefficient must "improvise" in order to remain faithful to the reality it stands in relation to.

The contemporary jazz community stands in a relation of constancy to the jazz tradition in such a way. In order to be faithful to that tradition—the compositions, history, and persons who make it up—contemporary jazz musicians must continually contextualize that tradition if they are to remain faithful to its history, *ethos*, and *telos*. That necessitates improvisation and innovation. Jazz musicians do no justice to the tradition if they function solely as "cover bands"—preserving and re-performing the music of the past for contemporary audiences. Granted, archiving and duplicating what has been done before is an essential part of keeping that tradition alive. However, preservation alone cuts the tradition off from its life in performance, where musicians bring the tradition into an active conversation with different times, audiences, and musical languages. It may be preserved in memory or in a museum, but to experience the jazz tradition only in that fashion would be not to experience it at all.

To stand in a constant relation to the jazz tradition, and to be faithful to its deep logic, requires the risk taking that is central to any act of innovation, improvisation or contextualization. Constancy and faithfulness understood as formal duplication of the past, or, in another more Torrancean sense, "mimetic correspondence to reality," is not intended. Constancy of purpose however is intended; and to remain constant to a *purpose* requires risk and innovation in engagement with the present and in anticipation of the future, not simply repetition and imitation of the past within the confines of the present.[16]

THE SOCIAL COEFFICIENT AS A JOINT AGENT OR FACTOR

Thirdly, and related, the term "coefficient" refers to that which acts together with another thing as a *joint agent or factor in producing an effect or result*. Semantic adjustments are due here as well if we are to understand the unique sense in which Torrance employs this term. For Torrance, the priority in the knowing relation is squarely placed upon the objective pole of the relation, with the subjective pole based in the human knower, certainly as a joint agent, but more specifically as a *responsive agent*. The creative subject is required, but that creativity should be exercised in the service of the objective pole of the relation and as such guided by it. For Torrance, ordering the relation in this way does not subvert the subjective pole of the knowing relation. Instead, it establishes and liberates the subjective pole by directing it toward its proper *telos*. Within that boundedness the subjective pole can truly be itself. It is a relation that is determinate without being determined.[17]

---

16. We think here of Peter's vision of the sheet filled with unclean animals, or of any intimate human relationship, where change is necessary in order to remain faithful.

17. As Torrance notes elsewhere, "Thus we may think of God as communicating himself to us within the structures of our personal and epistemic relations with one another in this world in such a way that, while in the Incarnation he adapts himself to the weakness of our creaturely structures of knowledge, in the mission and presence of the Spirit he uses them as the very means to lift us up and beyond ourselves to apprehend and love him in his Triune Being" (Torrance, *Reality and Scientific Theology*, 192).

What the terminology of coefficient does in this context is to disallow any consideration of the coefficient as true knowledge apart from the quantity it is meant to multiply or measure.[18] The coefficient is only valuable when it faithfully measures or multiplies the reality it stands in relation to. It cannot do this by drawing attention to itself as an object of knowledge, but only as a medium of knowledge; and not just knowledge, but the knowing relation it occurs in the midst of. The coefficient in this sense is cooperative or mediatorial in that it enables the knowing relation to take on a particular form even as it only has its form by standing in a faithful and responsive relation to the reality it reflects. The coefficient in this sense refers to the fact that it is partly the product of a subjective pole but also a product of objective features of reality.[19]

THE SOCIAL COEFFICIENT AND CULTURAL PLURALITY

Fourthly, the coefficient is a multiplier and measurement in social terms of a known or unknown quantity. This implies that any number of coefficients can be placed in a constant relation to the particular reality to be measured, and that different coefficients will measure that reality in different ways, while still serving as multipliers *of the same reality*. We think here of the Christian church, which Torrance understands as a social coefficient of the knowledge of God, and the various cultures and communities that serve as coefficients of the one reality of God—multiplying and giving measure to the mystery, wonder, and inexhaustibility of the triune God. This aspect of the social coefficient may be helpful in articulating a theology of cultural plurality, or of properly bounding the work of contextualization, and Torrance's reflections upon the relationship between the special and general sciences may be a way to explore further the relationship between cultures and sub-cultures.[20]

With this basic background in mind, let us go on to consider some additional nuances and components in Torrance's understanding of the

---

18. See Torrance's discussion of the difference between an "affect" and an "effect" mentioned below.

19. This is how Torrance understands all symbolic forms, as "partly the product of our creative imagination and partly the product of objective features and properties of reality" (Torrance, *Reality and Scientific Theology*, 98).

20. See Torrance, *Theological Science*, 106–40.

social coefficient of knowledge that will be important for the development of a theology of culture based upon his thought.

Developing the Term for Use in a Theology of Culture

In order to develop the term in a manner that will be helpful to our overall project we have chosen to draw Torrance's thought alongside that of sociologist Peter Berger[21] and missiologist Paul G. Hiebert.[22] We have employed this method earlier in this project in order to draw out some of the social implications of Torrance's thought that may not be readily apparent because the implicit social implications and dynamics of Torrance's thinking are couched in language that is common in the natural sciences. The use of the term "social coefficient" to describe what is essentially a community or tradition is a case in point, as Mark P. Achtemeier has noted.[23] This is not a violation of Torrance's thought, but rather a redirection and reorientation of his thought that unlocks the power of Torrance's trinitarian theology and directs it more explicitly toward concerns that may not have been central to Torrance's initial goals as he formed the concept. However, though not central to Torrance's explicit research goals, they are not outside the boundaries of his thinking.

We saw earlier that Torrance's understanding of "order" was in many respects similar in intent and function to an understanding of the "principalities and powers" as developed by social ethicist John Howard Yoder and missiologist Lesslie Newbigin. This opened up for us a new way of understanding and developing Torrance's thought, and we have the same goal in mind here. However, while our development of Torrance's concept of order was helped by its commonalities with understandings in the natural sciences, social ethics, and missiology, his concept of the social coefficient has more in common with similar concepts in the sociology of knowledge and cultural anthropology.

Since the particular character of the knowing relation determines the shape of the social coefficient, we will first consider how Torrance

---

21. See in particular Berger and Luckmann, *Social Construction of Reality*, as well as the essay on Berger's thought by James Davison Hunter in Wuthnow et al., *Cultural Analysis*.

22. See in particular the helpful survey in Hiebert, *Missiological Implications*.

23. Achtemeier, "Truth of Tradition," 360.

understands the knowing relation under the heading *The Formation of Social Coefficients*. In the process of discussing how social coefficients are *formed*, we will also necessarily discuss many of the *functions* of a social coefficient. For that reason, we will only take up the matter of how social coefficients function briefly, in order to note three of their more important and fundamental functions: the provision of semantic, participatory, and multi-leveled environments.[24] If we were to enumerate all the functions of a social coefficient we would find ourselves, not only covering much of the ground we are about to traverse here, but material covered in chapters 2 and 3 on Torrance's concept of order as well.

The Formation and Function of Social Coefficients

Social Coefficients are Formed Around Knowing Relations Established with Objective Reality

Social coefficients are formed around "knowing relations," which, for Torrance, are composed of an objective and subjective pole. At the center of any social coefficient there is a subject or knower (individual or corporate), and an object to be known. The object to be known exists apart from the subjectivity of the knower, even if the subjectivity of the knower plays an indispensable role in enabling and expressing the knowing relation. Recognizing that there are two poles, and maintaining a proper relationship between them, is essential to Torrance's concept of social coefficients and how they are formed.

The subjective and objective poles in the knowing relation are not the only variables that contribute to the shape of the social coefficient, the actual *relation* between the two poles is also a variable, and that relation can be healthy, translucent, and "apposite" or unhealthy and distorted. These three variables: the objective pole, the subjective pole, and the quality of the relation between them, act together to form particular social coefficients.[25] Social coefficients are driven and determined,

---

24. The knowing relation comes first only as a matter of methodological development since Torrance would not allow that the knowing relation comes first and the social coefficient of that knowing relation comes chronologically or even developmentally second. They arise together conjunctively. The relation between the two is symbiotic and dialectical even though the components of that relation are distinguishable.

25. See Torrance, *Reality and Scientific Theology*, 190ff., for a discussion of "the subject-object-relation model" as applied to an understanding of the Holy Trinity.

shaped and embodied, by the dynamic interaction that takes place in history between these variables. Perhaps the best way of picturing the centrality of this knowing relation is to understand it as the hub of a wheel or the cornerstone of a building, although these are mechanical and physical ways of understanding what is essentially a social, historical, and dialectical reality.

Consequently, it is not only necessary that there be an objective and subjective pole, it is also essential that the relation between them is properly ordered and structured.[26] In other words, the relation between the subject and the object must not only be in place, it must also be properly ordered, and in such a way that facilitates the disclosure of the objective pole, the transformation of the subjective pole, and an appropriate social embodiment that reflects both subject and object. The relation between the two poles is moral, not simply functional. The way the objective and subjective poles are related and aligned is essential and determines the kind of knowledge that is shared in the knowing relation (distorted or transparent) and the way that knowledge is embodied and expressed through the relation (the social implications of that knowledge).

The Social Coefficient of Knowledge as a Centered Set

Perhaps the best way of conceptualizing what Torrance refers to as a social coefficient of knowledge, and the role of these relations in their formation, comes from the field of set theory, concerned as it is with the formation and definition and sets.

In his essay "The Category *Christian* in the Mission Task,"[27] anthropologist Paul G. Hiebert draws upon set theory to explore how we form

---

26. Nicholas Wolterstorff, in developing the biblical concept of *shalom* for social ethics, notes that implicit in the concept is that human persons are responsible agents who exist in a network of relationships, specifically relationships with God, neighbor, and nature. Shalom is not simply the result of recognizing these relationships, or even of carrying out our responsibilities properly in each sphere. Rather, shalom results when these relationships are properly ordered, and our responsibilities are carried out, in such a way that "delight and joy" are the by-products. See Wolterstorff, *Until Justice and Peace Embrace*, 124. The same dynamic appears in Torrance's thought when he speaks of knowing relations in general and social coefficients specifically. There is a third factor involved in the knowing relation, namely, the relation itself and how it is aligned or ordered.

27. See Hiebert, *Anthropological Reflections*, 107–36.

and assign content to various cultural categories. Hiebert uses the term "Christian" to develop a proposal for how we should understand what belongs in this particular category and why it belongs there. Hiebert's discussion will be instructive for us as it points to a more constructive and accurate way of understanding both the open and determinate nature of cultural boundaries and hence, by extension, the formation and boundaries of various social coefficients.

Categories are formed when people or things are grouped together upon the basis of shared qualities. Consequently, the same item can be placed in a number of different categories depending upon which quality is assigned as the identifying mark of the person or thing. Will it be color? Shape? Size? When something is identified as being in one category as opposed to another, it determines how we perceive and relate to that item.

Drawing upon contemporary studies in mathematics Hiebert examines four types of sets, each with its own structural characteristics and logic. However, these four sets are formed upon the basis of two specific variables:

- *Variable #1*: Upon what basis do we assign items to one category over another? Extrinsic or intrinsic?

Do we assign membership in the category based upon the intrinsic or extrinsic qualities of the item? If upon the basis of intrinsic qualities then the set is formed "on the basis of the *essential nature of the members themselves—on what they are in and of themselves*."[28] Most nouns in the English language are examples of intrinsic sets.

Alternately, do we assign membership in the category based upon extrinsic or relational qualities? To do so would be to form the set, not upon what a particular item is intrinsically, but *upon its relationship to some other item or a common reference point*. Most kinship terms are sets of this nature.

- *Variable #2*: What is the nature of the boundary between one category and another? Fuzzy or bounded?

If the boundaries between one category and another are unclear or ambiguous, without any sharp demarcation, then you have a fuzzy set where one category flows into another and where there can be degrees

28. Ibid., 110.

of inclusion in a given set. If the boundaries are clear and sharp, then you have a well-formed or bounded set where items belong to the set or they do not. Taking the idea of race as an example, many Americans understand racial categories in terms of a bounded set where people are placed into categories such as white, black, or Hispanic and are treated accordingly. However, racial categories are more accurately understood as fuzzy sets where the boundaries between one race and another blend into each other and become, at times, imperceptible.

Drawing these two variables together results in the formation of four set types: Intrinsic bounded sets, intrinsic fuzzy sets, extrinsic bounded sets (centered sets) and extrinsic fuzzy sets. Hiebert's discussion of each set type, and the ramifications of understanding the categories of "Christian," "church" and "mission" in terms of each set, is instructive. However, our concern at this point is to note how one of the sets Hiebert discusses might illuminate Torrance's concept of the social coefficient of knowledge as a category for understanding and elucidating the concept of culture.

Hiebert notes that in the West, intrinsic bounded sets are the most common way we categorize the external world. They are "the basic building blocks of our reality" and as such "fundamental to our understanding of order."[29] Although we use fuzzy sets, such as adverbs and adjectives (green, greener, greenest), we use them primarily as qualifiers for "bounded-set nouns."[30]

Modern definitions of culture have tended to understand it as an intrinsic bounded-set category, however Hiebert's description of the dynamics of the extrinsic centered set may be a more appropriate way of understanding, not only Torrance's concept of the social coefficient of knowledge, but the formation and nature of culture itself.

In the extrinsic bounded set members of the set are included or excluded upon the basis of *their relationship to the center of the set*. Consequently, we will refer to this type of extrinsic set as a "centered set." Hiebert notes four characteristics of centered sets:[31]

29. Ibid., 113.

30. Hiebert notes that the predominance of bounded-set thinking in the West is to be traced back to the role of Greek culture in the formation of Western society, with its concern to understand "the intrinsic nature of things and the ultimate, unchanging structure of reality" (ibid., 114).

31. See ibid., 123–24 for further development of these characteristics.

- Centered sets are created by defining a center or reference point and noting the relationship of things to that center: are they moving away from, or toward, the defined center?
- Consequently, centered sets have dynamically and organically defined boundaries that are formed upon a relational or directional basis, not an intrinsic one. Boundaries can be ambiguous, overlapping, and fluid.
- Participation in the centered set is extended fully to all members upon the basis of their orientation toward the center, but some may be near the center while others are not.
- Finally, as a relational centered set, transformation and change are accommodated by (1) allowing those near the center to move away from it and *vice versa*, without leaving the set and (2) allowing those once in the set to depart from it or those outside the set to enter it based upon relational changes.

There is a great deal of correspondence between Hiebert's articulation of centered-set theory and Torrance's concept of the social coefficient of knowledge.[32] This correspondence is rooted in the fact that *both the centered set and the social coefficient are fundamentally defined, shaped, and bounded by their centers and the nature of the relationships and structures that form around those centers.* As Hiebert notes, each set theory has its own unique dynamics, structures, and logic.[33] The dynamics and logic of Torrance's social coefficient would seem most congruent with centered set theory.

At the center of the social coefficient is a relationship between subjective knowers and objects to be known. As mentioned above, there are three variables that together give the relation a unique quality that in turn is embodied in the social coefficient: the subjective pole, the objective pole, and the quality or nature of the relation between them. These three variables act as a "mold" that will determine how the relations are socially embodied. That form is determined from *within* the social coefficient (acting somewhat like human DNA does in the formation of a

---

32. Hiebert and Torrance also have a great deal in common when it comes to their epistemic commitments. See Hiebert, *Missiological Implications*, 68–96.

33. Hiebert, *Anthropological Reflections*, 110.

human being) as opposed to being stamped upon it from *without*. Let us consider briefly Torrance's understanding of each pole of the relation.

THE OBJECTIVE POLE DETERMINES THE MEANS BY WHICH REALITY IS ENGAGED AND KNOWN

A knowing relation is a relation established with some feature of the objective world. When Torrance speaks of the objective world he is speaking of both a divine and contingent order that exists as real apart from our perceiving or believing. The contingent world in particular has come into being through the creative will and act of God and carries within it a particular design and purpose. That design and purpose must be understood and respected if both the human and non-human creation are to realize their true ends as "priests of creation" and "hymn of praise" respectively.[34]

Essential to this cooperation is the moral obligation of the knower to allow the object to be known to dictate the means by which it is known, and to make sure that there is congruence between the means of obtaining knowledge and the knowledge to be obtained. The means used must be appropriate to the end pursued. In this sense there is a certain asymmetry in the knowing relation with a priority being given to the objective pole, in that it is to determine how it is to be known and under what conditions, and to a great degree also how that knowledge is to be embodied (symbolically, ritually, etc.) and therefore shared.[35] This is not to suggest that a genuine dialectic between the objective and subjective pole of the knowing relation is non-existent. An ongoing conversation between the subjective and objective pole is essential to the process of knowing and the construction of meaning. That granted we understand the asymmetry between the objective and subjective poles of the knowing relation in Torrance's thought to be based upon his understanding of the created order as a fallen reality. The human mind participates in this falleness and consequently holds within itself a certain tendency, and along with it a great deal of social momentum,

---

34. These are labels that Torrance frequently uses to describe the role of the creature and the goal of creation.

35. For instance, positing the triune God as the objective pole of a knowing relation dictates that we employ means of knowing that are personal in nature and that the embodiment and sharing of the knowledge gained be done through relational means.

to want to form the objective world around its own desires and perceptions as opposed to allowing the objective world to transform the way the human mind perceives reality.[36]

Apart from this theological conviction Torrance also notes that the history of thought is on his side as well: "As the history of thought has shown again and again . . . no sooner has full place been accorded to the agency of the human subject in knowledge than it tends to arrogate to itself far more than its share."[37] Subjective structures need to be kept in check and Torrance does so by allowing the objective pole of the knowing relation to have priority in determining how knowledge of that object is to be engaged, received, embodied, and shared. The character of knowledge cannot be wholly determined by the subjective pole—its demands, contexts, or goals. In this way, he recognizes both a theological truth and a historical reality.

The objective pole "speaks" to the subjective pole when aspects of the objective pole do not "fit" the subjective structures employed to understand, describe, and explore it. This is true in both the world of persons and the world of inanimate objects. In the case of the former one thinks of the power of prejudices in their ability to close us off from responding to, or even perceiving, qualities in another person that do not fit the subjective frame we employ for understanding that person. Stereotypes are useful in approaching an object of knowledge, but if those stereotypes are not allowed to change in response to the disclosures of the object of knowledge, then the subjective pole of knowledge is asserting itself upon reality and by so doing cutting itself off from reality to live in its own fantasy world. Like a parent that refuses to allow their child to grow up, insisting they conform to expectations set

---

36. An often painful process and part of Torrance's very understanding of how social coefficients are formed; they involve a "running conflict" between the objective world pressing in upon us, and our subjective structures of thought (culture) oppressing the voice of the objective world. See his discussion of the formation of Israel as "the womb of Christ," in Torrance, *Mediation of Christ* where he understands the conflict to be between divine revelation and Israel's "carnal mind" (10–12). The role and priority ascribed to the external world by Torrance is problematized by the fact that the created world, as well as the human mind, is a fallen reality. Perhaps this is why Torrance prioritizes the character of the "transcendent ground of meaning," which ultimately defines the social coefficient. Though the objective pole of the knowing relation is given a methodological priority, Torrance knows that this priority alone will not resolve the problems inherent in any human knowing that takes place in a fallen world.

37. Torrance, *Reality and Scientific Theology*, 8.

in stone a long time ago, the knowing relation morphs from one that should be characterized by trust, risk, and freedom and becomes one of fear, force, and control.

In the case of the latter, the world of inanimate objects, the same dynamic is true even if the "disclosure" of the object does not come in the form of speech *per se*. We know when some aspect of the world is "asking" us to view it in a different way. Is not the environment asking us to view it in a different way and engage it in a more responsible manner when we discover that our consumption of the earth's resources are creating conditions where both human and non-human life are unsustainable? Torrance himself notes that the creation of tools, conceptual and otherwise, is necessary in order to enable the inanimate world to "speak" to us in this way.[38] When these tools are created and employed properly they enable the inanimate world to "speak" to us, say, through the microscope or the telescope.[39] Upon reception of that "speech" the subject is under a moral obligation to the object of knowledge. That moral obligation requires that the subjective frame of reference be transformed in such a way as to accommodate the new knowledge, sometimes with revolutionary effects.[40]

---

38. Torrance, *Mediation of Christ*, 5–7.

39. For Torrance, one of the main responsibilities of the human person is to engage the created order in such a way that it is enabled to "speak" the praise of its Creator. The created order, by its very nature, is "mute," and it is only through the agency of the human person that it is enabled to "speak." The creation of tools, conceptual and otherwise, is essential to the fulfillment of this uniquely human and scientific task. See Torrance, *Ground and Grammar*, chapter 1. However, in order to enable the created order to address the Creator, one must also, to some extent, know the Creator the created order is meant to praise. This will be explored in greater detail shortly, when we discuss the role of the "Archimedean point" in Torrance's "social coefficient of knowledge." Elsewhere Torrance notes that the Archimedean point serves as a "fundamental clue" or "pattern of truth" and describes its orienting and heuristic power in terms of a jigsaw puzzle. See Torrance, *Mediation of Christ*, 4–5. For Torrance an example of one of these fundamental clues is the relation of oneness between the Father and the Son. This clue should guide all our thinking about the Christian faith.

40. As examples of a telescopic and a microscopic discovery of this nature, one thinks of the shift from a Ptolemaic to a Copernican view of the universe, or of the discovery of the human genome. The process involved in such shifts, and the personal trauma involved, are described by anthropologist Charles Kraft in terms of the phenomena of "culture shock." See Kraft, *Christianity in Culture*. The experience of culture shock is a form of speech, albeit not from the objective created world, but from the objectivated social world (to use Berger's term). This speech requires us to adjust our subjective frame of reference if we are to understand and negotiate a different social

Torrance sums up the nature of the knowing relationship, and the dynamics between the subjective and objective poles, in the following way: "We seek to understand something, not by schematizing it to an external or alien framework, but by operating with a framework of thought appropriate to it, one which it suggests to us out of its own inherent constitutive relations and which we are rationally constrained to adopt in faithful understanding and interpretation of it."[41]

The Subjective Pole Determines the Means by Which Reality is Received and Reflected

In spite of the priority Torrance gives to the objective pole of the knowing relation such an emphasis is not meant to cancel out the importance of the subjective pole nor to enslave it to the objective pole. Again, the priority given to the objective pole is based upon theological truth and historical experience, not any disdain Torrance has for subjective elements in the reception or expression of knowledge. Torrance has consistently affirmed that knowledge cannot be had, nor may a knowing relation be established or sustained, apart from the subjective pole of the knowing relation,[42] nor is that pole meant to be eclipsed in the knowing process. The subjective pole is enabled to receive, recognize, and interpret clues and organize those clues into a coherent system of meaning while allowing that system of meaning to be modified in the process. This is the power and the purpose of the subjective pole of the knowing relation.

"The power of the subject is also its power to grasp objective being, to receive the effect of its intrinsic intelligibility, recognize its intimations and interpret the clues to which it gives rise. And that in turn indicates that in its capacity to be affected and modified in the orientation of its social consciousness toward objective being, a society or community provides the semantic frame within which meaning emerges and is sustained, but as such it functions through suggestive

---

environment. If we refuse to make these adjustments and, say, keep speaking English when Spanish is required, we will suffer accordingly.

41. Torrance, *Mediation of Christ*, 3–4.
42. Torrance, *Theological Science*, 85–105.

reference in the mode of art-form rather than in the mode of explicit mathematical or logical form."[43]

It is a common stereotype that Torrance's thought leaves no room for the human subject, and that his quest for objective knowledge both explicitly and implicitly belittles the contributions of the human subject to the knowing relation.[44] This stereotype is based more in the nature of the subject matter Torrance has chosen to work with (the natural sciences), and the requisite language he has expressed his thoughts in, than any prejudice Torrance has regarding human subjectivity. The subjective pole of the knowing relation is essential to the reception and embodiment of the knowing relation and the distinctive character and purpose of social coefficients.

Social Coefficients Are Socially Constructed Matrices Formed through a Historical Process

For Torrance, a knowing relation is a relation that is dialogical and dialectical in nature. It takes place in history between an objective and subjective pole and the consequence of that dialogical relation is the social embodiment of the knowing relation. Torrance describes the process between God and the formation of Israel as a covenant people in these terms. This "covenant partnership between God and Israel involved a running conflict between divine revelation and what St. Paul called 'the carnal mind.'"[45] That "running conflict" took place within the

---

43. Torrance, *Reality and Scientific Theology*, 103.

44. We think here of the work of John Douglas Morrison, who asserts that Torrance's theological epistemology requires a flight from history into a "mystical and non-discursive cognitive or conceptual encounter" if true knowledge of God is to be had. See Morrison, *Knowledge of the Self-Revealing God*, 316ff., and my review of that work. It seems clear from Torrance's understanding of the nature and function of the social coefficient that knowledge of God comes to us in and through a historical process and cannot be had otherwise. This does not negate the accuracy or objectivity of that knowledge.

45. Torrance, *Mediation of Christ*, 10. The subjective pole of the knowing relation is described here in negative terms, as something that is "carnal" and as such constantly in conflict with divine revelation. For Torrance, this is rooted in the fallen nature of the human mind and not in any deficiency of the created order or the ability of history to mediate divine revelation. That this conflict takes place is a reminder that human persons are in need of redemption and transformation. It is not a general statement about the ultimate value of the subjective pole of the knowing relation, which Torrance

boundaries of the created order and involved, not only the thinking of a particular people, but their entire way of life. This "conflict" involved affirmation and validation as well as judgment and critique.

In an attempt to understand better what is involved in this dialogical and dialectical relationship, and to bring out into the open the implications of this process for a theology of culture, we will draw Torrance's thought on this subject alongside that of sociologist Peter Berger. It is hoped that this will serve to clarify the assumptions that stand as the basis for each person's thought in this area and will simplify our understanding of the dialectical process through which social coefficients are formed.

For Torrance social coefficients, and the epistemological projects or knowing relations they bear witness to, are sustained by a "circle of knowing."[46] The dynamics of this circle are very similar to the dialectical process that Peter Berger and Thomas Luckmann describe in their work *The Social Construction of Reality*.[47]

For Berger the process that stands at the center of his theory of culture is *dialectical* in nature. Sociologist Robert Wuthnow notes that Berger uses this term to carry a very specific meaning in specific contexts, but that it is roughly synonymous with the terms "interaction" or "interplay." However, Wuthnow notes, "what is critical to emphasize is the sustained and unremitting character of this interplay."[48]

The sustained and unremitting character of this interplay arises from incompleteness in the human organism and thus there arises a need for a continual process of negotiation between the self and the body, and the self and the socio-cultural world in an effort to complete the human person by externalizing the self into socio-cultural forms and structures. Wuthnow notes that it is the latter negotiation in particular that is at the center of Berger's theory of culture.[49] Consequently,

---

understands as both essential and good. This is rooted in Torrance's doctrines of creation and incarnation.

46. The dynamics involved in this circle of knowing are described throughout Torrance's work, but with particular detail and clarity in *Reality and Evangelical Theology*.

47. A more condensed version of the process described in Berger and Luckmann, *Social Construction of Reality* may be found in Berger, *Sacred Canopy*, 1–28, with a more condensed version still in Wuthnow et al., *Cultural Analysis*, 34ff.

48. Wuthnow, et al., *Cultural Analysis*, 38.

49. Ibid., 38.

the very existence of this dialectical process, and its unremitting character, are grounded in Berger's assumptions regarding the nature of the human person as an incomplete organism and the external world as a socio-cultural construction directed toward the completion of the human self. We have already argued that these are two important factors essential to determining the character of any theology of culture. Berger captures these two aspects of this dialectic when he notes: "society is the product of man and that man is the product of society."[50] How this statement holds true for Berger, and the dialectic it encapsulates, will be described presently.

There are three distinguishable steps or "moments" (as Berger refers to them) in the dialectical process that serve as the basis for Berger's theory of culture.

EXTERNALIZATION

Wuthnow notes that for Berger "externalization is the ongoing outpouring of individuals physical and mental being into the world necessitated by their biological underdevelopment. Externalization is the essence of human being."[51]

Human persons are not born with the instinctual or physical structures necessary for survival, so they must build those structures themselves by externalizing their needs into the physical and social world. Consequently, "externalization [becomes] an anthropological necessity."[52] "Man must make a world for himself."[53] This comes through clearly in the thought of Clifford Geertz: "We are, in sum, incomplete or unfinished animals who complete or finish ourselves through culture—and not through culture in general but through highly particular forms of it."[54]

The world that is constructed in an effort to complete the human organism is culture, and through the cultural process an environment comes into being that is specially suited to the needs of particular human organisms. Therefore, the fundamental purpose of human culture is "to

50. Berger, *Sacred Canopy*, 3.
51. Wuthnow et al., *Cultural Analysis*, 39.
52. Berger, *Sacred Canopy*, 4.
53. Ibid., 5.
54. Geertz, *Interpretation of Cultures*, 49.

provide the firm structures for human life that are lacking biologically."[55] Culture is then understood as "the totality of man's products."[56] There is no hint of a transcendent design or purpose in this understanding of culture, nor of the anthropology upon which it is based.[57] Culture is a product that begins and ends with the human necessity of externalization due to its biological incompleteness. As Berger notes: "Society, then, is a product of man, rooted in the phenomenon of externalization, which in turn is grounded in the very biological constitution of man."[58]

However, externalization is only one moment in the process of culture creation for Berger, even if it is the moment most grounded in, and under the control of, the human organism.

Objectivation

The second moment in the continuing dialectic of culture construction is objectivation. Objectivation refers to "the transformation of man's products into a world that not only derives from man, but that comes to confront him as a facticity outside of himself."[59]

Wuthnow notes that through this transformation the socially constructed world created through externalization attains "the character of an external and 'objective' reality, not as a reality only plausible to the individual but as one experienced in common with others."[60] The main consequence of this objectivation is that the world *constructed* by the human person now has the ability to *instruct* the human person, in that it achieves the capacity "to direct behavior, impose sanctions, punish deviance and at the extreme, destroy human life."[61] For Berger, the objectified world "consists of objects, both material and non-material,

---

55. Berger, *Sacred Canopy*, 6.

56. Ibid., 6.

57. This is largely because of Berger's methodological assumptions, where he brackets out his theological beliefs in the development of his sociological theories. Consequently, it is not that Berger does not have theological beliefs that might illuminate his theory of culture; it is simply that he considers it inappropriate to include them when developing his thoughts as a sociologist.

58. Berger, *Sacred Canopy*, 8.

59. Ibid., 8–9.

60. Wuthnow et al., *Cultural Analysis*, 39.

61. Ibid. 39.

that are capable of resisting the desires of their producer."[62] An example of the power of material objects would be the creation of a tool that must then be handled in very particular ways. An example of the power of non-material objects would be the creation of a value that produces guilt when violated, the creation of a social role that produces embarrassment when stepped outside of, or the attempt to resist the flow of power in an institutional structure.[63]

Another aspect of objectivation is that it produces objects *that can be shared with others*. Objectivation makes it possible to apprehend a world external to us and to share that world with others through the creation of physical goods[64] and non-material symbols. Through this sharing we become mediators of life and identity for others, for example, through the sharing of something as basic as food or as complex as the gift of language. These "objects" arise out of our engagement with the created world and with others. Subsequently, they are finally rooted in our creation in the image of God.

However, one final moment in Berger's dialectic needs to be noted for the whole circle that feeds, sustains, and directs the development of culture to be completed.

Internalization

For Berger internalization, the third moment in the dialectic, is much more than the subjective apprehension of the objective world. It is rather "the reabsorbtion into consciousness of the objectivated world in such a way that the structures of this world come to determine the subjective structures of consciousness itself. That is, society now functions as the formative agency for individual consciousness."[65]

---

62. Berger, *Sacred Canopy*, 9.

63. One is reminded at this point of the nature of the "principalities and powers" in that they are structures created with a purpose toward the enrichment of human life (they have an objective basis in the creative purposes of God), but that they are also socially constructed and directed and, therefore, are fallen and can subvert human life. The two poles of the powers also need to be correlated properly for the purpose of the powers to be realized.

64. For a detailed treatment of the role material goods play in the construction and continuity of the self, see Csikszentmihalyi and Rochberg-Halton, *Meaning of Things*.

65. Berger, *Sacred Canopy*, 15.

Society functions as a formative agent through the process of socialization. The consequence of this process is that "the individual not only comprehends the objective socio-cultural world but identifies with it and is shaped by it. The world becomes *his* world."[66] In becoming *his* world the social reality that a given person internalizes then comes to influence greatly his/her habits of thinking and acting in the world.[67]

Just as the world-building externalization of the human person occurs as a social enterprise so too the internalization of the socially constructed world is a collective project carried out through the process of socialization. Socialization is, according to Berger, "a life-long process whereby individuals are initiated into the meanings of the culture and learn to accept the tasks, roles, and identities that make up its social structure."[68]

Through the process of socialization the socially constructed world of one generation is passed on to the next generation, with greater and lesser degrees of success. The entire dialectic is a collective process within which the individual participates. This process is succinctly described by Berger in the following way: "It is through externalization that society is a human product. It is through objectivation that society becomes a reality *sui generis*. It is through internalization that man is a product of society."[69]

The dialectic that stands at the basis of Berger's theory of culture, with its three "moments" of externalization, objectivation, and internalization, may also be discerned in the thought of Torrance, particularly in his understanding of the formation and function of social coefficients of knowledge. This similarity extends not only to the actual dialectic itself, but also, to some degree, to the anthropological and cosmological assumptions upon which it is based.

---

66. Wuthnow, et al., *Cultural Analysis*, 39.

67. This is why, for Torrance, the social coefficient is both an identity structure and a legitimacy structure; for how we understand ourselves as agents will determine our action in the world. Additionally, how we morally justify our actions will also influence our relationships and the world-building activity that is based upon them. If the objectivated world is not congruent with the "real" world, then human agents, whose identities are formed in conversation with the objectivated world, will be mis-formed and directed toward a *telos* that is foreign to them, even if it serves the goals and imperatives of the objectivated world.

68. Wuthnow et al., *Cultural Analysis*, 40.

69. Berger, *Sacred Canopy*, 4.

For Torrance, the human person is a creature created in the image of God. As we noted in chapter 4, this means that the human person is constituted as a personal being through relation to God, to others, and to the world. To be constituted in such a way requires that the human person be open to that which is beyond him or herself.

Where Berger grounds the dialectic that stands at the basis of society in human biological incompleteness or "plasticity," Torrance would locate it in the creation of the human person in the image of the triune God and the vocation of the human person as a priest of creation. For Berger, the fundamental plasticity and sociality of the human organism leads to a diversity of social constructions and a willingness and ability to be formed by what the human organism creates.[70] For Torrance, the plasticity and sociality of the human person becomes the basis for the expression of the image of God and the fulfillment of human stewardship by enabling cultural plurality and by making it possible for the human person to take on a concrete cultural identity through the process of internalization/socialization. Torrance also understands that very plasticity and sociality to be just as much a threat to the human person as it is the very essence of the uniqueness and dignity of human persons created in the image of God. This is because the very openness of the human person to the world that this requires also opens the human person to being determined by the world they are open to. In order to set the human person free to be *determinate* without being *determined* a transcendent reference point is required.[71] For Torrance, this reference point is the triune God, and it is this reference point that safeguards the personal structure of human being even while safeguarding the plastic-

---

70. Torrance also recognizes the "plasticity" of the human person and understands this plasticity as a quality of personhood: "As person . . . man is the being who is open to others as well as to the world" (Torrance, *Reality and Scientific Theology*, 193).

71. Perhaps a reminder is in order here. Torrance fully affirms the goodness of being created a determinate being. This is not a negative quality of being human that must be transcended. As chapter 4 noted, the determinate nature of human life is rooted, not in the fall or human sin, but in the declaration of the created order as "good" by its Creator and the assumption, resurrection, and redemption of the created order through the incarnate Christ. For Torrance being *determinate* is good, for it means the realization of God's good purposes for the creature. However, being *determined* for Torrance takes on a different meaning, where the identity and ultimate purpose of the human creature is defined solely by is relation to the created order and not the Creator who brought it into being. Whether something is determinate or determined can only be discerned through an understanding of that object's *telos*.

ity of the human person from becoming a means of bondage as opposed to liberation and the fulfillment of its unique *telos*. Externalization and objectivation that is incongruent with the divine *telos* for the created world evolves into the determination and oppression of creaturely being and the subversion of the human vocation as priest of that created order. This is summed up by Torrance in the following way: "I submit that it is only through a divine Trinity who admits us to communion with himself in his own transcendence that we can be consistently and persistently personal, with the kind of freedom, openness and transcendent reference which we need both to develop our own personal and social culture and our scientific exploration of the universe."[72]

What Torrance introduces here is the idea that social coefficients, like the human organisms that generate them, are incomplete in themselves. They are teleological realities that require completion beyond themselves in order to fulfill their purpose for being. For Torrance, the purpose of the social coefficient is to mediate meaning, primarily by placing human persons in contact with an external world. However, the external world they are placed in contact with is also contingent, and as such cannot bear the burden of meaning without a transcendent reference point or orientation. At this point, we are introduced to two concepts that are central to Torrance's trinitarian realism:

- Social coefficients mediate and sustain meaning by placing human persons in contact with the real world.
- Social coefficients can only accomplish this semantic task when it is recognized that reality is multi-leveled in nature, and that meaning is ultimately lodged not in the created order, but in a "transcendent ground."

These are two ways of saying that social coefficients of knowledge are oriented toward a specific function and task that is semantic in nature, and the particular character and shape of the social coefficient will be determined by how it makes meaning, or how it fulfills this task. This brings us to the final component central to the formation of social coefficients: they are not only formed around knowing relations, nor only through a historical process; they are also formed in an effort to achieve or fulfill a particular goal or *telos*. That goal or *telos* is to mediate and

---

72. Torrance, *Reality and Scientific Theology*, 196.

sustain meaning and, consequently, the personal beings whose identities and projects are formed upon the basis of those semantic constructs.

Social Coefficients are Socially Constructed Matrices Oriented toward a Specific Telos

Social Coefficients Mediate and Sustain Meaning through Correlation, Congruence, and Translucence: Semantic Intentionality

The primary function of the social coefficient is to put the human subject in contact with an external world, and upon the basis of this contact to lodge meaning and significance in a place that is external to the self. This is accomplished through socially constructed matrices, with their symbols, rituals, and structures. As Torrance notes: "There is an inescapable need for a social coefficient of knowledge in order to establish and maintain semantic relations with the universe."[73] However, meaning itself is not socially constructed or contained, even if socially mediated. Meaning is grounded in an ordered dialogue between the two poles of the knowing relation, where the objective pole of the relation is given a degree of primacy and where the task of the subjective pole is to enable persons and communities to grasp, articulate, and socially embody the knowledge "received" from the objective pole of the relation. As Torrance continues, the social coefficient makes it possible for us "to be rightly related to [the] essential patterns and intrinsic intelligibilities [of reality] which are the ground of meaning."[74] In the context of this relationship with the created world the human subject encounters the "impress" of reality, an impress that seeks expression and realization "within the personal and social patterns of our human life."[75]

To accomplish this goal, the social coefficient must orient its members away from themselves as the locus of meaning towards the objective pole that defines their social life. The symbols, structures, and rituals that orient the members of a social coefficient must have a *semantic intentionality* that constantly refers them beyond themselves to the intelligible ground of reality where the true locus of meaning exists.

73. Ibid., 102.
74. Ibid.
75. Ibid., 99.

As Torrance notes, "it is this semantic intentionality that gives meaning to the whole framework of human life so that without it every culture slips away into meaninglessness."[76]

However, such an orientation does not come without struggle. As Torrance notes, "the social structure of human life struggles with adjustment to the insistent demands of intelligible reality, and is not infrequently found in flight from the self-criticism and discipline that knowledge of reality brings."[77] As mentioned above, social coefficients form through a dialectical process carried out in the context of history. When a cultural form becomes institutionalized or objectified, it takes on an objectivity and facticity of its own, which is then internalized by the human subjects who participate in the life of that institution. If these cultural forms are incongruent with the demands of reality, a painful transformation in the frame of human knowing must take place, where human social constructs are brought into a greater degree of correspondence and congruence with the objective pole of the knowing relation. This is a form of personal and social self-denial that comes through a process of great difficulty. It is not unlike the process of culture shock experienced by persons traveling to other cultures who must make numerous individual and social adjustments in order to adapt and flourish in a profoundly different environment.

Requiring that symbols orient the human subject away from their own cultural embeddedness if they are to obtain and sustain meaning is not a form of semantic colonialism or cultural homogenization, where order and significance are impressed upon a community or culture from without and through a single source. What Torrance is suggesting is not a mimetic reproduction of "the regularities and invariances disclosed in the frame of created reality," but rather a *correlation* between our diverse symbolic and cultural forms and created reality. What Torrance suggests is a *correspondence or congruence* that effectively transforms our symbols and structures from being merely reflections of our own

---

76. Ibid.

77. Ibid., 100. For Torrance, this struggle is exemplified in the life of Israel. See Torrance, *Mediation of Christ*, 10–12.

in-turned self-consciousness to conceptual tools[78] that are suggestive[79] and translucent.[80]

As Torrance notes, ultimate reality "acts *creatively* upon us, not to reproduce itself in our formalizing activities, but to call them, as it were, into contrapuntal sequences and patterns of an open texture through which it can reverberate or resound in the human spirit."[81]

The language of improvisational music is most helpful in understanding the dynamic between subject and object that Torrance is describing here. As a musician engages a piece of music he or she is called upon not only to reflect accurately the particular qualities that make the piece of music this piece and not another, but also to bring something of him or herself to the piece in a fresh and creative way. This is done via improvisation, tempo, differing arrangements, various musical settings, etc. A dialogical relation between the composition (objective pole) and the musician (subjective pole) exists, but without the expectation that there is going to be a mimetic correspondence between composition and performance. In fact, with jazz music in particular, for the composition to be rendered in a mimetic fashion would be a "violation" of the "semantic intentionality" of the piece, if in fact it was composed in such a way as to generate improvisational music. In addition, to so "flourish" the piece as to make it unrecognizable would also be a violation of the composition by granting the subjective pole a freedom and autonomy beyond its purpose and bounds. In the first instance, the objective pole overshadows the subjective, and in the second instance the subjective

---

78. For an explanation of this term, see Torrance, *Mediation of Christ*, 6.

79. This is a term used with reference to art in particular but can apply to all symbolic forms. See Torrance, *Reality and Scientific Theology*, 98.

80. "Translucency" is a quality that results when the appropriate correspondence has been achieved between a cultural form and external reality. When this occurs, the cultural form may be described as "translucent." This does not mean the cultural form loses its particularity, but rather that the cultural form fulfills its purpose. See Torrance, "Christian Apprehension," 126ff., where he refers to the appropriate role of linguistic forms as "transparent media" or "open analogies," through which "the truth of God may disclose itself to us and through which the Word of God himself may sound through to us and be heard by us, and not some word of ours that we have projected into God's mouth" (129). See also Torrance, *Reality and Evangelical Theology*, where language is described as a "transparent medium" (64), and where linguistic forms, in dialogue with intelligible reality, are to serve as "apposite ways of representing the structured objectivities of the universe" (62).

81. Torrance, *Reality and Scientific Theology*, 99; italics mine.

pole overshadows the objective. Torrance will have neither. The relation between the subjective and objective poles of the knowing relation requires the same kind of fluidity and nuance as Torrance's conception of contingence considered earlier. The subjective pole of the knowing relation is affirmed in its particularity and finds its freedom only in its dependence upon, and faithfulness to, the objective pole of the knowing relation.

Torrance is not interested in mimetic reproductions of reality in our social life. His doctrine of God as triune and creation as contingent will not allow for such an understanding. It must be remembered that though meaning is located in the objective pole of the knowing relation, that objective pole has been brought into being by the creative activity of a triune Creator and is characterized by a contingence that cannot be captured by any single form of social life. The created contingent order is "infinitely suggestive"[82] and consequently there need be no fear that locating meaning there will homogenize cultural activity or cultural forms.[83] However, if social coefficients are meant to put human persons into touch with created reality, and by so doing to sustain their personal being, then we can expect some normative features to be present in human cultural constructs.[84] For Torrance, these normative features cannot be solely located in an impersonal created order, but in the transcendent ground of that order, a ground that is personal in nature. To ultimately locate meaning in any other place is to invite the slow erosion of that which is distinctly personal. It is to cut human persons adrift from the personal and transcendent ground of their being.

---

82. This is a phrase used by jazz guitarist Pat Metheny when he was asked about his repeated performance of the Antonio Carlos Jobim song "How Insensitive." Metheny responded by saying that this particular song has a quality that makes it "infinitely suggestive" and therefore an inexhaustible vehicle for improvisation. We propose that the contingent created order, and the God who has brought it into being, may also be so characterized.

83. Even though this common engagement will result in physical and social structures that are universal and normative for human life, and which make broad structures of human understanding and community possible. See Augsburger, *Pastoral Counseling across Cultures*, 48–58.

84. Many of these normative features are noted in Augsburger, *Pastoral Counseling across Cultures*, chapter 2.

Social Coefficients Require an Archimedean Point in Order to Fulfill Their Distinctive *Telos*: The Transcendent Ground of Meaning

If, as suggested above, we are to understand social coefficients of knowledge as relational centered sets, then we must also affirm that these sets form as the members of the set congregate or crystallize around distinctive centers or objects of knowledge. The boundaries of the set do not emerge by imposing order upon the object of knowledge. Rather, the boundaries of the set emerge through varied relations with the object of knowledge at the center of the set. It is the center of the social coefficient that confers upon it a distinctive character and form, just as a DNA strand is the source of the distinctive characteristics of a living organism.

However, we are still here speaking of relations between an objective and a subjective pole, where both poles are located within the boundaries of the created order. We mentioned earlier that the center of the social coefficient has three variables: the subjective pole, the objective pole, and the quality of the relation that exists between them. Perhaps at this point we can suggest a fourth variable: where the social coefficient locates its transcendent ground of meaning, or how it identifies its "Archimedean point."

Torrance notes frequently in his writing on the social coefficient of knowledge that "we need an Archimedean point far beyond us, and indeed beyond the world, through which we can be levered out of our rigid fixations and social mechanisms, and liberated for the pursuit of pure science concerned with reality for its own sake, and for the free and open-structured society that is correlated with it."[85]

Torrance mentions the need for an Archimedean point for reasons that are rooted in his doctrines of creation and humanity, and further identifies this Archimedean point as the triune God of Jesus Christ. He continues:

---

85. Torrance, *Reality and Scientific Theology*, 117. With the social coefficient of knowledge Torrance is certainly developing an implicit social theory of his own, and by grounding scientific activity (understood in its broadest sense) in a social coefficient of knowledge, which in turn demands "faith in a transcendent reality," he clearly suggests an outline for a theology of culture. Later, when Torrance identifies this transcendent reality as the triune God, the components for a theology of culture that is distinctly trinitarian in nature are in place.

> It is not enough for us ... to have in view the kind of transcendence we have to do with *in* the world ... We need to have in view the infinite transcendence of God *over* the world, who, as the Creator of the universe and its immanent rational order, is the ultimate ground of all transcendence within the universe and to whom the universe as a whole is left open at its boundary conditions ... It is, of course, with the Transcendence of God that we are primarily concerned here. He is the one Archimedean point beyond the universe to whom the universe as a whole is so related that it is given authentic meaning ... and the one Archimedean point to whom we are so related ... that we are constantly emancipated from ourselves and enabled to transcend the structures of our scientific and social activities.[86]

When we speak of the social coefficient as forming around a subjective and an objective pole and the relation that exists between them, we are still only speaking of "the kind of transcendence we have to do with *in* the world." When Torrance introduces the idea of an Archimedean point of transcendence beyond the kinds of transcendence we experience in our encounters with the created world he introduces a fourth, and pivotal, variable in the formation of social coefficients: all meaning must ultimately refer to a transcendent ground of meaning, or Archimedean point. Torrance identifies this Archimedean point as the triune God of Jesus Christ.[87]

Two questions immediately emerge: First, why must we recognize an Archimedean point as an essential component and variable of the social coefficient? Second, why identify that Archimedean point as the God of Jesus Christ? We will address each of these questions in turn.

The Archimedean Point as a Tuning Fork: Its Function

For Torrance, the central function of the Archimedean point is that it serves as a fulcrum, a fulcrum through which we may escape "our rigid fixations and social mechanisms." This "fulcrum" will set us free from the threats of social determinism, not by enabling us to transcend

---

86. Ibid., 117; italics original.

87. We are here reminded that for Torrance meaning and rationality are multi-layered. Each social coefficient must reflect and/or recognize this "texturing" of reality and meaning. Each of these layers must be properly tuned to the others, and the only way of doing so is by recourse to an Archimedean point. This "texturing" of reality and meaning will be discussed below as a feature of the social coefficient.

the historical character of human life, but by enabling us to discern its meaning, purpose, and *telos*. As noted previously, the historical character of human life is rooted in our creation in the image of a triune God and the created order as contingent. Human life as intended by God is to be lived within the coordinates of space and time. However, when we situate human life within coordinates that are strictly rooted in the created order itself we lose our way in the world. It is as if we are orienting ourselves upon the basis of a faulty compass or mis-drawn map. When this disorientation occurs, the social environment externalized and objectified by the human person undergoes a transformation. With no transcendent reference, a society closes in upon itself and becomes a product of its "rigid fixations"—its unquestioned values, goals, and gods. An environment meant to sustain and nurture human life in freedom becomes a "social mechanism," with detrimental effects on human life, and indeed the entire created order.

Colin Gunton, in his book *The One, the Three and the Many*, notes that the loss of a transcendent reference point has detrimental effects upon how we relate the particulars of life to each other without extinguishing them or escaping from them. He cites the words of Vaclav Havel with approval: "I believe that with the loss of God, man has lost a kind of absolute and universal system of coordinates, to which he could always relate everything, chiefly himself. His world and his personality gradually began to break up into separate, incoherent fragments corresponding to different, relative coordinates."[88]

For Gunton the language of "coordinates" is important, for it "implies a system in which particulars are truly related to one another, and yet in such a way that 'space' remains between them."[89] Such coordinates, and the "space" they offer, are necessary "if we are to know who we are and what our world is" and if we are to have "a perspective from which to view and assess our various interests and actions."[90] Gunton is not only concerned to maintain the appropriate space between things in the world, but also between human persons and the divine. Without an appropriate set of coordinates created life becomes fragmented, and the very ecology that allows for the flourishing of created life, in all its diversity and interrelatedness, is placed in jeopardy.

88. Gunton, *The One, the Three and the Many*, 71.
89. Ibid.
90. Ibid.

Torrance introduces the Archimedean point as a way to address this destructive dynamic. The Archimedean point, when properly identified, "liberates" the cultural process (described by Berger in terms of externalization, objectivation, and internalization) by orienting the human agent beyond itself. Human cultural activity therefore, is no longer rooted in what Ernest Becker has referred to as "the denial of death"[91] but rather a transcendent source of meaning and purpose. The Archimedean point in this way serves both a purpose of particular interest to Torrance ("the pursuit of pure science concerned with reality for its own sake"), but also a goal of importance to us all (a "free and open-structured society that is correlated with it"). For Torrance, "science, faith in transcendent reality, and the free society are inseparately interlocked together."[92] Though Torrance's work has been largely devoted to exploring the relationships between "science" and "faith in a transcendent reality" it is clear that he sees both of these as deeply connected to cultural development and transformation towards the end of producing and protecting a "free society."

Torrance uses mechanical imagery when he describes this "transcendent reality" as an "Archimedean point." What he describes however, when discussing the social coefficient of knowledge and the role of the Archimedean point in it, is a very personal and relational process, involving a number of variables that need to be properly oriented, not only to the Archimedean point, but to each other as well. This is true of Colin Gunton's comments as well, with his language of "space" as being necessary for the proper relation of one thing to another. Perhaps the use of different imagery would clarify further the specific dynamic that Torrance and Gunton are seeking to describe.

To refer back to the musical imagery employed in the previous chapter, we might understand this fourth variable (the Archimedean point) as a "tuning fork" that serves to keep the relations between the objective and subjective poles of the knowing relation "in tune." For instance, if a group of musicians desire to gather together around a particular piece of music (piece of music = objective pole), they must first agree how they are going to be related to that piece of music (tempo, key, etc.) as well as to each other (subjective pole). Agreeing that they will perform "All Blues" in a particular key is one thing. They then need

---

91. Becker, *Denial of Death*, chapters 1 and 2.
92. Torrance, *Reality and Scientific Theology*, 117.

to "tune up" by making sure that each of their instruments is properly tuned—not only in relation to themselves, but also to each other. This cannot be done in isolation. An "objective" standard must be recognized, a "tuning fork" that serves to orient further the musicians and particularly their relations with each other.[93] Consequently, there are two points of orientation for the subjective pole of the knowing relation: the object of knowledge itself (which is infinitely variable), and the transcendent ground of meaning or Archimedean point, which serves to orient the subjective pole to the objective by referring both to a point beyond the dyadic relation itself.

The Archimedean point is not variable in a functional sense. All social coefficients operate with one, whether implicitly or explicitly. However, it can be identified in any number of ways. Torrance himself asserts that only the triune God of Jesus Christ can faithfully serve as the Archimedean point for our relations in the world in a way that "humanizes" and "personalizes" them and moves them toward God's purposes for creation. The triune God then becomes a "tuning fork" for orienting our relations with each other, with God, and with the created order in such a way that they approximate God's intentions for the world. Freedom, purpose, meaning, and a "free society" are the by products we experience as we approximate and embody these intentions in our social worlds.[94] Our social worlds are "legitimated" by reference to the various coordinates in the social coefficient and the Archimedean point used to orient them all to each other.

At this point, let us summarize our argument thus far. We will then move on to consider why Torrance insists that the only Archimedean point adequate to serve as a tuning fork for the various social coefficients in the world is the triune God of Jesus Christ.

Torrance's anthropology requires that we affirm two realities: First, the necessity of social coefficients of knowledge if human persons are

---

93. In a jazz ensemble the piano is commonly used as the point of reference for tuning the instruments to each other. Another example would be the way in which the drummer serves as a point of reference for maintaining the time signature of the piece.

94. University of Chicago social psychologist Mihaly Csikszentmihalyi notes in his book *Flow* that the things we desire most in life (freedom, joy, and contentment) are only found as by-products of our full engagement in other tasks and not in directly pursuing these things in themselves. Nicholas Wolterstorff notes that the by-products of shalom are "joy and delight." See Wolterstorff, *Until Justice and Peace Embrace*, 124ff.

to "be at home in the universe."⁹⁵ These social coefficients are created through the cultural activity of persons created in the divine image, and function to provide the human creature with a semantic web of significance that confers upon the human creature a sense of being "at home." Second, the necessity of a transcendent ground of meaning or "Archimedean point" to orient those social coefficients and the persons that indwell them. The human person, as a contingent being created in the image of God, is just as open to the world at its boundary conditions as the created order itself. This openness to the world is essential to our constitution not only as cultural beings, but also as personal beings. Yet, the very openness that makes personhood possible is also the same ground that makes the subversion of that personhood an ever present threat, unless personhood is ultimately grounded beyond the contingent order in a triune God who upholds it, even while doing so through the social structures that threaten to subvert it. With this Torrance recognizes the following truths:

First, *we are creaturely beings* who stand in solidarity with the rest of the created order, a solidarity Ray S. Anderson refers to as "the solidarity of the sixth day."⁹⁶ As such, "we need a world with determinate conditions and limitations in which to live as rational persons."⁹⁷

Second, that *we are social beings* who bring into existence these "determinate conditions" not only by recognizing the nature and limitations of the physical world, but by constructing social worlds that provide for us "universal conceptions and public language through which we may communicate intelligibly with one another" and "order our behavior in universally acceptable ways."⁹⁸ In other words, social coefficients of knowledge "enable us to be *at home* in the universe."⁹⁹ However, as social beings we are also "subject to the constraints of rigid patterns of law and exposed to the tyranny of necessitarian structures."¹⁰⁰ The social gives rise to the personal, since "as person,

---

95. Torrance, *Reality and Scientific Theology*, 114.
96. See Anderson, *On Being Human* 22.
97. Torrance, *Reality and Scientific Theology*, 192.
98. Ibid.
99. Ibid., 114; italics original.
100. Ibid., 193.

man is the being who is open to what is beyond himself, open to others as well as to the world."[101]

Third, *we are personal beings*. If it were not for the fact that human beings are also personal beings, open to the world and to others, the physical and social construction of a determinate world would not be problematic for the human subject. However, as personal beings we have been brought into being according to a particular design and given a particular identity and task. This identity and task cannot be exclusively located within the coordinates of space and time. Consequently, when the determinate world we have socially constructed is incongruent with our creation as personal beings "[the] rational human being feels his freedom threatened [and] his personal structure being undermined."[102] The personal structure of humanity is sustained in a matrix composed of the relationships between created reality, social structures, and a transcendent ground of meaning. When the relations between these variables are "misaligned" or "out of tune," human personhood is threatened. Therefore, Torrance asserts that "a transcendent relation or openness to what is beyond it is necessary for the existence of authentic personal being . . . and it is precisely this kind of openness that is created through the intensely personalizing interaction of the triune God."[103]

Consequently, what needs to be posited is a transcendent ground for personhood and meaning that is not simply functional and rooted in human subjectivity, but that is congruent with the particular identity and task assigned the human person. For Torrance, this can be none other than the triune God of Jesus Christ, even if other transcendent grounds may be recognized: "I submit that it is only through a divine Trinity who admits us to communion with himself in his own transcendence that we can be consistently and persistently personal, with the kind of freedom, openness and transcendent reference which we need

---

101. Ibid.

102. Ibid.

103. Ibid. Torrance also discussed the role of Christ as "the personalizing Person" and the "humanizing Man," in Torrance, *Mediation of Christ*, 67–72. At its heart, Torrance's theology is profoundly concerned with the personal: its identification, redemption, sustenance, and embodiment. This is a theme of Torrance's thought that has been little explored, and that we shall have more to say about shortly. For Torrance the triune nature of God, the personal nature of humanity, and the existence of a free society belong together.

both to develop our own personal and social culture and our scientific exploration of the universe."[104]

The Archimedean Point as the Triune God of Jesus Christ: Its Identity

Why is the proper identification of this Archimedean point so crucial for Torrance? If we were to draw a few conclusions from the material just cited, the ontological integrity of the human person, the health of our personal and social worlds, and our progress in scientific knowledge are, for Torrance, dependent upon the proper identification of this Archimedean point. It also seems clear from Torrance that this Archimedean point must be identified as the triune God of Jesus Christ if we are to realize and sustain any of the above things in a consistent fashion. The common factor here is that only the triune God of Jesus Christ is a personal God who binds himself to human persons, thus making them open for relations beyond themselves, both with God and with created reality. This openness to the other is essential to Torrance's understanding of both divine and human personhood[105] and all human projects, whether personal, social, cultural, or scientific. Such openness is only possible through "the intensely personalizing interaction of the Triune God."[106]

However, to note such things is to be speaking at the surface level of Torrance's thought. As Torrance himself would no doubt encourage us, we should try to discover the deeper connections between these assertions. We should attempt to elucidate the inner-logic that unites these truths. Why do these things work together in this way? Why does Torrance insist upon making connections between the triune God of Jesus Christ, the ontological integrity of the human person, the health of our personal and social worlds, and our progress in scientific knowledge? Answering this question will take us into the heart of Torrance's evangelical theology.

---

104. Torrance, *Reality and Scientific Theology*, 196. This is yet another indication that for Torrance the social coefficient of truth has implications much broader than for the development of particular research traditions or paradigms.

105. We should clarify here that for Torrance divine personhood is rooted in the eternal *perichoretic* relations of the Father, Son, and Spirit and not in any necessary relation with the created order, personal or otherwise.

106. Torrance, *Reality and Scientific Theology*, 193.

Torrance would also assert that intuitive and heuristic leaps are often necessary in order to get to the deep logic of some reality. We will suggest that the deep logic of Torrance's thought is not only evangelical and doxological, but also sociological, where matters of identity, agency, sociality, embodiment, and worship are woven together, providing rich soil from which to grow a theology of culture. By employing the thought of other thinkers these assumptions will be made more explicit, and will be found to repose ultimately upon Torrance's doctrines of God as triune, creation as contingent, and human persons as stewards in the image of God.

Let us first consider some of the reasons for Torrance's identification of the Archimedean point with the God of Jesus Christ.

EPISTEMOLOGICAL REASONS: REVELATION—In Torrance's 1992 essay "The Christian Apprehension of God the Father," we have perhaps the most concise statement of Torrance's theological epistemology and what is involved in his understanding of divine revelation.[107] Central to this epistemology is the being and agency of the triune God and the fact that God addresses, in revelation, human persons created in the image of this God.

Torrance notes that knowledge of God is only possible as God "enters into actual relations with us as human beings and reveals himself to us ... within the frame of our human speech in the world."[108] Such a movement of God into the world, and into our frame of knowing, would not be possible apart from the triune agency of God in revelation.[109] Torrance notes in particular the work of the Son and the Spirit in the mediation of revelation: "This [the revelation of God within our frame of knowledge] would not be possible for us apart from the *Word* of God become flesh in Jesus Christ, for in him God addresses us in such a way as to create in us the ability to hear him beyond any creaturely capacity we may have in ourselves."[110]

---

107. Torrance, "Christian Apprehension," 120–43.

108. Ibid., 122.

109. See also Torrance's understanding of the relation between general and special revelation in Torrance, *Karl Barth: Biblical and Evangelical Theologian*, chapter 5. These themes are developed further, in conversation with Barth and Torrance, in Anderson, "Barth and a New Direction."

110. Torrance, "Christian Apprehension," 122; italics original.

God's address to humanity, and our ability to hear that address, is rooted in the creative work of the incarnate Son. However, it is also rooted in the agency of the Spirit. Torrance continues: "Nor would it [the revelation of God within our frame of knowledge] be possible for us apart from the *Spirit* of God, for God through his Spirit graciously makes himself present to us within the littleness and lowliness of our creaturely existence and sustains us from below in relation to himself, thereby opening our hearts and minds toward him and enabling us to receive his Word and understand his self-revelation."[111]

For Torrance, there is an indissoluble relation between the triune being and agency of God and the knowledge of God we are able to have within the coordinates of space and time. Put most simply, there would be no knowledge of God to *receive* apart from the work of the Son, and there would be no way for us to *respond* to that knowledge (or to go on responding to it) apart from the work of the Spirit. Neither would be possible apart from a specific social and historical location. This is another way of saying that through the work of the Son and the Spirit God establishes and sustains a knowing relation with human persons; a knowing relation where the social and cultural matrix of the human subject is incorporated into the very self-giving and self-revealing of God: "[God] establishes and upholds a *human co-efficient* in the knowing relationship, and really makes us partners with himself in this two-way relationship. Thus the act of God's self-revealing to us takes our human speaking, hearing, and knowing into its concrete realization within God's personal interrelation with us, and so there is necessarily included within it an *anthropomorphic* component."[112]

This would certainly seem true if we are speaking of theological knowledge, in particular knowledge of the God of Jesus Christ embodied in the particular social coefficient of the Church.[113] Apart from the triune agency of God knowledge of God would be neither accurate, nor distinctly "ours," since it would not be grounded in God nor in our

---

111. Ibid., 122; italics original.

112. Ibid., 124; italics original.

113. Torrance is not saying that we cannot have knowledge of God unless we recognize the triune being and agency of God in revelation. He is only asserting that if we are to move from grounds located in the most basic and incipient forms of knowing to a higher level of synthesis, then the triune nature of God is essential to a doctrine of revelation.

particular social coefficients apart from the agency of the Son and the Spirit.

However, is the triune being and agency of God just as central to our knowledge of this-worldly objects? Torrance seems to think so. In fact, he does not even mention its importance for the church in particular until after asserting its importance for our personal and social projects in general.[114] Obviously, correctly identifying the Archimedean point is essential, and this is not possible, in Torrance's view, unless that Archimedean point is the triune God of Jesus Christ, for reasons just described.[115]

More directly however, we must identify the Archimedean point with the triune God of Jesus Christ for salvific reasons. This brings us to our second point.

SOTERIOLOGICAL REASONS: SALVATION—Torrance notes that "the social coefficient of human knowledge has immense advantages," the most basic being that it "enables us to be *at home* in the universe."[116] This sense of being at home in the universe has more to do with semantic structures than physical ones.[117] We are at home in the universe because we are able to "make sense" of the world we inhabit. The primary tool we use to accomplish this task is language, for it enables us to interpret, categorize and arrange our experiences of the world in an orderly and coherent fashion, usually in a way that is congruent with our deepest values and presuppositions. Through language, we *inherit* a meaningful world and through language we *maintain* the meaningfulness of that world. As Torrance notes: "The web of meaning that is found lodged in human language is significant, for language, as Heidegger used to say, is the house of being, and it is through language that reality shows itself to us and we become familiar with it."[118]

---

114. Torrance, *Reality and Scientific Theology*, 196.

115. This epistemological point will become important for reasons of sanctification and doxology shortly, for it is toward this point and around this center that society is healed and enabled to glorify its Creator.

116. Torrance, *Reality and Scientific Theology*, 114; italics original.

117. However, it is quite clear in Torrance's writings that he also believes that the cosmos, as our *physica*l home, has been finely crafted to support our biological life and to encourage our vocation as stewards created in the image of God.

118. Torrance, *Reality and Scientific Theology*, 114.

It is clear at this point that human language, for Torrance, must have a realist component to it. If it is to function authentically as a "web of meaning" and in such a way that we find ourselves "at home in the universe," it must place us in contact with a reality external to ourselves, not simply a "reality" that makes sense in a purely subjective fashion. Torrance continues: "This [realist] function of language is basic to what we have been calling the social coefficient of knowledge, as it enables us to be *rightly related* to the intelligible world around us."[119]

In other words, the objective and subjective poles of the knowing relation must be properly related, balanced, and tuned in order for the kind of meaning that will make us "feel at home in the universe" to emerge. The coordinates necessary for the emergence of meaning lie not only in language and the subjectivity of the human agent, but also in an objective world. The function of language then, as the carrier of a "web of meaning," is to place us in a proper relationship to this world so that the intelligible world can "shine through into our understanding," making meaningful human action in the world a possibility.[120]

When language functions in this translucent manner, "we are not left to grope our way singly in the dark."[121] Apart from this translucent function of language and the "comprehensive outlook" upon the world embodied in it, "we would be rather blind and would not be able to recognize or identify significant aspects of reality."[122] What we are offered implicitly through the acquisition of language is not only a "com-

---

119. Ibid., 114; italics mine.

120. Language carries with it implicit concepts, presuppositions, and values which are internalized by those who acquire the language, but which remain at an implicit level. However, at this implicit level they profoundly guide our perception of, and action in, the world. We may *think about* the various things we use language to describe (such as "reality"), but language also gives us the implicit conceptual tools that we *think with* (an assumption that this term refers to an external orderly world as opposed to something I can only experience through the loss of my sense of self). Consequently, the presuppositions we think with are rarely examined, except through the most rigorous scientific means or through encounters with others who speak a different language and thus entertain different core presuppositions.

121. Torrance, *Reality and Scientific Theology*, 114. Torrance's realist understanding of language is an outworking of his theological anthropology and his doctrine of creation as contingent. The created order has no inherent ability to "speak" to us unless through the cultural activity and stewardship of the "priest of creation" it is enabled to speak, and not just enabled to speak, but to speak in such a way as to bring glory to its Creator: the triune God of Jesus Christ.

122. Ibid., 114.

prehensive outlook" upon the world, nor simply a "web of meaning" but more importantly a *predisposition* "toward explicit apprehension of the rational order intrinsic to the nature of things."[123] Torrance refers to this as "the social sub-structure of our thought."[124] We inherit and are meant to sustain a flexible and dynamic framework for our ongoing engagement with the world, the sustenance of personal life within it, and its transformation toward the ends of God. This is the function of the social coefficient and this is its responsibility to whatever object of knowledge stands at its center.

The ultimate question then, in terms of social ethics, becomes: how are we to know when these frameworks are fulfilling their function and when they are not? To return to the imagery of Heidegger, how are we to know when the house of being has become a *prison* house? How are we to know whether the windows in that house are translucent, enabling us to see the external world accurately, or whether they are mirrors, reflecting only the subjective structures of our individual minds? As mentioned above, the realist function of language must be maintained if the "house" built with this language is going to sustain the kind of personal beings that we are. If this realist function is lost or distorted then a key coordinate for relating us rightly to the intelligible world around us is lost and our personal being subverted. The social and the ontological are intimately interrelated in Torrance's thought.

This is clearly seen when Torrance describes what happens when the translucent windows in the house of being turn into mirrors, or when "the social sub-structure of our thought [becomes] self-contained."

The social sub-structure of our thought "can grow in upon itself and thus lose its openness to the vast intelligibility of the universe. It has the tendency to develop an independent life and momentum of its own, and to assume power in prestructuring our life and thought ... This can happen when under pressure from below, the knowing relation becomes inverted and the creative source of intelligibility is located in the human consciousness itself instead of in objective reality when it takes on a categorical and absolute character which cannot be modified by further experience."[125]

---

123. Ibid. This is perhaps as close as Torrance gets to describing what many would refer to as a "worldview."

124. Ibid.

125. Ibid., 114–15.

What we have here is an epistemological and sociological description of the fall, the dynamics of which sound very similar to those in Peter Berger's theory of culture mentioned above. For Torrance, the social coefficient[126] becomes "self-contained" when the proper relation between the objective and subjective poles of the knowing relation become inverted. This is due in no small part to "pressure from below," which we understand to mean pressure from the subjective pole of the knowing relation, but perhaps more specifically, the objectivated cultural world that nurtures and sustains the subjective pole of the knowing relation and, as mentioned above, determines how the objective pole of the knowing relation is embraced and embodied.[127] Consequently, momentum in the objectivated world could close us off from a genuine embrace of the objective world and its appropriate embodiment, as opposed to opening us out toward it. Torrance is more concerned about the subjective pole overshadowing the objective and thus gives the objective pole a certain priority in the knowing relation.[128]

---

126. Torrance refers to the social coefficient with a number of other phrases. In the essay we are presently exploring, it is also referred to as a "cognitional structure of social consciousness," an "articulate framework of thought," an "operational framework of thought," and as the "social sub-structure of our thought."

127. See Torrance, *Reality and Scientific Theology*, 114–15. Torrance's language is a bit confusing here. Why is the hierarchical language "from below" employed? We can see how this language would be appropriate when discussing the divine Archimedean point, but is it also appropriate when referring to this-worldly points of transcendence? Is he speaking of the subjective pole strictly as the interpersonal structure of the human person (image of God), or is he also including the objectivated social world? If only the subjectivity of the human person, then how does that "gain an independent life and momentum of its own"? It would seem that Torrance is speaking of the two as integrated and inseparable realities.

128. The reasons for this were discussed earlier in the chapter. This could be a potential weakness in Torrance's thought, and the reason for his use of hierarchical language when describing the knowing relation; for in spite of the fact that Torrance constantly asserts the necessity of anthropomorphic elements in human knowing, they are always subject to the demands of objective reality. In the view of this author, the role of the subjective pole in the knowing process needs to be more explicitly developed lest it be overshadowed by the demands of "objective reality." Torrance has reminded us that granting such a priority to the subjective pole of the knowing relation has historically proven disastrous, but simply acknowledging the fact that subjective elements will always be involved in the knowing process as long as humans exist hardly seems adequate. These concerns seem to be at the heart of many of Torrance's critics (Anderson, Morrison, etc.). Perhaps describing this relationship in terms of "parity" as opposed to "priority" (of objective pole over subjective) is to be preferred.

It would seem at this point that Torrance is entertaining a very deterministic view of the world, in which the human person (subjective pole) is wholly dependent upon its social environment for the sustenance of personal being. If social arrangements put us in genuine contact with the objective world, and we respond accordingly, then personal being is sustained. However, if social arrangements refer us only to the subjective structures of our social consciousness then we are cut off from objective reality and personal being is subverted. This relation between the social/cultural and the ontological/personal is suggested when Torrance states that "the articulate framework of thought with which we operate is grounded in the ontological substructure of our social existence, [and] it is that social existence that needs to be changed if any new outlook is to be achieved."[129]

Let us develop this through the use of a series of bullet points.

- Being rightly related to the objective world is essential to our personal being.[130] Human personhood is sustained through its relations to God, others, and creation.

- We cannot be rightly related to the objective world apart from a specific cultural "outlook" or "articulate framework of thought." This might be described as the *surface level of culture* of which we have an explicit or focal awareness.[131]

- This "articulate framework of thought" is mediated to us through our "social existence" in the world. This might be described as the *deep level of culture* of which we have an implicit or tacit awareness. This is what Torrance refers to as the "social coefficient of knowledge." Social coefficients mediate to us, not explicit conceptual knowledge, but a "predisposition" toward reality.[132] This pre-

---

129. Torrance, *Reality and Scientific Theology*, 115.

130. We understand "personal being" here to refer to phrases in Torrance's thought such as "ontological substructure," "interpersonal structure of being," or "image of God."

131. There seems to be a pattern in Torrance's development of the various levels of social existence that roughly follows his understanding of the multi-leveled nature of truth. See Torrance, *Christian Doctrine of God*, 84ff.

132. "The social coefficient of our knowledge, or the cognitional structure of our social consciousness, does not generate in us concepts of reality, nor does it provide our knowledge with informational content, but it does predispose us toward explicit apprehension of the rational order intrinsic to the nature of things through the informal, inarticulate way in which it reflects it" (Torrance, *Reality and Scientific Theology*, 114).

disposition enables us to interpret and organize our experiences into meaningful patterns, which are then embodied in surface level cultural forms.

- The "ontological substructure" of our social existence is a reference to Torrance's understanding of the *imago Dei*. This might be described as the *ontological substructure of culture*.[133]

- There would be no social existence or social coefficients apart from this ontological structure of personal being, however the ontological structure of personal being is sustained through our social existence and the "articulate frameworks of thought" that emerge from them.

- Because of the dialectical relation between the ontological structure of personal being and our social existence, it becomes vitally important that our social existence is congruent with the ontological structure of human personhood. While the two aspects of personal life may be distinguished, they cannot be divided.

- As mentioned above in chapter 4, the image of God is an eschatological image, which means that the ontological substructure of our social existence has been brought into being for a purpose. Embedded in that substructure is a specific *telos* that is prior to the particularities of our social existence, even if dependent upon them. That *telos* must be approximated in our social existence if the ontological substructure of our personal being is to be sustained and not subverted.[134]

- The socio-cultural matrix (composed of the surface and deep levels of culture) can gain a momentum of its own that disorients

---

133. Torrance elsewhere refers to the image, and the cluster of relations involved in understanding it, as the "interpersonal structure of being." See Torrance, "Soul and Person, in Theological Perspective," 109, 115. Ray S. Anderson understands the image of God as referring to a "core social paradigm." See Anderson, "Socio-Cultural Implications," 500–503.

134. The surface and deep levels of culture, and the ontological structure that births and sustains them, are roughly akin to Torrance's "levels of truth," which together form a "multi-leveled organic structure" and with each level serving a critical purpose whose ultimate goal is to make sure that all three levels are coordinated with and congruent with each other. See the discussion in Torrance, *Christian Doctrine of God*, 82ff. There is much more work that could be done here in teasing out the implications of Torrance's stratification of truth for a theology of culture and as a basis for social ethics.

our relations to the objective world, thus subverting personal being, orienting it towards a *telos* incongruent with its nature. To refer again to Berger's theory of culture, this disorientation is then externalized by human persons, objectivated in our social existence, and internalized by the human subject. This is how the socio-cultural matrix gains its momentum, perpetuating and deepening the subversion of personal being. Torrance is correct to note then, that our social existence needs transformation if the coordinates necessary for the sustenance of personal being are to be properly related to each other.

However, dependent as we are upon the socio-cultural matrix for our engagement with the external world, we are unable to tune these relations ourselves. Realizing that these social structures are necessary for the sustenance of personal being, but also that they are in need of transformation, Torrance asks, "How do we break free from the social structures which regulate and shape our intellectual development from below, and so gain new insights into a larger whole of which the old framework of thought is found to be only a partial and distorting reflection?"[135]

For Torrance, the mere shattering of these old frameworks alone will not secure the desired liberation, for "we cannot even begin to advance toward the new without some guidance derived from the old."[136] However, our attempts to heal and transform the old solve some problems while creating others. The root of the problem lies not only in the cultural system, but also in the cultural agent as a sinful and fallen being whose relations with God, creation, and others are deeply disoriented as the result of an aboriginal act of disorder. This disorder is consistently externalized and objectivated in our social existence through human agency. The human person and the social order are in need, not only of transformation, but also of salvation. As Torrance notes: "Human society

---

135. Torrance, *Reality and Scientific Theology*, 116.

136. Ibid. This is another way of recognizing the dialectical relationship between the ontological substructure of culture (the image of God) and the deep (tacit) and surface (focal) levels of culture. We cannot find freedom as cultural beings through attempts to be a-cultural beings, nor is it possible autonomously and instantaneously to throw out the old and introduce the new through a revolutionary act. Freedom is found in and through the socio-cultural matrix, but only as it refers us beyond itself to the true end of our being.

cannot be transmuted into an authentic community of personal being merely through a redisposition of its diseased in-turned structures … Such a transmutation can take place only through the reconciliation of people with God and with one another and through the healing of personal and inter-personal structures in their ontological depths through participation in the creative source and fullness of personal being in the Communion of the Holy Trinity."[137]

Consequently, what is required is not simply a "movement of thought" but "a movement of personal response and commitment in worship, obedience and love in which a transformation of our mind or a spiritual reorganization of our consciousness of God takes place."[138]

Such a movement is "initiated by God, informed by his personal address to us in his Word, and sustained through the presence of his Spirit in our personal response to his Word."[139] Here we have an epistemological and sociological description of justification by faith through grace. We might refer to this as Torrance's "gospel of the Archimedean point" for it is only through the initiative of the triune God of grace that we

- Find a point beyond the contingencies of life that is not merely a product of those contingencies.
- Find a point that is congruent with our ontological and teleological design as personal, social, and cultural beings.
- Find a point that will freely, graciously, and redemptively enter the boundaries of our lives, heal the ontological substructure of our personal being, reconcile the relations that sustain them, orient us toward our true end, and empower us to approximate that end within the contingencies of our creaturely life.[140]

---

137. Ibid., 197. This emphasis can also be found in Torrance, *Mediation of Christ*, 30–31.

138. Torrance, *Christian Doctrine of God*, 88.

139. Ibid., 88.

140. We have here, in more nuanced language, the classic tension between the finite and infinite embodied in the human person. However, mere finiteness is not the problem for Torrance, it is rather a tension between the *telos* of the human person as created in the image of God and the socio-cultural environment where that *telos* is either sustained or subverted. It is a tension between ontology and society. Further discussion regarding the tension between the finite and the infinite may be found in Niebuhr, *The Nature and Destiny of Man*.

Given that we are creatures created in the image of God, our relations with God, others, and the created world are mediated by a socio-cultural matrix. However, due to the fall, that socio-cultural matrix has lost its translucency, and thus its ability, to refer us beyond itself and to orient properly the relations that sustain personal life. Consequently, we cannot reach beyond our linguistic and symbolic worlds, and in our attempts to do so we only end up referring obliquely to ourselves. The human being as a social and cultural being stands in need of salvation, and in particular a salvation that is rooted in a divine initiative, not a human one. We are in need of one who will reach into our linguistic and symbolic worlds and open them up or, to use musical terms, "tune them" in ways that will liberate and personalize them—setting them free to realize their true ends. For Torrance, this is only possible through the initiative and agency of the triune God of Jesus Christ as the Archimedean point and transcendent ground of meaning for all our social projects. The semantic projects that orient and govern our lives have no ultimate meaning, and cannot fulfill their true end, apart from the salvific activity of the triune God.

The triune God "is the one Archimedean point beyond the universe to whom the universe as a whole is so related that it is given authentic meaning throughout all its immanent structures, and the one Archimedean point to whom we are so related within the universe and all its science and social structure that we are constantly emancipated from ourselves and enabled to transcend the structures of our social and scientific activities."[141]

That "emancipation" has been secured in an objective sense through the work of the triune God in salvation and reconciliation, but is a constant and ongoing project through the work of the Spirit in sanctification. Torrance does not mean to say that the transmutation of our social structures is not necessary; simply that transmutation alone does not go deep enough. It does not alter the fact that the real problem is ontological, and is thus beyond the ability of human persons to diagnose and heal. The initiative and agency of God in salvation is necessary because the disorder rooted in creation is ontological, not simply sociological. As Torrance asserts: "The redemption of the universe from

---

141. Torrance, *Reality and Scientific Theology*, 117.

disorder requires more than a rearrangement of form ... [it requires] the radical undoing and defeat of evil."[142]

This "radical undoing and defeat of evil" is secured in the incarnation and resurrection of Jesus Christ, for in him both the disordered depths of human personhood and the disordered depths of the entire created order have been redeemed, reoriented, and set upon a new basis. The work that has resulted is, in an objective sense, complete.

However, the triune God of Jesus Christ not only saves, but also redeems, sanctifies, and consummates what has been objectively reconciled. Consequently, Torrance posits the triune God of Jesus Christ as the Archimedean point not only for purposes of revelation and salvation, but also sanctification.

ESCHATOLOGICAL REASONS: SANCTIFICATION—What has been objectively secured through the work of Christ must be subjectively realized within the boundaries of the created order through the agency of the *"Spiritus Creator"* who comes to us from the Father through the Son. Again, as with Torrance's doctrines of revelation and salvation, the triune agency of God is essential for it is only the triune God of Jesus Christ who has (1) *revealed* to us the true end of the created order and our role in it, (2) *reconciled* the disoriented relationships that keep us from approximating that true end, and (3) *orients and empowers* us to approximate those ends within the boundaries of space and time, so that through our activity as "priests of creation" and "mediators of order" the created and contingent order we indwell, with its intrinsic intelligibility, harmony, and beauty, "is discerned to derive from and ultimately to repose in the uncreated Rationality and eternal Love of the Creator."[143] This is the task of sanctification, and it cannot be accomplished apart from the gift and agency of the Holy Spirit.[144]

While the salvific work of God entails much more than "a rearrangement of form," one should not conclude that the "rearrangement of form" is inconsequential to the fulfillment of God's purposes. It is, in fact, essential. Torrance's comments above simply highlight the fact that the rearrangement of form alone cannot bring about redemption

---

142. Torrance, *Christian Frame of Mind*, 103.
143. Torrance, *Reality and Scientific Theology*, 198.
144. See the discussion of the Spirit's identity and work in chapter 1.

nor can it fulfill God's purposes for creation. Social engineering cannot save.

However, the focal work of atonement is undertaken with the tacit awareness that it will enable the fulfillment of God's purposes for creation, of which the rearrangement of form is an essential part. Just as there is a deep connection between justification and sanctification, the work of the Son and the work of the Spirit, so too there is a deep connection between reconciliation, redemption, and consummation. Each presupposes the other.

For Torrance, the Archimedean point for all our social projects must be the triune God of Jesus Christ for only this God has given to us the Spirit. It is this Spirit, as discussed in chapter 1, whose work is carried out upon the basis of Christ's work and who (1) bears witness to Jesus Christ as the revelation of God's purposes for creation, (2) enables our participation in God, and (3) orients and empowers human agents so that their activity in the world may advance the purposes of God. Such is the nature of the perfecting and consummating work of the Spirit that is sanctification.

The social coefficient, by reference to an appropriate transcendent ground of meaning, "can be given an open-textured disposition within which people are prompted to rise above the patterns of social and religious consciousness, to be transported in wonder, and in wonder to think ahead of concept and word."[145] This is the essence of Torrance's conception of "participation," a dynamic made possible only through the presence and agency of the Holy Spirit and upon the basis of the past and present priestly work of Christ.

To "think ahead of concept and word" brings us to Torrance's understanding of the role of doxology in the transformation of social coefficients.[146]

DOXOLOGICAL REASONS: GLORIFICATION—Finally, it is for *doxological reasons* that the triune God of Jesus Christ be identified as the tran-

---

145. Torrance, *Reality and Scientific Theology*, 125.

146. For Torrance, this does not mean that we think *without* concept and word. To do so would mean that we are no longer cultural beings. It refers instead to Torrance's interest in understanding concepts and words as tacit tools that must enable us to be focally aware of the objects we seek to know. In other words, we can only think ahead of words and concepts when they function in a translucent fashion. That is accomplished through the work of the Spirit.

scendent ground of meaning for all human persons and projects. This is perhaps be the most comprehensive reason why Torrance asserts the necessity of the triune God as the transcendent ground of being. His doxological reasons are three-fold:

- *Regarding Human Identity*: Human persons become what they behold or worship. They identify themselves in relation to that which they consider ultimate.[147]

- *Regarding Human Agency*: Human identity and human agency, being and act, are intimately interrelated. This is an explicit assumption in Torrance's Christology and seems no less important here when speaking of social coefficients of knowledge.

- *Regarding Moral Legitimacy*: That which is ultimate not only forms personal identity and guides human action but also legitimates both by referring human persons to a moral order. This moral order legitimates human identity and action by providing a design and purpose for the created order and human life in it.

Though Torrance himself does not explicitly develop these particular points, they seem to be operative assumptions in all his thinking about social coefficients of knowledge (their formation and function) and the Archimedean points that orient them. We mention them now for purposes of orientation, but will develop each in subsequent headings. Presently we will consider in greater detail the assumption that human persons are transformed by what they worship, and we will do so in conversation with theologian Robert Jenson and economist Bob Goudzwaard.

Robert Jenson has noted that the human person may be uniquely described as "the praying animal."[148] As a social and personal animal, those prayers are offered in a variety of ways,[149] drawing together every

---

147. Torrance, after Calvin, understands the *imago Dei* as a mirror that has been uniquely designed to take on the imprint of whatever stands consistently in front of it. That object will seek expression in the patterns of life available to it. Torrance refers to this same reflective dynamic when speaking of human culture. It too is a mirror for the world's self-understanding. Peter Berger would agree, using the terms "objectivation" and "institutionalization" to refer to the processes by which the self-understanding of a particular group takes social form. This dynamic is noted by Torrance when he speaks of the Church in the world as well. See Torrance, *Reality and Scientific Theology*, 119.

148. Jenson, *Systematic Theology* 2:58–61.

149. Jenson also notes that it matters not if the addressee of the prayers is misidentified; the doxological and uniquely human nature of the act remains intact. Ibid., 59.

dimension of human existence, not simply the "spiritual." Jenson notes in particular that "we respond to God's address not only in language but with a wide repertoire of gestures and objects"[150] that result in ritual activity, which, as we will note shortly, is a cultural activity that is central in the construction of social worlds. With this ritual activity human persons engage in an act that "gives visibility to wishes directed beyond themselves."[151] Along with Paul Tillich, Jenson asserts that cultural activity is inherently religious. It is a secularized act of doxology, and this is precisely why it is so important for Torrance to identify concretely the ultimate addressee of these secular prayers, for that which is addressed in these secular prayers will ultimately determine the character of our social and personal life.

Bob Goudzwaard, in his *Aid for the Overdeveloped West*,[152] captures succinctly the logic of these secular prayers and why Torrance is concerned that the triune God of Jesus Christ be their proper focus. Goudzwaard notes three "biblical laws":[153]

- Every person is serving a god or gods. To decline such divine service is not an option for "the praying animal."

- Every person is transformed into an image of the god(s) he or she worships. As created in the image of God we are, by design, open to the world in a way that we take on the shape of the world we create and indwell.

- Human persons then create a social structure in their own image, as a reflection of the values and world-view they have formed in conversation with the particular deity they worship.[154] The struc-

---

150. Ibid.
151. Ibid., 61.
152. Goudzwaard, *Aid for the Overdeveloped West*.
153. Ibid., 14–15. These "biblical laws" might come just prior to the threefold dialectic central to Berger's theory of culture mentioned above (externalization, objectivation, internalization).
154. Goudzwaard's interest in the conversation between these three "laws" is economic in nature. To put it in more generic terms, our ultimate concerns ultimately define not only who we are, but also the social structures we construct to support, sustain, and forward that vision, whether economic, political, or otherwise. For an interesting collection of essays looking at economic underdevelopment in terms of cultural values, see Harrison and Huntington, *Culture Matters*.

tures of society become a reflection of their own beliefs, hopes, faiths, and commitments.

The line between idolatry and genuine worship is defined by the object of worship itself, or the transcendent ground of meaning we functionally or explicitly identify as the basis for our actions. Persons are deeply transformed by what they worship, and if what they worship is incongruent with both who they are, and the created order they have been placed within, then it is ultimately their personal being and social life that will be subverted.[155] Implicit in Torrance's thought is a trinitarian social ethic and central to that social ethic is this dynamic.

A triune God who takes the initiative to reveal himself and redeem creation by entering the conditions of space and time is essential if cultural and social determinism is to be barred from becoming a feature of human social life. This is the social import of a doctrine of revelation, a feature of Christ's prophetic role, and yet another reason why merely creaturely points of transcendence will not do, as all points of this nature suffer from their own self-enclosure due to their finiteness and falleness—which in turn are rooted in the very creature who brings these structures into being.[156] An Archimedean point, a transcendent ground of meaning far beyond our material and social world, and yet active within it, is a defining mark of Torrance's thought.

Social Coefficients Orient, Mediate, and Sustain Our Knowing Relations

Social coefficients are matrices through which we receive from and respond to the intelligible ground of reality. They enable human subjects to do so by providing two primary structures: semantic and participatory. Through these webs of thought and action, human subjects are

---

155. If it could ever be said that God is the tempter of the human race, it is because God has created a world so profoundly good that it is so easily confused with the divine Creator himself.

156. This is why "the strange new world of the Bible" functions unlike any other cultural or social world we may encounter, as it uniquely points beyond itself to the unique Archimedean point that personalizes human life and culture. Cross-cultural encounters, as enlightening and self-revealing as they are, are still only this-worldly points of reference *in* the world, as opposed to *beyond* it.

oriented in relation to the objective world and knowing relations with it are mediated and sustained.

By Providing Semantic Structures: A Symbolic Environment

For Torrance, "the culture of language, in spoken or written form, is essential to the development of personal and social being."[157] This is primarily because it is through language that human persons "are able to achieve a measure of transcendence over nature for it is by means of language that they can represent things to themselves."[158] This grants human persons "a position of independence over the object world of their knowledge and the environment of their activities."[159]

Human language and symbols enable the human person to achieve a degree of transcendence over the created world that is essential to personhood. This is so because symbol systems are the primary means we use to identify, label, organize, interpret, and share our experience, and consequently are the building blocks of all social life. Language is the means by which we order human life and share meaning, and for Torrance, how social life is ordered has everything to do with personal being. As Raymond Williams notes, following the definition of culture by Clifford Geertz, culture functions as "a signifying system through which a social order is communicated, reproduced, experienced and explored."[160] Torrance's understanding of symbol systems, while congruent with that of both Williams and Geertz, reflects his critically realist epistemology: "Symbolic systems . . . are formal instruments of thought enabling us to cope more adequately with the world of our actual experience by extending the range and power of our thought beyond what we would be capable of without them. [They are] used to deepen and

---

157. Torrance, *Reality and Scientific Theology*, 194.

158. Ibid.

159. Ibid. At this point Torrance introduces a discussion about the relationship between "word rationality" and "number rationality" that is important but reflects the concerns already discussed above about the relation between the objective and subjective pole of the knowing relation needing to be properly ordered and balanced.

160. Williams, *Sociology of Culture*, 13.

widen the bearing of our thought upon empirical reality and to enable us to grasp its intrinsic intelligibility at a deeper level."[161]

For Torrance, symbols are generated through the convergence of two forces: the creative imagination of the human mind and objective features of an external world. As Torrance notes, all symbolic forms are "partly the product of our creative imagination and partly the product of objective features and properties of reality."[162] Some of these symbolic forms are formal and explicit in nature and others, like art, are suggestive.[163] Important to note is that Torrance understands the knowing relation to be bi-polar in nature, with an objective and subjective pole, and that signs should mediate and signify both poles of that relation.

A similar critically realist understanding is found in the writings of Paul G. Hiebert, who bases his work upon the thought of philosopher Charles S. Peirce and his work on semiotics.[164] We will follow here Hiebert's interpretation of Peirce's work.

For Peirce, signs mediate our perceptions of reality and are triadic in nature, having three parts:[165] (1) an exterior form (the *signifier*), (2) a mental concept or image (the *signification*), and (3) the reality the sign refers to (the *signified*). This triadic relation is meant to "link mental images to realities, real or imagined, by means of words, gestures, sounds, and other signifiers. If only two dimensions are present, it is not a true sign."[166]

Torrance's understanding is very similar. He notes the objective and subjective poles in the knowing relation and develops the nature of this relationship extensively.[167] Torrance refers frequently to "the sign" and "the thing signified" in his writings about the sacraments, language for God, and social coefficients of knowledge. Though it appears that

---

161. Torrance, *Reality and Evangelical Theology*, 62.

162. Ibid., 98.

163. Torrance's understanding of the unique features of the "suggestive form" he calls "art" may be found in ibid., 98ff.

164. See in particular Hiebert, *Missiological Implications*, 69ff.; and the work of Peirce in Peirce, *Philosophical Writings of Peirce*. Hiebert's work is similar to Torrance's at many points. In addition to his understanding of signs and his critically realistic epistemology Hiebert also develops a multi-leveled model of "mental construction" that is very similar to Torrance's "levels of truth." See Hiebert, *Missiological Implications*, 83.

165. See the discussion in Hiebert, *Missiological Implications*, 71ff.

166. Ibid., 71.

167. See Torrance, *Theological Science*, 75–105.

Torrance has only accounted for two of the three dimensions necessary in order to have what Pierce calls "a true sign," in fact Torrance's work in developing his concept of the social coefficient of knowledge is meant to refer to the product of the subjective and objective poles of the knowing relation. Together the objective and subjective poles produce what Pierce calls the "signification" or the mental concept or image that subsists in the minds of persons and communities. The interesting aspect of Torrance's thought is that the "signification" is never an isolated individual possession, nor even simply a mental one, but a social one, held not in the minds of isolated individuals but in the social community to which the individual belongs. In the context of this community the "signification" is embodied, legitimized, and passed on to other members. Understood in this light, Torrance's thought is triadic in nature as well. However, where Pierce posits a relationship between signifier, signification, and thing signified, Torrance might refer instead to a signifier (the sign itself), a social coefficient (the community that assigns the sign meaning and function), and a thing signified (the reality referred to). This is due to the fact that the social coefficient not only creates the signifier but is also formed by the thing signified, and is thus the product of both "our creative imagination" and "objective features and properties of reality." The social coefficient then becomes the signification and more weight is given to the social embodiment and effect of the mental concepts and images it lives by and, most importantly, the knowing relation that nourishes it. This reflects not only Torrance's interest in a critically realistic understanding of language, but also a relational and trinitarian understanding of God, creation, and human persons. This in turn renders each of these factors (signifier, signification, and thing signified) as much more complex in nature and function, and focuses their relationships to each other upon a more fundamental knowing relation established with reality. This has consistently been a feature of Torrance's thought. For Torrance, we should think in terms of relations, not simply the grammatical or semantic rules that mediate those relations. When we make this subtle shift, we allow the relation to determine the content, form, and function of our linguistic rules and signs and not the other way around. This is a more complex way of saying that the object to be known must determine the method by which it is known. Signification then requires social embodiment and social relations, and any attempt to translate a sign apart from the social coefficient that produced and perpetuates it is mistaken. As Torrance notes: "Nowhere, perhaps, have dualist modes of thought been more deeply entrenched in our cultural tradition than in our understanding of language."[168] Also, any attempt to equate meaning or relation to the combination of certain linguistic signs, grammatical rules or mental constructs is mistaken and is to cut ourselves free of the objective pole of the knowing relation, preferring to substitute our socially constructed sign systems for the knowing relation with the objective world they are meant to mediate.[169] In *Reality and Scientific Theology* Torrance notes how this took place in the romantic period in the fields of art, literature, painting, and music. What took place there was "a considerable shift in orientation away from the intentionalities of our existence toward the ultimate ground of reality, to the view that the content of art is predominantly subjective and personal."[170] Such a shift in orientation is inevitable in any field of human discourse where "the referential and intentional relations with reality [are] cut or damaged."[171] The relation between the subjective and objective poles of the knowing relation are symbolically mediated and balanced.

The creation of a symbol attaches a socially constructed form to a feature of the objective world. A semantic and symbolic relationship emerges between the socially constructed form and the objective world referred to. In the process, the socially constructed form takes on its own objectivity. Experiences and ideas are now shareable through the medium of the symbol as long as the agreed upon meaning for that symbol is intact. It is *where* that meaning is located that is an important facet of Torrance's thought. Meaning is located in the objective world and in the quality of our relations with it, not simply upon social agreements. This means that reality exists apart from the symbolic constructions of the human mind or collective agreements of society. The locus of meaning is in the external world and the burden of the symbol is to keep persons in touch with that external reality—allowing it to shape our symbolic constructions and their semantic content.

---

168. Torrance, *Reality and Evangelical Theology*, 61.

169. This is a mistake committed by George Lindbeck. See the critique by Elmer Colyer in *Nature of Doctrine*, 127 n. 157.

170. Torrance, *Reality and Scientific Theology*, 100.

171. Ibid.

Locating meaning in an external world and making it imperative that symbol systems accurately reflect that external world is a primary concern of Torrance. This is due in large part to his understanding of order, described in chapters 2 and 3 above. Human persons have been created in a particular way and for a particular purpose that human persons may not define for themselves without impunity. Symbol systems are essential in orienting human persons in the created world. Torrance would agree with anthropologist Paul G. Hiebert that "we cannot perceive nature or think or communicate about it without language, but language, to a great extent, also molds what we see and how we see it."[172]

This "molding" function of language is of particular concern to Torrance. We will see the world around us, ourselves, and others in terms of the cultural categories we inherit, and will act in ways appropriate to those categories. If they are not "apposite" or "translucent" then we will act in a way that is incongruent with reality and by so doing subvert our true being and purpose in the world. Torrance, in agreement with Heidegger, notes that "the web of meaning that is found lodged in language is significant, for language, as Heidegger used to say, is the house of being, and it is through language that reality shows itself to us and we become familiar with it. This function of language is basic to what we have been calling the social coefficient of knowledge, as it enables us to be rightly related to the intelligible universe around us."[173]

BY PROVIDING PARTICIPATORY STRUCTURES: A RITUALIZED ENVIRONMENT

Social coefficients are inhabitable worlds that are integrated and unitary. They can be indwelt not only mentally, or even spiritually, but also physically. An example of this aspect of the social coefficient may be found in Torrance's writings on Israel as the "womb of Christ" as found in his *The Mediation of Christ*.[174] In this instance "God's revelation came to Israel in such a way that it intersected and integrated its spiritual and physical reality."[175] This process resulted in an "embodied

---

172. Hiebert, *Cultural Anthropology*, 119.
173. Torrance, *Reality and Scientific Theology*, 114.
174. Torrance, *Mediation of Christ*, in particular chapter 1, "The Mediation of Revelation."
175. Ibid., 15.

revelation," with the consequence that "physical behavior is tied up with faith in God."[176]

It is also on display in Torrance's frequent observation that a child, by the age of five, knows a great deal about physics simply through his or her repetitive interactions with the physical world, even though that knowledge is only tacit and cannot be conceptualized by the child.[177] The same truth applies to the social worlds children indwell: identities, values, and ultimacies are communicated most profoundly through ritual performance.[178] In the words of Polyani, we often know much more then we can tell, and what we know in this fashion is acquired through ritual participation. This is due in large part to the fact that our social environments and communities are a more or less integrated pattern of symbols and rituals of the most sacred and mundane sort. The integrated nature of the world the child inhabits makes it possible for him/her to acquire accurate knowledge of the world before being able to conceptualize that knowledge. Again, as Torrance notes in the case of Israel, "divine revelation did not just bear upon the life and culture of Israel in some tangential fashion, rippling the surface of its moral and religious consciousness, but penetrated into the innermost centre of Israel and involved itself in the concrete actuality and locality of its existence in time and space."[179]

This involvement of divine revelation in "the concrete actuality and locality of its existence in time and space," which I understand to refer to culture, is the reason why ritual participation in a community is so powerful and formative and why the values communicated in this way are so intuitive and constitutive of personhood.

David Morgan, commenting upon the role of images in human societies, notes that images legitimate the social order in various ways,

---

176. Ibid., 16.

177. "Just as each of us comes to know far more about the physical or moral order of the world than we can ever tell by the time we are five years of age, so we early acquire an ability to read what is engendered in us by the structure of social consciousness in which we grow up" (Torrance, *Reality and Scientific Theology*, 104). See also Torrance, *Christian Doctrine of God*, 89.

178. This is why, in the jazz tradition, improvisational skills are passed on through apprenticeships established in the context of a learning community. See Berliner, *Thinking in Jazz*, chapter 2: "Hangin' Out and Jammin': The Jazz Community as an Educational System."

179. Torrance, *Mediation of Christ*, 15.

but primarily by "tirelessly repeating what we have always known, as if *the ritual act of repetition might transfigure a belief into a condition of nature*."[180] Roy Rappaport, in his book *Ecology, Meaning, and Religion* agrees when he asserts that ritual is "*the* basic social act" because societies and cultures are founded upon shared understandings of reality that are constituted ritually, that is through shared performance, long before they come to be privately or inwardly believed.[181] Torrance would no doubt take issue with Rappaport if the "constitution" of reality that takes place through ritual performance were understood in a way that sought no congruence or correspondence with an external objective world. However, the power and place that Rappaport assigns to ritual would be strongly affirmed by Torrance, not only because Torrance understands the social coefficient as a participatory structure but also because the social coefficient is an integrative structure. We cite Grenz and Franke's synthesis of Rappaport's thought to make this point: "Ritual brings together what language, by its very nature, divides . . . Whereas the distinctions of language 'cut the world into bits—into categories, classes, oppositions, and contrasts'—ritual unites or reunites 'the psychic, social, natural, and cosmic orders which language and the exigencies of life pull apart.'"[182]

Ritual performance, like language, has a world-ordering and subject-orienting function that is central to the construction and maintenance of cultural and social reality.[183] It accomplishes this function by integrating symbols and actions into a confessional performance that

---

180. Morgan, *Visual Piety*, 9–10; italics mine.

181. Rappaport, *Ecology, Meaning, and Religion*, 174, 197. Our discussion here follows that in Grenz and Franke, *Beyond Foundationalism*, 145–46.

182. Grenz and Franke, *Beyond Foundationalism*, 146.

183. See Driver, *Magic of Ritual*. Driver notes in part 3 of his book that ritual offers us many social gifts; however, three of the most central are order, community, and transformation. Driver sees all of these gifts as interrelated: "Social order is not an end in itself but is necessary to make possible the benefits of communal love. But even love is not an end in itself unless, allied with justice, it is devoted to freeing individuals and groups from the forces that oppress them" (132). Torrance would want to affirm what Driver has said but also to assert that any socially constructed order must be congruent with the created contingent order as a reality brought into being by a triune God with a design and purpose all its own. That design and purpose should to be reflected in ritual as a medium of social order if genuine justice is to be realized and sustained. See his essay "The Concept of Order in Theology and Science," in Torrance, *Christian Frame of Mind*, 17–34.

orders the world and orients the subjects who perform the ritual. By so doing, rituals, both sacred and mundane, create and preserve specific forms of order that are culturally construed and will reflect varying degrees of correspondence with the intelligible grounds of reality.

For Torrance, the social coefficient of knowledge provides for human persons a participatory structure, as it "constitutes from generation to generation the sensitive matrix within which our all-important informal relations with reality are evoked, and thus constitutes the medium in which those relations while not formally communicable are nevertheless communicated through common participation in the affected modification of social consciousness."[184]

By Providing Multi-Leveled Structures: A Textured Environment

The idea that the social coefficient is to provide its members with a semantic and participatory environment links Torrance's vision of the social coefficient strongly with contemporary anthropological understandings of culture. However, it is here that we may begin to note some divergences, if not in actual content, then in emphasis, between Torrance's thought and that of contemporary definitions of culture. It also reminds us that Torrance's primary concerns are with scientific methodology and exploration, and only in a secondary sense with the nature and function of cultures.[185] It is hoped that we have shown that the steps necessary to get from one place to the other, based on Torrance's thought, are not many, and will enrich our understanding of the nature and function of culture in the process.

Torrance notes, upon the basis of his doctrine of God, creation and humanity, that "our interpersonal relations with one another have an open-ended, transcendent relation built into them, which is constitutive of our personal and social reality."[186]

---

184. Torrance, *Reality and Scientific Theology*, 104.

185. We have attempted to show throughout that there are many convergences between Torrance's language and the language more familiar to social scientists in general and anthropologists in particular. Torrance's understanding of the human person is a case in point. He describes the primary human vocation as "scientific" in ways very similar to the anthropologists' or sociologists' description of the human vocation as "cultural."

186. Torrance, *Reality and Scientific Theology*, 111.

However, the "open-ended, transcendent relation" that is built into our interpersonal relations with one another leave the human person open to, not only proper objects of worship, but inappropriate objects of worship as well, objects that have the power to subvert human personhood: "As person ... man is the being who is open to others as well as to the world. It is indeed through this openness of being to the world that he can easily become enslaved to the determinate patterns of nature. But what he needs in this state of affairs is an openness that transcends the power of the determinate world to fix him in its rigid structures and suppress his freedom. He requires a transcendent reference, an Archimedean point beyond him and beyond the power of his own sophisticated technology to control or master."[187]

We have discussed the importance of this Archimedean point earlier. It is now important to note that the social coefficient of knowledge is to provide the human person with a heuristic, dialogical, and multi-leveled structure that refers the openness of the human person not only to the objective created world or to other persons but also to an objective and transcendent ground of meaning. In this way the formation of the human person and the construction of human culture takes place in a conversation between an objective created order and a transcendent ground of meaning, just as the human person and the transcendent ground of meaning are embodied through the agency of the human person as priest of creation. The result is a fertile ground where plurality, both personal and social, of the richest sort may flourish.

However, the plurality that arises from this fertile soil, whether economic, political, social or moral, has a particular function, direction, orientation, and *telos*, and that is the formation, sustenance, and expression of the personal. This *telos* cannot be accomplished apart from the recognition that the world the human person indwells is a textured and multi-leveled one, and that the recognition of these levels and the relation of one level to another is essential for the affirmation and preservation of the personal. As noted earlier, it is through the correlation of these "levels of truth" that human freedom and a free society arises. When these levels are not recognized the human person is understood in a reductionistic sense, whether primarily as a spiritual being, a social being or a creaturely being. As a result, the personal in all its richness is lost through a severance of the vital relations that make human persons

187. Ibid., 193.

what they are. An understanding of Torrance's concept of levels of truth is essential to his understanding not only of human personhood, but also of the tri-unity of God,—since both are onto-relational concepts.[188]

The reason for this may become clearer through a consideration of Torrance's distinction between the social coefficient as an "affect" as opposed to an "effect." Torrance is adamant in pointing out that a social coefficient is an affect and not an effect. As an *effect,* the social coefficient is cut off from its source and *telos* in objective reality and socially objectified as its own semantic base, where it becomes its own Archimedean point. Semantic intentionality is lost since there is no further living contact with the reality the coefficient refers to (other than the initial causation that brought the effect into being) or that formed and nourished it. In this understanding, the relationship between reality and a social coefficient is purely causal, and, once brought into being, reference to the first cause is no longer necessary to fill the social coefficient with meaning. The social coefficient is then "free" to determine and construct its own meaning and *telos* unbounded by the constraints of reality.[189]

However, when the social coefficient is understood as an *affect,* expression is given to a dynamic, dialectical, and multi-leveled relationship that the social coefficient participates in with reality itself. In such an instance there takes place a mutual modification that is ongoing and has a goal, *telos,* and character that lies outside of its own social construction of reality, its own cultural values, imperatives, goals, goods, and evaluative criteria. As an effect, the social coefficient is closed in upon itself and its heuristic power is lost. As an affect it is open, it becomes a system based upon faith, in that it is open to a reality external to it, while an effect is a reality closed in upon itself and, as such, lives only according to its own possibilities. As an affect, it is determined in faith by another. As an effect, it is determined by its own boundaries and socially conceivable possibilities. Consequently, the social coefficient as effect cannot change, cannot be transformed, cannot make the heuristic leaps or form a tacit dimension through which openness to reality would provide it with new knowledge and new possibilities. As an *effect,* the social coefficient can only play the musical notes it has

---

188. Torrance develops the idea of "levels of truth" in Torrance, *Christian Doctrine of God,* 73–111.

189. See further Colyer, *Nature of Doctrine,* 99.

written for itself. As an *affect*, the social coefficient is freed to improvise and imagine new possibilities within old forms while maintaining the integrity of a specific piece of music.

The social coefficient, by reference to an appropriate transcendent ground of meaning, "can be given *an open-textured disposition* within which people are prompted to rise above the patterns of social and religious consciousness."[190]

Social Coefficients Express and Embody Our Knowing Relations

Not only does the social coefficient orient, mediate, and sustain knowing relations with the intelligible ground of reality, it is also the means by which those knowing relations are expressed and embodied in the social and material world. The expression and embodiment of knowing relations is not something that may or may not occur. Knowing relations will be socially embodied regardless of the quality of those relations. This is a social fact we mentioned above in conversation with Peter Berger, who noted that one of the primary drives of the human organism is the completion of the self through the act of externalizing the self into the world. We also noted that God has so created the human person in his image that the externalization of human subjectivity into the world is rooted ultimately in God's desire and will. Since the subjective pole of any knowing relation is a human subject, the externalization of that relation is not an option but rather a human imperative. This is one of the primary reasons we noted for the characterization of the human being as a cultural being in chapter 4. The social coefficient of knowledge becomes an expression and embodiment of knowing relations in the following ways:

By Integrating the Subjective and the Objective

For Torrance, all knowing relations have at least three components: (1) the objective pole, (2) the subjective pole, and (3) the quality of the relation between them. The knowing relation takes on a concrete form when the objective and subjective poles of that relation are integrated,

---

190. Torrance, *Reality and Scientific Theology*, 125; italics mine.

where subjective factors enable the expression and embodiment of an objective reality. For instance, when an objective reality is described using a specific language, subjective factors (language) are being integrated with (or attached to) objective factors (reality). Another example would be when a written piece of music (objective factor) is given expression through the various subjective factors a musician brings to the piece.

The best example of this integration is how Torrance understands the incorporation of "anthropic elements" (subjective factors) into the service of divine revelation, and the best treatment of how and why this process takes place may be found in Torrance's essay "The Christian Apprehension of God the Father," in *Speaking the Christian God*.[191]

The integration of subjective and objective factors takes place within the context of a dialogical relationship that God both initiates and sustains. For Torrance, "our knowing of God (objective factor) takes place within the two-way movement in which his revealing of himself and our knowing of him in that self-revelation are interlocked. He [God] thereby establishes and upholds a human coefficient in the knowing relationship."[192]

The inclusion of subjective factors in the knowing relationship is a consequence, not of necessity or even pragmatics, but God's free will and good pleasure, for it is God who initiates and sustains the dialogical relationship and includes a "human coefficient" in his self-disclosure.

The result is that God's act of self-revelation, God's objective self-giving, is mediated through media supplied by human persons responding subjectively to that self-giving. As Torrance notes: "The act of God's self-revealing to us takes our human speaking, hearing and knowing into its concrete realization within God's personal interaction with us, and so there is necessarily included within it an *anthropomorphic* component."[193]

Though Torrance here uses the language of necessity, the integration of subjective factors in the process of revelation is not fundamentally rooted in the necessities or pragmatics of communication, but in a prior affirmation of the value of the human person with whom God seeks to communicate. This human person, as we have considered above, has been created in the image of God and thus in such a way as

---

191. Kimel, *Speaking the Christian God*.
192. Ibid., 124; parentheses mine.
193. Torrance, "Christian Apprehension," 124; italics original.

to generate the reality we refer to as "culture," which is, in the language of Peter Berger, fundamentally rooted in the externalization of human subjectivity into the world. On one level, "necessity" is an appropriate way to discuss the incorporation of anthropomorphic components into divine revelation. However, on a deeper theological level the incorporation of human subjectivity into the process of divine revelation seems more deeply correlated with God's being as love and God's affection for the human creature created in his image. A human coefficient is included in God's self-giving as a loving affirmation of humanity, a humanity that, by God's design, is essentially social and thus inextricable from its cultural environments. As Torrance notes: "Since God has purposely created and formed man for partnership and fellowship with himself, there is no genuine reciprocity between them without the inclusion of a distinctly anthropomorphic ingredient."[194]

This would seem to be why Torrance introduces a second factor in his discussion of the integration of subjective and objective elements in divine revelation, namely, *theomorphism*. God welcomes and desires anthropomorphic/subjective elements in the mediation of his revelation. However, not all anthropic components are adequate for this task, and many need to be transformed before they can be adequately employed in the service of God's revelation.[195] Anthropic elements employed in God's revelation must be rendered *transparent* so that knowledge of the objective pole of the relation may shine through the subjective elements employed for the purposes of its reception and expression. For Torrance, such transparency is only possible if the relation between the subjective and objective poles of the knowing relation is properly ordered.[196] As mentioned above, for this relation to be properly ordered a

194. Ibid., 128.

195. Referring specifically to our language of God, Torrance notes that "self-critical and self-corrective processes" are necessary. Through these tools our "thinking and speaking of God are pruned of inappropriate anthropomorphisms and illegitimate subjective features." These tools serve as "corrective devices" that we may use to "check the objectivity of our knowledge and the ontological reference of its conceptual content in order to obstruct the intrusion into our trains of thought of any distorting images and extraneous analogies projected out of our own self-analysis and self-understanding onto God." See ibid. Thus we must develop conceptual tools that keep us from projecting our inappropriate images of fatherhood onto our understanding of God as Father. The fatherhood *of God* should qualify and define our understanding of father, not the other way around.

196. Speaking of the function of symbolic systems Torrance notes: "Symbolic or formal systems are not invented for their own sake, but are used to deepen and widen

certain priority must be given to the objective pole of the knowing relation. In the case of divine revelation, and in particular of language used to refer to God as triune, Torrance describes the proper ordering of this relation in the following way: "The Creator/creature relationship in being and knowing cannot be reversed. Accordingly, far from God being conceived in the image of man, man is to be conceived as formed after the image of God. It is this biblical theomorphism, understood in this irreversible way, that must be taken into account in assessing the place of any anthropomorphism in our thinking and speaking of God."[197]

Implied in the integration of subjective and objective factors in God's self-giving is that God remains transcendent over them even while working through them. However, this prioritization of the objective pole of the knowing relation does not mean that the subjective pole is of no concern. Nor does it mean that the only value the subjective pole holds is that it gives concrete expression to an objective reality. For Torrance, a proper relation to the objective pole upholds the integrity of the subjective pole. If that relation is not properly mediated and oriented through the use of appropriate anthropic elements, then not only will we lose touch with the objective pole of the knowing relation, the integrity of the subjective pole will also be subverted.

The work of God through anthropic elements is pluriform, and the role of the presence of the Spirit is of particular interest to Torrance at this point. The transformation of anthropic elements takes place through the sanctifying agency of the Holy Spirit, for "the presence of the Holy Spirit empowers, integrates and establishes the [frail forms of contingent rationality with which we are endowed]."[198]

Because of God's transcendence over the anthropomorphic components employed in his self-revelation, and due to the particular pres-

---

the bearing of our thought upon empirical reality and to enable us to grasp its intrinsic intelligibility at a deeper level. In order to perform that function they have constantly to be purified and refined so that they may become more and more apposite ways of representing the structured objectivities of the universe as these become disclosed through our inquiries. Everything goes wrong, however, if the formal language does not prove to be an apposite system of representation, or if the relation between the symbols we employ and the realities upon which they are meant to bear is damaged, for then the symbolic systems break loose from the objective control of reality and bear upon it only in an indirect, ambiguous and misleading way" (Torrance, *Reality and Evangelical Theology*, 62).

197. Torrance, "Christian Apprehension," 125.
198. Torrance, *Christian Doctrine of God*, 220.

ence and agency of the Holy Spirit, these anthropic elements are adopted, critiqued, transformed, and integrated into God's self-revelation, some in such a way that they become normative for any attempt to participate in a knowing relation with the God who has revealed himself through them. The best example of this is the role Israel plays as a social coefficient of God's self-revelation, the importance of the language of Father, Son, and Spirit in naming and addressing God, and the indispensability of Holy Scripture in the life of the Church. In each instance, we see the profound and deep integration of God's objective self-giving and that self-giving being expressed and embodied through subjective elements brought to the table by those who hear and respond to that revelation. It is this integration of the subjective and objective that makes both Israel and the Church a unique people, and a manifestation of a particular knowing relation.

By Orienting and Aggregating Human Relations

The expression and embodiment of knowing relations is a communal affair. Social coefficients arise and are sustained, not by formal signification systems, but by communities that continue to use those symbol systems to understand, describe, order, and act in the world in a specific way. There is no integration of subjective and objective apart from the agency of specific human communities.

Therefore, the work of the Spirit also entails the formation of reciprocal relationships between the object to be known and those who seek to know it. Through these reciprocal relationships the knowing relationship is sustained, expressed and embodied. This is accomplished as participants in these communities allow themselves to be oriented to, and aggregated around, the object to be known. Participants in these communities are oriented to the object to be known through the symbolic language and ritual practices of the community, through which an understanding of the object to be known is communicated as well as appropriate forms of response to it. Consequently, what emerges is a social coefficient that provides the coordinates by which participants in this community orient themselves to the object to be known and, by necessity, to each other. The by-product is a tangible, communal expression of the knowing relation.

For Torrance, the intersections of two relational axes are involved in this process: the horizontal and the vertical. Speaking specifically of the work of the Spirit in the Church, Torrance notes that the Spirit not only integrates the objective and the subjective, but does so as the Spirit of reciprocity, through whose agency a vertical relation with God is given expression through our horizontal relations with others. Where the objective pole of the knowing relation is the God of Jesus Christ, the Christian Church emerges as the social coefficient of this knowing relation. In the Christian Church, the subjective responses of its members are to bear witness to the object of knowledge at the center of its life. For Torrance, the fellowship or *koinonia* of the Christian community with God is actualized within the space-time structures of this world, in our horizontal relations with others: "In *koinonia* the community of reciprocity which we have with God is actualized within the reciprocities we have with one another in human society, but in such a creative way that our reciprocities with one another are organized and informed by the intelligible presence of God through his Word and Spirit indwelling the Church, and are at the same time deployed in the service of God's love and will for all mankind."[199]

There is no reciprocity, with God or with one another, apart from the creation and use of symbols, where subjective factors are employed to refer to objective realities and to share meaning. In addition, there are no symbolic languages that are not created and communicated apart from specific communities and their ritual practices.

However, this stock of cultural symbols is not static. They do not contain meaning in themselves but are "conceptual tools" that bring us into contact with objective realities. The main purpose of cultural symbols is to orient human persons in relation to objective realities and to

---

199. Torrance, *Reality and Scientific Theology*, 119; italics original. On another occasion Torrance noted that our communion with God and with others is rooted in God's communion with himself as personal and triune "since it is God as a Communion of personal Being who communicates himself to us through Christ and in his Spirit, it is a community of persons in reciprocity both with God and with one another that is set up. In other words, the person constituting interaction of God with us calls into being a church as the spatiotemporal correlate of his self-giving and self-revealing to mankind. Correspondingly, the church constitutes the social coefficient of our knowledge of God" (Torrance, *Reality and Evangelical Theology*, 46). The purpose of the social coefficient is to express and embody knowing relations, and in that sense the Church as a social coefficient should be ordered in such a way as to give expression to the reality it seeks to know, namely, the triune God of Jesus Christ.

aggregate human relations in such a way that objective realities may be expressed more accurately through those relations, so that a dynamic and living relation between subject and object is expressed and sustained through their use. Both subject and object are actively involved in this process.

Torrance's understanding of the dynamics of the social coefficient accord well with recent thinking in the field of cultural anthropology, where culture is viewed less as a static reality "out there" that orders and integrates human relations through external force, and more as something that is constantly evolving under the impact of social actors actively involved in the reception, transmission, and transformation of culture.[200]

For Torrance, culture as simply a static deposit of human knowledge is a positive hindrance to human freedom and fosters a determinism of the worst sort, for it cuts human persons off, individually and collectively, from positive and dynamic engagement with the objective world, rendering the objective world mute and the human person adrift in the world without positive coordinates to orient and sustain its life.[201] Torrance's words are instructive: "No social coefficient of knowledge, no infra-structure of connections in community life, and certainly no axiomatic system of ideas can have ultimate meaning if it is closed in upon itself. Any meaningful rational system must have indeterminate areas where its formalizations break off and retain their consistency only through controlling organization from a higher frame of reference."[202]

It is not enough that human subjectivity finds expression in a world of symbols, those symbols must properly orient the human person *vis-à-vis* God, the created order, and other human persons. Ultimately, the accomplishment of this task requires an Archimedean point, and the character of that Archimedean point will determine the character of the social coefficient that crystallizes or aggregates around it.

Symbols and rituals result from the integration of subjective elements with an objective world. They are also the primary means by

200. See the discussion in Grenz and Franke, *Beyond Foundationalism*, 134ff.

201. When we speak of aggregating we also call to mind the model of the centered set (and also effect and affect): people aggregate around certain centers; they are not pushed into those centers from without.

202. Torrance, *Reality and Scientific Theology*, 124. We are reminded here that the social coefficient is, as discussed above, a "multi-leveled structure" for semantic reasons.

which human subjects are oriented before God, the world, and other persons. This orienting function is accomplished as symbols (linguistic, visual, etc.) and rituals aggregate human persons into macro and micro communities, which in turn bear witness to the object these communities seek to know and the quality of their relationship to that object. If the relations of this community are properly oriented to the object of knowledge, that object will be disclosed to that community in ever greater depths, and they will in turn be increasingly transformed by it.

By Ordering the Social and Material World

Social coefficients of knowledge, whether micro or macro in scope, emerge through our interaction with an objective world and are formed as we respond to the impress of that world upon us. This very dynamic entails the integration of subjective and objective factors in the knowing process and it involves the one seeking knowledge to be oriented in a specific way before the object to be known. That orientation is provided by the community of which one is a part and the stock of cultural symbols that community uses to describe their relationship to the object of knowledge.

However, these factors not only determine one's orientation to an object of knowledge, they also determine how we are to respond, individually and collectively, to that object of knowledge within the boundaries of the spatio-temporal world. Consequently, how we respond to the object of knowledge will have an effect upon the social and material worlds we indwell.

Clifford Geertz, speaking of the function of religion in society, notes that religion is essentially a symbolic system that functions to "synthesize a people's ethos ... their most comprehensive ideas of order."[203] Those comprehensive ideas of order are embodied in, and nourished by, the religious outlook of a people and serve to orient persons not only before God but also before one another. Their orientation in turn guides their actions toward both God and others in the context of their social and physical surroundings.

Like a painter using a palette of colors and textures to express and embody on canvas what he or she is seeing in the objective world, so too human beings as cultural beings draw upon a palette of cultural

203. Geertz, *Interpretation of Cultures*, 89.

symbols and rituals to describe and embody in their social relations and physical environments their vision of the world and their role in it. While for the painter the paint on the canvas becomes the expression and embodiment of an artistic vision, for human persons the communities they indwell and the cultural stories they create become expressions of their most comprehensive ideas of order. Telling those stories entails our action in the world, so that the order expressed in the stories becomes socially and materially embodied in our life together.

For Torrance, telling the story of God's work in the world involves the embodiment and expression of God's purposes for it. This story cannot be told apart from the formation of specific communities and their concrete action in the world. When human persons act in the world they function, implicitly or explicitly, as "mediators of order." They cannot escape the fact that their actions have a purpose and that purposeful action is rooted in an overarching and comprehensive conception of order. As Torrance notes: "Order presupposes an ultimate ground of order, with which we operate at the back of our mind in all rational activity."[204] If we are to acknowledge the truth of Torrance's statement (and Geertz's as well) then ultimately every form of order (whether "scientific" or "theological") is in some way religious and moral in nature.

These dynamics come through clearly in Torrance's essay "The Concept of Order in Theology and Science."[205] In this essay Torrance notes that "science and theology are each dedicated in their own way, not only to clarifying and understanding order, but to achieving order, not only to probing into and disclosing the order of things as they actually are, but to the actualizing and realizing of order in our interaction with nature and with one another. That is to say ... we are concerned with *the kind of order that ought to be*."[206]

Here Torrance introduces an eschatological and ethical element into an understanding of human cultural activity, scientific and theological alike, and he is correct in doing so. As Christian Smith notes, every human culture is the embodiment of a moral order, for each constitutes a "living narrative" that is eschatological and moral in nature.[207] Those narratives are dramatized repeatedly through our actions in the

204. Torrance, *Christian Frame of Mind*, 17.
205. Ibid., 17–34.
206. Ibid. 18–19; italics original.
207. Smith, *Moral, Believing Animals*. See chapters 2 and 4 in particular.

world. Scientific and theological communities not only seek greater *understanding* of the objective world, but are called upon, through their collective activities, to *transform* it as well.

The social and material world, like a piece of clay on a potter's wheel, is something human agents work with and mold, and they do so with a particular vision in mind, whether implicit or explicit.[208] What results on the turning wheel as the finished product is, more or less, a representation of the vision entertained in the artist's mind and the particular limitations and qualities of the material the artist is working with. In the words of Peter Berger, the result is both the externalization and objectification of the subjectivity of the artist.

The same may be said of both small and large human communities. The way in which these communities actualize and realize order is guided by a comprehensive vision and purpose that is ultimately religious in nature. That vision guides and legitimates our ordering activities.[209]

Consequently, the way in which human communities order their social and physical environments becomes a form of "embodied worship,"[210] a living and concrete witness to their most comprehensive ideas of order, value, and purpose formed in conversation with a real and objective world. Our relationships with others, the created order, and God form the fundamental basis upon which this activity takes place. The quality of these relationships will also determine whether the result of that activity (a socio-cultural environment) will sustain or subvert the very relations upon which it is built. For Torrance, those relations, and the cultural environments they produce and sustain, can only be morally legitimated as they enable the embodiment of God's purposes for the created order and by so doing sustain the personhood and integ-

---

208. The limitations of this analogy are apparent. As stated earlier, human agents do not stand apart from the cultural process, but are fully implicated in it at all times. However, that does not falsify the truth that we are also active shapers of our social and cultural worlds as well.

209. See Hall, *Imaging God*, chapter 1. Hall's text offers a description of how human agency is informed and legitimated by specific interpretations of the *imago Dei*. His particular concern is to show that our misinterpretation of this Christian symbol has led human agents to act in the world in such a way as to subvert our real calling, work contrary to what the created order is "telling" us, and thus sow disorder in our relations with the created world.

210. This is a description that can be found in Dyrness, *Earth Is God's*, 159ff.

rity of human agents created in God's image.²¹¹ This is the inner-logic of Torrance's theology of culture, an inner-logic that is also present in what Nicholas Wolterstorff refers to as "shalom" and William Dyrness refers to as "embodied worship."

However, Torrance is enough of a realist to assert that not all comprehensive visions of order are accurate, and where those conceptions are flawed, so too will our action in the world bring about the embodiment of disorder. We considered this above in chapter 4 when discussing the ideas of evil and disorder in Torrance's thought.

Referring back to our fictional potter as an example, this might occur when the artist has a vision for a clay structure that the properties of the material itself will not allow. At that point the artist must simply recognize the limitations of the material he or she is working with, or alter that material in some way to allow his or her vision to become a reality.

Another example could be offered from contemporary debates in athletics over steroid drug use. A given athlete may desire to perform at ever increasing levels. In order to achieve these goals a number of different techniques could be employed to help the athlete achieve this goal: more rigorous training programs could be undertaken, better equipment obtained, a new diet adopted, etc. However, at some point, when all other techniques are exhausted, the athlete will come to a place where he or she must face the raw limitations of his or her physical gifts and abilities. A number of athletes have chosen, when confronted with this limitation, to alter their body chemistry through the use of anabolic steroids. By so doing, their vision of what they want to achieve requires them to sacrifice the very integrity of the body they need in order to obtain those goals. The clay of the potter is asked to perform tasks it was not created to perform, and, in an attempt to achieve those goals, the integrity of the clay is subverted in order to do so.

For these reasons Torrance will not allow us to say that our cultural activity is bounded only by our imaginations, or that we can order the world in whatever fashion we desire, using whatever means we see fit to employ. The "order that ought to be" is not something we subjectively imagine and then impose upon a neutral or generic world.²¹²

---

211. As discussed earlier, there is no way of discerning God's purposes for the created order, or human life in it, apart from an Archimedean point of some kind.

212. Torrance would reject Richard Niebuhr's definition of culture as "the artificial,

Rather, through our cultural tools and activity, we must "relate actual order to the ultimate controlling ground of order from which all order proceeds." The "order that ought to be" emerges from this activity. Our cultural activity and cultural environments should enable us to correlate and relate actual order to the ultimate ground of order. Only as we perform this task will the "order that ought to be" become embodied in our socio-cultural worlds. The "order that ought to be" arises as we seek ever greater correlation and congruence between "actual order" and "the ultimate ground of order." Consequently, human persons are not blank slates to be socially programmed as we wish, nor is the created order passive material that we can arrange as our needs and socio-economic goals dictate. There is an order already present in reality, created into it by "the ultimate controlling ground of order" prior to our ordering activities. Our task is to create cultural/conceptual tools that enable us to discern that order so that we may cooperate with it, not impose ourselves upon it. This is simply Torrance's theological science applied to the social and material world.

---

secondary environment which man superimposes on the natural" (Niebuhr, *Christ and Culture*, 46).

Toward a Trinitarian Theology of Culture
Persons, Powers, and Pluralities

HAVING SPENT SOME TIME DISCUSSING THE NATURE OF THE SOCIAL coefficient of knowledge in Torrance's thought, its trinitarian basis and congruence with sociological and anthropological thought, we will now conclude this study with a consideration of two social coefficients that Torrance refers to frequently in his writings, followed by a brief summary of the argument and accomplishments of the project as a whole.

The Social Coefficient of Knowledge: Examples

In Torrance's thought social coefficients serve two primary macro-roles, which are based upon the functions we have just described. Torrance has developed his concept of the social coefficient of knowledge primarily in conversation with developments in the philosophy of science. However, it is through his application of this conceptual framework for understanding the identity, formation, and mission of Israel and the Christian Church that the broader implications of this concept may be noticed. As applied to Israel and the Church the social coefficient of knowledge is both an embodiment and expression of truth and a social witness to the totality of Christ's claims upon human life (the Church as culture). However, as a culture it is also serves as a transforming matrix (the Church transforming culture) as its mission is not only to express and embody the truth, but also, as such, to engage and transform every culture and cultural sphere it comes into contact with.

With regard to the latter, Torrance is quite clear. The Church as a social coefficient of God's self-giving and self-revealing is called upon to penetrate deeply into God's self-giving in order to develop "appropriate modes of conceptuality through which [this self-giving] can be brought to expression."¹ The goal of this task is to enable God's self-giving to "exert [its] creative power upon the whole range of human life and thought. Far from schematizing Christian theology into the patterns of the prevailing culture, this should have the opposite effect of transforming the very foundations of culture."²

We note here how these two roles are developed in Torrance's thought, as they will further illustrate the many parallels between Torrance's social coefficient of knowledge and contemporary anthropological definitions of culture, while also hinting at Torrance's trinitarian social vision and the role of the Church in that vision.

The Social Coefficient as Embodied Truth: The Church as Culture

Israel as the Womb of Christ

In chapter 1 of *The Mediation of Christ* Torrance sets out to "consider the mediation of Christ from the perspective of his intimate and intense involvement with Israel."³ Through God's historical dialogue with Israel a "structure of mediation"⁴ develops that will be essential to the proper understanding of Christ's person and work for all times and places. This structure is composed of a collection of conceptual tools, which Torrance refers to as "adequate modes of thought and speech,"⁵ that will be necessary in order to apprehend and grasp the significance of Christ's person and work and the nature of God's work through him. Torrance describes the purpose of this process in the following way: God "took Israel into his hands . . . in order to provide the actual means, a whole set of spiritual tools, appropriate forms of understanding, worship and expression, through which apprehension of God could be made accessible to human beings and knowledge of God could take root in the soil of humanity. A two-way movement was involved: an adaptation of divine revelation to the human mind and an adaptation of articulate forms of

---

1. Torrance, *Reality and Evangelical Theology*, 47.
2. Ibid.
3. Torrance, *Mediation of Christ*, 5.
4. Ibid.
5. Ibid., 6.

human understanding and language to divine revelation. That is surely how we are to regard God's long historical dialogue with Israel."[6]

This historical dialogue resulted in the embodiment of the oracles of God in the very life of Israel through "a unique cultural integration of its thought and religion."[7] In other words, Israel was formed into a social coefficient of the knowledge of God through a historical dialogue initiated for teleological reasons by Yahweh, and resulting in normative semantic and participatory structures that refer beyond themselves to the coming of the ultimate self-disclosure of God in Christ.[8] Hence, Israel is described by Torrance as "the womb of Christ"[9]—a place of formation, preparation, and anticipation—and even the "corporate counterpart to the self-revelation and self-communication of God to mankind."[10] What has taken place through this historical dialogue with Israel is both an affirmation and transformation of cultural forms, which has resulted in structures of life and thought so normative that if we would know Christ we must "go to school with Israel."[11]

Torrance's understanding of Israel as "the womb of Christ" is a rich and instructive example of the formation, function, and purpose of a particular social coefficient of knowledge.

THE CHURCH AS A ROYAL PRIESTHOOD

Israel as a social coefficient of the knowledge of God cannot function adequately in isolation from the Christian Church, which Torrance also understands as a social coefficient of knowledge. For both historical and theological reasons the Church is not understood to function as "the womb of Christ," but rather as "a royal priesthood." The formation and function of the Church as a social coefficient is no different from the formation and function of Israel as the same, however, the identity of the Church is different because the objective pole of the knowing relation has undergone a change. This change has to do with the way in which the objective pole is made available to those who

---

6. Ibid., 7.
7. Ibid., 9.
8. Ibid.
9. Ibid., 18–19.
10. Ibid., 14.
11. Ibid., 12.

form the social coefficient, and not so much with the actual content of that objective pole. The God of Israel, of Abraham, Isaac and Jacob, is revealed to be the God of Jesus Christ, present to the world through the priesthood of the Church and as a consequence of the agency of Christ and the Spirit.

Torrance notes another important shift that took place between the Old and New Testament conceptions of priesthood: where the cultic activity of the community of Israel was once allocated solely to the Aaronic priesthood, it has now been allocated to the entire body of Christ through the gift of the Spirit, with the gift of the Spirit and the ministry of the Church being grounded objectively in the Royal Priesthood of Christ.[12]

Of particular importance to Torrance are shifts that took place in the understanding of two words used to describe the identity and mission of the Church: *leitourgia* and *latreia*.

With regard to the former, Torrance notes that the words *leitourgein* and *leitourgia* in the Greek Old Testament "were used almost exclusively of the sacrificial *cultus*. But in the New Testament there is a decided change. As Christian terms they are used with priestly and even sacrificial *nuance*, but they are no longer used of ceremonies or religious observances. They are used of the ministry of the whole Church vis-à-vis the heavenly ministry of Christ."[13]

Consequently, in the New Testament Christ is spoken of as the *Leitourgos*, while those who minister in his name are *leitourgoi* or "servants," the ministry of the latter being grounded and shaped by the ministry of the former. Since the sacrificial *cultus* has been fulfilled through the Person and work of the Great High Priest the Church is now called upon to offer a different form of worship, one not rooted in ceremonies or religious observances, but rather in the grateful offering of one's entire life to God in service. Such an offering now incorporates both the sacred and the mundane. We see this shift of emphasis in the writings of the Apostle Paul, who understands the liturgical action of the Church to consist in spending herself for the sake of the Gospel and in the ministry of love from one person to another: "This liturgy of life and love in the Gospel he [Paul] sees as the embodied liturgy of

---

12. Torrance, *Royal Priesthood*, chapter 1.
13. Ibid., 16. Italics original.

thanksgiving to God. This is liturgy done into the flesh, enacted in the body, as sacrificial oblation to God."[14]

We offer our "sacrificial oblation to God" in grateful response to the sacrificial act of Christ on our behalf. Our grateful response, our "embodied liturgy of thanksgiving to God," incorporates the entire ecology of our lives, and by so doing "[the] sacrificial act of Christ once and for all performed and enduring in His endless life in the presence of God, is realized in the life of his people, not by repetition of His substitutionary sacrifice, but by their dying and rising with Christ in faith and life, and by the worship of self-presentation to God."[15]

One is reminded at this point of William Dyrness's understanding of culture as "embodied worship," for that is precisely what is being asked for when we are invited to respond to Christ's work by offering ourselves to God in worship. Our service in the body, our cultural activities and engagements, are liturgical acts that God both desires and delights in.

Thus, and now picking up on the second word of interest to Torrance, our *latreia* or service to God is integral to what it means to worship God, in particular when that service is offered in gratitude and acknowledgment of Christ's sacrifice. The finished work of Christ and the gift of the Spirit have redefined worship, transforming it from a strictly ceremonial activity performed in a temple to all activities in which one's whole self, and the entire ecology of one's life, are offered to God and to others in the name of Christ.[16] Such a redefinition of worship would not be possible apart from a trinitarian understanding of God, where the finished work of Christ and the gift of the Holy Spirit are pivotal to the worship of the Church as Christ's earthly-historical form in the world. For Torrance, "the great characteristic of this *latreia* is that it envisages a relation between the worship on earth and in body to worship in the heavenly realm."[17]

---

14. Ibid., 17.

15. Ibid.; emphasis original.

16. "The *latreia* of the New Testament is rather different from the *latreia* of the Old Testament, because here [in the New Testament] we have the reality of Christ through the Spirit, so that the forms of worship come under judgment by that reality. What is supremely important is obedience to Christ who takes our place and whose sacrifice once and for all displaces us and relativizes all cosmic forms of worship" (ibid., 21).

17. Ibid., 19.

It is this relation, between our embodied worship "on earth and in body" and the worship of Christ our High Priest that is essential to the Church as a royal priesthood and social coefficient of the knowledge of God. Apart from this relation we know not who we are, apart from this relation we cannot offer *latreia* in gratitude, and apart from this relation we have no knowledge of God or of God's purposes for the created order. The God of Jesus Christ is the object of knowledge that stands at the center of the Church and defines both her identity and mission.[18] If that relation is construed properly, that identity and mission will thrust her into the world as a royal priesthood, whose activity in the world of culture will not only bear witness to the God she worships, but will advance God's mission in the world through cultural transformation. This does not mean that our worship on earth is to be "a transcription of the heavenly reality, but a pointer in observable form to a higher reality."[19] As the Church (the particular social coefficient of the knowledge of God) bears witness to this higher reality she fulfills her mission, which is "so to live and think within human society that it enables people individually and corporately to live and think in modes of being and thought that are open to change and advance by way of response to given and transcendent realities in the world, and to the transcendent Reality of God himself over the world who is its creative ground and all-sufficient reason."[20]

The particular mission of the theologian, vis-à-vis the Church, is precisely the same.[21] We will explore this particular function of the

---

18. For Torrance, "The pattern for the Church's worship and its relation to the heavenly worship is to be discerned in the Suffering Servant (cf. Jas. 5.10). The way in which the Church draws near to God is the way of the Son of Man" (ibid., 21). Parentheses original.

19. Ibid. 20. Here Torrance's particular concerns are with how we understand and structure priesthood in the Church, but the implications are far greater. The Church as a social coefficient of knowledge is an expression and embodiment of God's will and purposes, not a uniform transcription of them that must take the same shape in every time and culture. As such, our earthly worship and service, at its best, serve only as "a shadow cast ahead" by a coming eschatological reality, secured in the past and approaching in the future, but nevertheless active in our midst right now, generating rich forms of order that serve as embodiments and reflections of the God we worship through service.

20. Torrance, *Reality and Scientific Theology*, 120.

21. Ibid., 118, 121ff.

social coefficient presently, as it is deeply implied in both the mission of Israel and the Church as social coefficients of the knowledge of God.

The Social Coefficient as Transforming Matrix: The Church Transforming Culture

The Church as social coefficient serves not only as a lens or matrix through which objective realities (specifically, the God of Jesus Christ) are socially embodied, but also as yeast or leaven in the midst of human societies and cultures.[22] As Torrance notes, theological thought must move back and forth constantly "between the distinctive social coefficient of theological knowledge (the Church) and the general coefficient of our knowledge of the intelligible world around us. They are inevitably interconnected, for the former intersects the latter from above, and the latter interpenetrates the former from below."[23]

Like ripples in a body of water, there are numerous social coefficients, each with distinctive centers and each, in one way or another, ultimately overlapping by reference, implicitly or explicitly, to an ultimate ground of order. The mission of the Church is to point out this ultimate ground of order, and by so doing, to transform the very roots of human culture.

In Torrance's thought this service has been rendered on behalf of Western culture in a number of ways, but ultimately in the rejection of dualist modes of thought, a rejection rooted in the thinking together of central Christian doctrines, particularly the doctrines of the Trinity, creation, and the incarnation. This thinking together of central Christian doctrines, and their leavening influence on Western cultural presuppositions, has resulted in the transformation of ideas that are central to the development of Western culture. We mention two in particular: the idea of the "person" as an onto-relational category, and the three masterful ideas that led to the development of Western scientific culture.

---

22. There are many emphases in Torrance's thought that would place him on a Niebuhrian continuum as an advocate for the "Christ Transforming Culture" type. While this type may seem to be the best fit, no single type adequately captures the many dynamics involved in Torrance's theological and social thinking. Elmer Colyer notes that Torrance's realism and interest in the transformation of culture differentiates his understanding of the nature and function of doctrine radically from that of George Lindbeck. See Colyer, *Nature of Doctrine*, 127 n. 157.

23. Torrance, *Reality and Scientific Theology*, 121. Parentheses mine.

The Doctrine of the Trinity and the Concept of Person

Stanley Grenz has recently noted that one of the distinctive contributions Torrance makes to contemporary thinking about the triune nature of God is his concept of "onto-relations."[24] For Torrance, onto-relations refer to being-constituting relations, or relations between two realities that make them what they are and would not otherwise be apart from their relatedness. A prime example of this is the onto-relations between the Father, Son, and Spirit in the Holy Trinity. The very existence and identity of each Person is preserved through their relations with the others. The understanding of personhood as an onto-relational category was developed as the Christian Church came to conceptual terms with its experience of God and its affirmation of the deity of Jesus Christ: "The concept of person, which was not found before Christianity, is the direct product of the way in which the Church found it had to understand Jesus Christ and the distinctive relations in the Triune God as intrinsically personal."[25]

As the Greek Fathers thought together the implications of the self-revelation of God as Father, Son, and Spirit a new understanding of the nature of God came into view. Two terms in particular underwent important transformations as they were taken into the discourse of the Christian Church and transformed through the theological activity of the Church: *ousia* and *hypostasis*.

The Christian Church did not invent these terms *ex nihilo*. The terms *ousia* and *hypostasis* were widely used and understood during the time, particularly among students of Greek philosophy. They were terms rooted in the language and culture of a given society and a particular academic discipline. In Aristotle's *Metaphysics* the term *ousia*, for instance, is a metaphysical and static concept, translated variously by the terms *essentia* and *substantia* in Latin.[26] It is a term that is impersonal in nature, referring to that "which is and subsists by itself."[27] Torrance notes that Patristic theologians did not reject this understanding of the term entirely, but took the term "as-is" and, under the impact of divine revelation, transformed its primary reference when used to refer to the

---

24. Grenz, *Rediscovering the Triune God*, 208.
25. Torrance, *Mediation of Christ*, 48.
26. Torrance, *Christian Doctrine of God*, 116.
27. Ibid.

triune God of Jesus Christ. This was accomplished through the theological activity of the Church, the effects of which rippled out into the broader culture, at its deepest levels, and with significant effects.

This same process of theological reflection and cultural engagement was applied to the term *hypostasis*, a term taken from general cultural use and semantically tailored to refer to the divine Persons of the Holy Trinity and the intensely personal nature of God. This process is described by Torrance:

> In its theological deployment, the term *hypostasis* was not taken over from Greek thought unchanged, but was stretched and transformed under the impact of God's trinitarian self-revelation through Christ and in the Spirit to such an extent that it became suitable to express the identifiable self-manifestation of God in the incarnate economy of divine salvation as Father, Son, and Holy Spirit—that is, as three distinctive hypostatic Realities or Persons. This change from a Hellenistic impersonal to a Christian personal way of thinking is very evident in the penchant of early Church theologians to qualify words for "God," "Word," "being," "life," "authority," etc., by attaching to them the expression for "oneself" . . . in order to stress the intensely personal nature of God's interaction with us through the presence and power of his Word and Spirit.[28]

Through this process the terms *ousia* and *hypostasis* were transformed and employed by the Christian Church to refer to a distinctive experience and understanding of God, an experience and understanding that required the terms *ousia* and *hypostasis* to be modified and "stretched" if they were to serve as appropriate conceptual tools for referring to the objective reality of the triune God.[29] Semantic nuances

---

28. Ibid., 156. Colin Gunton notes that one of the great Cappodocian contributions to the doctrine of God as personal was the "desynonymizing of *ousia* and *hypostasis*: of making what were synonymous terms into words of distinct meaning" (Gunton, *The One, the Three and the Many*, 191).

29. This is one of the primary tasks of the social coefficient, of whatever form. Social coefficients not only give embodied expression to the object of knowledge at the center of their life but are constantly forming and refining conceptual tools that more accurately refer to the object of knowledge. Through the very process of forming such language, they are both giving expression to the object of knowledge within the boundaries of specific cultural forms and concurrently transforming those cultural forms and the social framework that invests them with meaning. Altering the language of a social group in this way is akin to altering the DNA of a biological organism. The change itself seems insignificant and slight, but the effects are significant.

were added to the terms through the theological activity of the Church, and a novel and powerful conception of God as personal and triune emerged.

This conception of the personal as being inherently relational was formed in the context of the Christian Church and her experience of God, as well as her determination to allow the reality of God's self-giving in Christ to determine the semantic content of the terms she used to refer to God. Since the "distinctive social coefficient of theological knowledge and the general coefficient of our knowledge of the intelligible world around us overlap through their various points of interconnection," it was inevitable that when the Church took an important cultural symbol and transformed it the effects would be felt not only in the Church, but in the culture at large.

It is the responsibility of the Church as a social coefficient to maintain the specific semantic reference of these terms if she is to be a faithful embodied witness of the God she worships and seeks to know. However, just as the Church transforms culture, so too broader streams of human culture (and other social coefficients) also exert a great deal of power in forming the language of the Church. This is also clearly seen in the term "person," which, in the West, has taken on a meaning quite incongruent with the intentions of those who originally crafted the term to refer to the personal as inherently relational, while in Western culture it has since come to refer to the person as an autonomous individual.

Western Science and the Three Masterful Ideas

In chapter 3 of *The Ground and Grammar of Theology*, titled "Creation and Science," Torrance discusses the intimate relation between Christian thought and the development of the Western scientific tradition.[30] His particular interest in this chapter is in the way conceptions of creation play formative roles in the development and practice of both empirical and theological science. In reference to the latter, Torrance notes that "an understanding of the *world* enters into the coefficients of theological concepts and statements."[31]

However, the same truth applies in the case of the former: Christian theological understandings of creation have entered into the coefficients

---

30. Torrance, *Ground and Grammar*, 44–74. See in particular pages 52–62.
31. Ibid., 45; italics original.

of scientific concepts and processes as well, particularly in the West. So much so in fact that Torrance can assert, and persuasively demonstrate, that "far from theology being based upon natural science, the opposite, if anything, is nearer the truth."[32] Tapio Luoma refers this to in his book *Incarnation and Physics*, as Torrance's "Idea of Contribution."[33]

We have just discussed this dynamic with regard to how the word "person" developed under the impact of both Christian revelation and broader cultural forces. We will now look briefly at how this dynamic was at work in the rise of Western science.

Torrance notes in the Preface to *The Ground and Grammar of Theology* that his project in the book is not only theological, but cultural as well. The second chapter of the book in particular is devoted to discussing "the underlying ground of dualism which has so deeply affected historic and modern thought, and which needs to be understood clearly, since it lies at the root of our present problems in [our] split culture."[34]

The only way to address the problems posed and perpetuated by the various dualisms present in Western culture is through "the breaking down of these dualisms in a switch to a unitary (but non-monist) and realist outlook in science and theology." This project will involve "a deep integration of thought" that Torrance says must begin with "certain masterful conceptions basic to both science and theology, which developed out of classical Christian theology as it sought to think through the relation between the incarnation and the creation of space and time."[35]

Torrance refers to these masterful conceptions elsewhere in the book as the "three masterful ideas"[36] that originated in Christian thinking about God and creation but have had a profound influence on the development of Western science and culture. Those ideas are:

---

32. Ibid., 44.

33. Luoma, *Incarnation and Physics*, chapter 1. In addition to "contribution," Luoma adds the ideas of "compulsion" and "reminder" to describe the dynamic that exists between the Christian faith and the natural sciences in Torrance's thought.

34. Torrance, *Ground and Grammar*, x.

35. Ibid.

36. Ibid., 52.

- The rational *unity* of the universe.[37]
- The contingent rationality or *intelligibility* of the universe.[38]
- The contingent *freedom* of the universe.[39]

Through the development of these ideas the Christian Church found herself at the center of a "radical reconstruction of the foundations of ancient philosophy, science and culture."[40] It is clear from Torrance's work that he thinks the development of these ideas were rooted not only in a desire to think faithfully about God's revelation in Jesus Christ, but also a missiological goal, that goal being to create an intellectual/cultural environment where the Christian Gospel could take root in the civilized world, transforming society until it was "brought within the Kingdom of Christ."[41] Faithful theological reflection was understood to be a missiological imperative of the Church and perhaps the most radical form of cultural engagement and transformation.

The only reason this is not so today is because the Christian Church is no longer being faithful to its proper object, no longer developing "new concepts that are in fundamental conflict with the paradigms of the community and that cannot be assimilated to them without a revolutionary change or conversion."[42] Instead of thinking ahead of the cultures in which it finds itself, the Church has taken the course of relevance, which is for Torrance no more than making the Gospel understandable to the modern mindset, and, in the process, fitting the Gospel message within the pre-existing paradigms held and affirmed by a specific cultural group. Thus, "while science advances through changing our thought, the preaching and teaching of the Church become more and more obsolescent. Is that not why . . . the more we have tried to make the Gospel relevant, the more it has become irrelevant to our contemporaries, while theology has fallen into the deep fissures that have opened up in our split culture?"[43]

---

37. Ibid.
38. Ibid., 53.
39. Ibid., 57.
40. Ibid., 47.
41. Ibid.
42. Ibid., 48.
43. Ibid.

So, it is clear that for Torrance the theological activity of the Church should be directed toward the transformation of the world, and that at a very deep and radical level. For an example of how this missiological task is to be carried out faithfully Torrance points to the Early Church: "[She] undertook the enormous task of recreating the very foundations of human philosophy, science, and culture so that the Gospel could take deep root and develop within human society in such a way as to evangelize and convert it."[44]

As the Church was faithful in this task she would fulfill her mission, which Torrance understands as involving a distinctly "cultural role" in the midst of human society, that role being the clarification and unification of "all human knowledge and life under the creative impact of God's self-revelation in Christ and the ordering power of his love."[45] The Early Church began her work with the very concrete revelation of God in the Person of Jesus Christ, thinking through the relationship between this event and the creation of the world out of nothing. What emerged were the three masterful ideas mentioned above. As these ideas, and the realities they refer to, were embodied in the social coefficient Torrance refers to as the Church, what emerged was not only a peculiar people with a distinctive way of thinking and acting, but a cultural force that revolutionized the very foundations of human thought and culture at the time. The knowing relation embodied and expressed through the Christian community positively engaged and transformed the culture she found herself in the midst of. The result, for the Christian Church, was "embodied worship," a gathering up of all human knowledge and life under the creative impact of God's self-revelation and love.

Upon the basis of these ideas Torrance finds the presence of epistemological dualism a fundamental threat to not only the Christian Church but also to human life, and this is why it is so vigorously opposed in his writings. It is the primary feature of Western culture that he has sought to engage and transform through his theological and scientific work.

---

44. Ibid., 49.
45. Ibid.

Project Summary and Accomplishments

The central goal of this project has been to sketch the contours of a trinitarian theology of culture, and to do so in conversation with the thought of Thomas F. Torrance. We have sought to accomplish this goal by following a line through Torrance's thought, a line that both originates and terminates in his understanding of God as triune. That line took us through many features of Torrance's theological work, particularly into extended discussions of his doctrine of God as triune Creator, the created order as contingent, fallen and redeemed, the human person as created in the image of God and entrusted with a task that is cultural in nature and doxologically motivated, and finally an exploration of an important and very suggestive concept in Torrance's thought: the social coefficient of knowledge. We then suggested that this final concept builds upon the trinitarian foundations of Torrance's thought (specifically in his doctrines of God, creation, and humanity) while integrating its various features in a way that strongly suggests the contours of a theology of culture that is trinitarian in nature.

It is now time for us to "improvise" a bit within this theological framework, and suggest more explicitly what a trinitarian theology of culture, rooted in Torrance's theological vision, might look like. The best way to do so is through an explanation of the title we have chosen for this project: *Persons, Powers and Pluralities*. An explanation of the title will serve as both a basis for summarizing the accomplishments of the project and for suggesting directions for its further development.

The Persons of the Trinity and the Purpose of Human Culture: A Design for Living

The inner-logic of Torrance's theological work is grounded in his doctrine of God as triune. No particular feature of Torrance's theological project can be understood apart from a deep appreciation of this truth. Intimately bound up with this is Torrance's belief that an affirmation of God's tri-unity requires us also to affirm that God is personal. Only where we find relations between persons do we find that which is truly personal.

That God is personal (and thus free, loving, and dynamic in his very Being) exercises a controlling influence upon how God exercises his creative power. Our particular interest in chapter 1 was to demonstrate that the tri-unity of God stands as the basis for God's creative activity, not only in the act of creation itself, but in all of God's activity *ad extra*. For Torrance, the Creator of the world is a triune Creator and all of God's creative activity flows from "a fellowship in creative activity"[46] that would not be possible apart from the particular identities and functions of the Father, Son, and Holy Spirit. Because of this the creative agency of God is, in essence, *perichoretic*.

As *perichoretic*, the identities and functions of each divine Person are essential to a proper understanding of God's creative agency. Torrance highlights both the unity and plurality of God's creative agency through a statement made by St. Basil: "Basil distinguishes the work of the Father as 'the original cause of all things that are made,' and the work of the Son as 'the operative cause,' and the work of the Spirit as 'the perfecting cause.'"[47]

We are granted access into the Being and character of God, as well as the character and *telos* of the created order (as a product of God's creative agency), only as we consider the *perichoretic* relationships between the Father, Son, and Spirit in their creative activity. This was the burden of our investigation in chapter 1.

However, that God's Being and creative activity are rooted in *perichoretic* relationships between Father, Son, and Holy Spirit also means that the very Being of God is personal. This is perhaps the most important, yet understated, feature of Torrance's thought, and the most suggestive for further development, not only for a theology of culture, but for any assessment of Torrance's thought. If the line we have been following through this project originates and terminates in Torrance's doctrine of God as triune, it does so because for Torrance the tri-unity of God is a truth about the nature of God as fundamentally personal. As personal, the very relations that obtain between the Father, Son, and Spirit make God who God is. They are "onto-relations." Only if God is personal can we affirm that God's creative power is exercised in both freedom and in love and for the purposes of redemption. God's creative power is exercised in the context of a "fellowship": from the Father, through the Son and in the Holy Spirit: "Within a trinitarian perspective, the power or almightiness of God is revealed to be essentially personal, defined

46. Torrance, *Theology in Reconstruction*, 220.
47. Ibid., 221.

by God's triune Nature and Being as Father, Son, and Holy Spirit. This personal power of God is not power that overrules the creature, not power that negates the freedom of the creature, but the power of the love God is, power therefore that sustains the relation and freedom of the creature before God, for it is always creative, and in relation to his human creatures always personalizing and humanizing power."[48]

Of course, that God is triune and thus personal is not a truth discovered or validated through reflection upon the created order, but rather through the witness of both the Son and the Spirit to the Father. Not only is God triune, but the means by which we know this God takes a trinitarian shape as well.

However, it is the means by which we discover, not only the nature of God, but also the character and *telos* of the created order. As Torrance notes: "The reason for the creation is theologically traced back to the free, ungrudging will of God's love to create a reality other than himself which he correlates so closely with himself that it is made to reflect and shadow forth on its contingent level his own inner rationality and order."[49]

For Torrance, a triune and personal God has brought into being a reality with a specific design and purpose, and has done so in freedom and love and with the desire that it reflect his own rationality and creative purposes. If the created order is in any way a reflection of the inner rationality and order of its Creator it is because it has been ordered in such a way as to sustain and foster *personal* life, since the triune Creator is, in his very Being, personal and the fount of all that is personal. This seems clearly implied in the biblical narrative, particularly in the opening chapters of Genesis, where the climax of the creation narrative is the formation of a creature created in the very image of God as male and female. This creature is placed in an environment specifically designed to sustain its particular form of life and given a task that they alone have been uniquely enabled to fulfill. In the context of their relation with God, their relations with each other, and their relation with the created order they are to exercise "dominion" over the earth, cultivating it in such a way that these personal and non-personal relations are not only sustained, but also ordered in such a way as to advance God's purposes. When God's purposes are advanced, God is "glorified."

48. Torrance, *Christian Doctrine of God*, 206.
49. Torrance, *Divine and Contingent Order*, 35.

We will discuss in greater detail the particular constitution of the created order and the human creature in the following two points. Here it is enough to say that a theology of culture developed upon the basis of Torrance's theological work must begin with the triune God of Jesus Christ, for here we discover that God is a communion of Persons, and thus personal in his very Being. It is this God who is the Creator of heaven and earth. It is this God in whose image human creatures have been made. It is this God who has entrusted the human creature with a task and responsibility that can only be fulfilled in the context of relations with God, other human persons, and the created order.

However, to say that God's creative activity has been exercised in these specific ways is to say that God has designed the world with a very specific purpose in mind. As Torrance notes: "The created order reflects to a certain extent the God who has brought it into being, since its intent and purpose for being is the glorification of the Creator."[50]

This project has sought to demonstrate that the accomplishment of this specific purpose (the glorification of the triune Creator) is enabled through the creation of a world that is meant to sustain and nurture personal life, and that personal life, as irreducibly relational and social, is possible only through the cultural activity of its most problematic inhabitants: the human creature.

The connection between the Persons of the Trinity and the purpose of human culture are many, but the most basic is this: human cultural activity is only possible because our triune Creator has given us the capacity to create by forming the human person after his image. When human persons create they are engaged in cultural activity. The purpose of human culture then is to sustain and nourish an environment where the personal is sustained and nourished through human cultural activity. For Torrance, this fundamental goal is approximated only as human creatures attend to, and cooperate with, the will and purposes of their triune Creator.[51] They succeed or fail in this vocation depending upon how they order their social and material worlds, and which "design" they utilize to guide their cultural activity. If it is a design that is at odds with the will and purposes of their Creator, or the structure of the cre-

---

50. Torrance, *Trinitarian Faith*, 93.

51. The will and purposes of the triune Creator are revealed through the Son and in the Spirit, and as human persons (through their cultural activity) interact with the created world as "scientists" and "priests."

ated order he has brought into being, then that which was intended to sustain the personal, will in fact subvert it. This, at the very least, is the overwhelming thrust of Torrance's thought when brought to bear on the question of the purpose of human cultural activity.

The Contingency of Creation and the Powers of Human Culture

As designed by God with a specific purpose in mind, the created order has built into it a definable structure, a structure that reflects the creative purposes of a triune God. Chapters 2–4 of this project paid particular attention to the broad contours of this structure. We did so by exploring two areas of Torrance's thought: his understanding of the created order as contingent (chapters 2–3) and his understanding of the human person as a creature with a particular identity (image of God) and vocation (mediator of order). This was the accomplishment of chapter 4.

As contingent the created order is structured in such a way that it is both *dependent upon God* for its very structure and being, but also *independent from God*, in that it is a distinct reality of its own. Torrance summarizes this dynamic in the following way: "The independence of the world depends entirely upon the free creative act of God to give it being and form wholly differentiated from himself, but that is then an independence that is delimited by the dependence that anchors the world beyond itself in the freedom of the Creator."[52]

The created order, so understood, is characterized by an intelligibility, freedom, and stability that are all contingent. Consequently, the created order cannot be ultimately understood without reference to God (contingent intelligibility), the multi-variability and open nature of the created order cannot be understood apart from reference to the freedom of God (contingent freedom), and the stability and regularity of the created order cannot be understood apart from the faithfulness of God in upholding its distinct structure (contingent stability).

If, as we asserted in the previous point (and in chapter 1) the created order has been brought into being to facilitate a specific purpose (the glorification of its triune Creator), then the nature of the created order as "contingent" must serve that end. In Torrance's doctrine of

---

52. Torrance, *Divine and Contingent Order*, 35.

creation, contingency sums up his understanding of how the created order can not only be traced back to "the free, ungrudging will of God's love" but also how it is so closely correlated with God "that it is made to reflect and shadow forth on its contingent level his own inner rationality and order."[53]

However, more must be said if we are to be faithful to the full implications of Torrance's thought as both trinitarian and personal, in particular if we want to bring it to bear on a theology of culture where the purpose of cultural activity is the affirmation of the personal through the glorification of God.

The contingency of the created order in itself does not serve as a reflection of God's purposes. As we concluded in chapter 3, the created order itself is ambiguous, suffering under the conditions of both falleness and redemption. However, it remains the environment for the embodiment and realization of God's purposes, primarily through the cultural activity of the creatures created in God's image and upon the basis of the reconciling work of the Son and the sanctifying work of the Spirit. These realities and conditions characterize the created order, giving it a determinate shape and distinctive dynamic. Torrance refers to these structures and conditions as "God given normative patterns" that have to do with "the intrinsic truth or objective intelligibility of contingent being."[54]

Chapter 3 suggested that these "God given normative patterns" are similar in nature to the "principalities and powers" referred to frequently in the Pauline corpus and utilized by those in the field of social ethics to refer to a broad range of natural and social structures that make created life possible. These structures are part of God's good design for the created order, and exist in order to enable the fulfillment of God's purposes for creation. However, they are also fallen, and, as such, can be utilized and directed in such a way as to thwart God's purposes instead of advancing them. Through the initiative of the triune God, through the Son and in the Spirit, these powers have been redeemed, and as such continue to have an abiding role in God's design for the created order. However, this is still an objective truth that is in need of subjective fulfillment. Torrance's doctrine of creation affirms the reality and importance of these "principalities and powers," understood as the

53. Ibid., 35.
54. Ibid., 37.

structures of space and time that give shape to cultural activity even while they are the very presupposition of that activity. It is at this point that our attention must turn to the human person, the third area of Torrance's thought, explored specifically in chapter 4.[55]

The Identity and Agency of Humanity and the Plurality of Human Culture: Designs for Living

God has ordered and structured the world in a particular way and for a particular purpose. The created order is contingent so that it may reflect, through its own distinct reality, the reality and purposes of its Creator. And yet, because the created order and its powers are contingent, and thus independent from God in their dependence, they cannot fulfill this purpose apart from the presence and agency of the creature created in God's image. The created order is, as Torrance frequently notes, "mute." It has been the suggestion of this project that the created order has been constructed in such a way that it requires the presence and agency of human persons as cultural beings to fulfill its *telos*. If that *telos* is, as Torrance claims, the glorification of its Creator, then that *telos* can only be approximated through the cultural activity of human persons: "Nature itself is mute, but human being is the one constituent of the created universe through whom its rational structure and astonishing beauty may be brought to word in praise of the Creator."[56]

In chapter 4 we noted that, not only has the created order been created in a way appropriate to its purpose and calling, but so has the human creature. By unpacking Torrance's theological anthropology we discovered that the human person is fundamentally a social and cultural being that completes itself through engagement with the world, and by completing itself through engagement with the world, also enables the created order to fulfill (or not fulfill) its *telos*. The by-product of that activity (as well as its presupposition) is human culture. Consequently, God has so ordered the world, and the human creature placed in its midst, as to enable the human creature as a steward of creation and mediator of order to manipulate and order the world in such a way as to

---

55. The previous two being his doctrines of God and creation. Together with his doctrine of humanity they form a triadic relation that informs much of Torrance's theological method.

56. Torrance, *Christian Doctrine of God*, 213.

generate a pluriform cultural witness to God's reality, glory, and purposes. This is accomplished through the formation of social coefficients.

As the particular subject of chapter 5, Torrance's conception of "the social coefficient of knowledge" was suggested as a way to conceive of the nature and purpose of human culture understood within a trinitarian theological framework. As was shown, Torrance's social coefficient of knowledge is firmly rooted in his doctrine of God as triune, the created order as contingent, and human persons as stewards created in the image of God. For Torrance, a social coefficient of knowledge is the social embodiment of a knowing relation established with some aspect of the objective world. As such, it is constructed through a sustained historical process that occurs between the subjective and objective poles of the knowing relation. What results is a social matrix that mediates the mutual modification of both poles of the knowing relation by properly orienting the relation that exists between them.

A problem occurs when one pole of the knowing relation is imposed on the other. Of particular concern to Torrance is when the subjective pole of the knowing relation is imposed upon the objective pole. At this point God is turned into humanity, persons are turned into things, or the created order is turned into a commodity. For Torrance, this inversion of the knowing relation is a result of the fall. Consequently, instead of social coefficients reflecting and advancing God's purposes for both human creature and created order alike, they turn in upon themselves and reflect only the will and purposes of the human creature. The created order is commodified and utilized as a means for the advancement of *teloi* constructed by fallen humanity and not those revealed by God. The result is the subversion of the powers of the created order and human personhood, which can only result in social determinism and the eclipse of God. In sum, the basis for a free society is lost.

As the origination point for this project, Torrance's doctrine of God as triune has been pervasive throughout. It has been integral to every feature of Torrance's thought, and no less so when considering the social coefficient of knowledge. Here the triune God of Jesus Christ is introduced as a necessary and fundamental component of every social coefficient, not only because the created order and human personhood are ultimately unintelligible apart from the reality of a triune Creator, but also because human agents as cultural beings must orient themselves to an appropriate Archimedean point if the created order and the human person are to realize their respective *teloi*. That Archimedean point is the God of Jesus Christ.

For Torrance, the Archimedean point serves a number of functions, whether it be identified with the God of Jesus Christ or not. In particular, the Archimedean point of each social coefficient plays a role in the identity formation of human agents. How a human agent identifies him or herself vis-à-vis the world in turn orients and guides their engagement with that world (cultural activity). Finally, that activity in the world is ultimately legitimated by recourse to the Archimedean point as the basis for both social and moral order. For all these reasons the identification of the Archimedean point that guides human agency is all-important, and for Torrance, it is essential that that Archimedean point be identified as the God of Jesus Christ.

In sum, we have suggested that a trinitarian theology of culture fashioned within the boundaries of Torrance's theological framework will require one to assert that the purpose of human culture is the glorification of the triune God of Jesus Christ. This purpose is accomplished as the created order is enabled to bear witness to this God through the unique constitution, agency, and vocation of the human person as a cultural being.

However, as a cultural being the human person must engage the powers of the created order in order to fulfill both the calling of humanity and the *telos* of the created order as disclosed through the revelation of God in Jesus Christ. The human person, through the power of the Spirit and upon the basis of the completed work of Christ, must relate actual order to the ultimate controlling ground of order from which all order proceeds. Through cultural activity we are invited to participate in the subjective realization of God's purposes for creation.

However, that participation assumes not only that we are social and cultural beings, nor simply that the created order has been created in such a way as to allow our understanding and manipulation of it. Rather, it assumes that we have some understanding of "the ultimate controlling ground of order from which all order proceeds." Since that ultimate controlling ground of order is the triune God of Jesus Christ, who has created an open and multi-variable world, and human persons who complete themselves through their relations with each other and their social and physical environments, it seems safe to postulate that cultural plurality of the most magnificent sort will be the consequence of relating the actual order of this world to the ultimate controlling ground of order—the triune God of Jesus Christ.

We conclude with a portion of Torrance's writing that captures much more than the thrust of his intellectual work, but it seems to me, the entire movement of his being:

> It is now the role of man in union with Christ to serve the purpose of God's love in the ongoing actualization of that redemption, sanctification and renewal within the universe ... Thus man has been called to be a kind of midwife to creation, in assisting nature out of its divinely given abundance constantly to give birth to new forms of life and richer patterns of order. Indeed, as the covenant-partner of Jesus Christ man may be regarded as the priest of creation, through whose service ... the marvelous rationality, symmetry, harmony and beauty of God's creation are being brought to light and given expression in such a way that the whole universe is found to be a glorious hymn to the Creator.[57]

---

57. Torrance, "Goodness and Dignity," 387.

Appendix: Project Outline

Chapter 1: Torrance's Doctrine of God: The Triune Creator

The Tri-unity of God as the Basis for the Creativity of God

The Creativity of God Is Signified by the Fatherhood of God

- THE FATHER SIGNIFIES THE TRIUNE BEING OF GOD
- THE FATHER SIGNIFIES THE ETERNAL BEING OF GOD
- THE FATHER SIGNIFIES THE CREATIVE BEING OF GOD
- THE FATHER SIGNIFIES THE PERSONAL BEING OF GOD

The Identity of God as Father and Creator Is Signified by God the Son

- THE SON'S UNITY IN BEING AND ACTION WITH THE FATHER: *HOMOOUSION*
  - *The Epistemological Significance of the* Homoousion
  - *The Soteriological Significance of the* Homoousion
  - *The Eschatological Significance of the* Homoousion
- THE SON'S DIFFERENTIATION IN IDENTITY AND OPERATION FROM THE FATHER: *PERICHORESIS*

The Work of God the Father, Mediated by God the Son, Is Signified by God the Holy Spirit

- THE BEING AND IDENTITY OF THE SPIRIT
  - *The Spirit Is Divine: The Spirit of God*
  - *The Spirit Is Translucent: The Spirit of Christ*
  - *The Spirit Is Lord: The Holy Spirit*
    - THE SPIRIT IS PERSONAL
    - THE SPIRIT IS FREE

The Agency and Activity of the Spirit

*The Spirit Creates and Sustains the Created Order:
The Creative Work of the Spirit*
*The Spirit Orients and Directs the Created Order:
The Eschatological Work of the Spirit*
*The Spirit Transforms and Consummates the Created Order:
The Sanctifying Work of the Spirit*

Chapter 2: Torrance's Doctrine of Creation I: Order as Contingent

The Inner-Logic of Order

Order as a Theological Concept: The Ground and Purpose of Order in God the Father

Contingence: Introducing and Defining the Concept
Contingence: Its Interlocking Nature and Dynamic
Contingence: Its Reflective Purpose

The Creation of the Powers: the Legislative Activity of God
The Language of the Powers: Structures and Patterns
The Function of the Powers: Mediating and Maintaining Order
The Purpose of the Powers: Temporal Analogues, Empirical Correlates, and Social Coefficients

Chapter 3: Torrance's Doctrine of Creation II: Order as Redeemed

Order as a Relational Concept: The Revelation and Reconciliation of Order in God the Son

Order as Fallen: Human Agency and the Subversion of Order
Order as Redeemed: The Divine Economy and the Redemption of Order

The Ultimate and Penultimate Function of the Law
The Divine Economy and the New Covenant

RESTORATION AND NEW CREATION IN CHRIST
- *The Incarnation and the Power of Identification*
- *The Resurrection and the Power of Love and Grace*
- *The Ascension and the Power of Pentecost*

Order as an Eschatological Concept: The Orientation and Sanctification of Order in God the Spirit

A Pneumatological Order: The Participatory and Sanctifying Work of the Spirit

THE ESCHATON AS BASED UPON A RELATION WITH THE ESCHATOS
- *The Cosmic Sphere*
- *The Corporate Sphere*
- *The Individual Sphere*

THE ESCHATON AS THE SPHERE OF THE SPIRIT'S SANCTIFYING WORK

An Ecclesiological Order: Through the Agency and Mission of the Church

An Ambiguous Order: Relating Actual Order to the Order that Ought to Be

A Sacramental Order: A Doxological Response to the Lord of Space and Time

A Heavenly and Earthly Order: In Anticipation of His Final Act

Chapter 4: Torrance's Doctrine of Humanity: Priests of Creation and Mediators of Order

Part One: Humanity as a Multi-Stringed Instrument

- *String #1: Humanity as Embodied Being*
- *String #2: Humanity as Personal Being*
- *String #3: Humanity as Relational Being*
- *From Creation to Incarnation, Crucifixion, and Resurrection*
- *From Resurrection to Ascension and Glorification*

Part Two: Tuning Up and Knowing the Score
   Humanity as an Eschatological Being
   Humanity as a Cultural Being

Chapter 5: Torrance's Theology of Culture: A Social Coefficient of Knowledge

Torrance's Social Coefficient of Knowledge

  Introducing the Term
  Defining the Term
   THE SOCIAL COEFFICIENT AS A MULTIPLIER AND MEASURE
   THE SOCIAL COEFFICIENT AS SIGNIFYING A RELATION THAT IS CONSTANT
   THE SOCIAL COEFFICIENT AS A JOINT AGENT OR FACTOR
   THE SOCIAL COEFFICIENT AND CULTURAL PLURALITY
  Developing the Term for Use in a Theology of Culture

The Formation and Function of Social Coefficients

  Social Coefficients Are Formed Around Knowing Relations Established with Objective Reality
   THE SOCIAL COEFFICIENT OF KNOWLEDGE AS A CENTERED SET
   THE OBJECTIVE POLE DETERMINES THE MEANS BY WHICH REALITY IS ENGAGED AND KNOWN
   THE SUBJECTIVE POLE DETERMINES THE MEANS BY WHICH REALITY IS RECEIVED AND REFLECTED
  Social Coefficients Are Socially Constructed Matrices Formed through a Historical Process
   EXTERNALIZATION
   OBJECTIVATION
   INTERNALIZATION

Social Coefficients Are Socially Constructed Matrices Oriented toward a Specific Telos

SOCIAL COEFFICIENTS MEDIATE AND SUSTAIN MEANING THROUGH CORRELATION, CONGRUENCE, AND TRANSLUCENCE: SEMANTIC INTENTIONALITY

SOCIAL COEFFICIENTS REQUIRE AN ARCHIMEDEAN POINT IN ORDER TO FULFILL THEIR DISTINCTIVE *TELOS*: THE TRANSCENDENT GROUND OF MEANING

The Archimedean Point as a Tuning Fork: Its Function
The Archimedean Point as the Triune God of Jesus Christ: Its Identity

EPISTEMOLOGICAL REASONS: REVELATION
SOTERIOLOGICAL REASONS: SALVATION
ESCHATOLOGICAL REASONS: SANCTIFICATION
DOXOLOGICAL REASONS: GLORIFICATION

Social Coefficients Orient, Mediate, and Sustain Our Knowing Relations

BY PROVIDING SEMANTIC STRUCTURES: A SYMBOLIC ENVIRONMENT
BY PROVIDING PARTICIPATORY STRUCTURES: A RITUALIZED ENVIRONMENT
BY PROVIDING MULTI-LEVELED STRUCTURES: A TEXTURED ENVIRONMENT

Social Coefficients Express and Embody Our Knowing Relations

BY INTEGRATING THE SUBJECTIVE AND THE OBJECTIVE
BY ORIENTING AND AGGREGATING HUMAN RELATIONS
BY ORDERING THE SOCIAL AND MATERIAL WORLD

Chapter 6
Persons, Powers, and Pluralities: Toward a Trinitarian Theology of Culture
The Social Coefficient of Knowledge: Examples

The Social Coefficient as Embodied Truth: The Church as Culture

ISRAEL AS THE WOMB OF CHRIST

THE CHURCH AS A ROYAL PRIESTHOOD

The Social Coefficient as Transforming Matrix: The Church Transforming Culture

THE DOCTRINE OF THE TRINITY AND THE CONCEPT OF PERSON

WESTERN SCIENCE AND THE THREE MASTERFUL IDEAS

Project Summary and Accomplishments

The Persons of the Trinity and the Purpose of Human Culture: A Design for Living

The Contingency of Creation and the Powers of Human Culture

The Identity and Agency of Humanity and the Plurality of Human Culture: Designs for Living

Bibliography

Achtemeier, Mark P. "The Truth of Tradition: Critical Realism in the Thought of Alasdair MacIntyre and T. F. Torrance." *Scottish Journal of Theology* 47 (1994) 355–74.
Anderson, Ray S. *Historical Transcendence and the Reality of God: A Christological Critique.* Grand Rapids: Eerdmans, 1975.
———. *On Being Human: Essays in Theological Anthropology.* Grand Rapids: Eerdmans, 1982.
———. "Barth and a New Direction for Natural Theology." In *Theology beyond Christendom: Essays on the Centenary of the Birth of Karl Barth*, edited by John Thompson, 241–66. Allison Park, PA: Pickwick, 1986.
———. *Theology, Death, and Dying.* Oxford: Blackwell, 1986.
———. "Socio-Cultural Implications of a Christian Perception of Humanity." *Asian Journal of Theology* 2 (1988) 500–515.
———. "On Being Human: The Spiritual Saga of a Creaturely Soul." In *Whatever Happened to the Soul? Scientific and Theological Portraits of Human Nature*, edited by Warren S. Brown, et al., 175–94. Theology and the Sciences. Minneapolis: Fortress, 1998.
Arnold, Clinton E. *Powers of Darkness: Principalities & Powers in Paul's Letters.* Downers Grove: InterVarsity, 1992.
Augsburger, David W. *Pastoral Counseling across Cultures.* Philadelphia: Westminster, 1986.
Barth, Karl. *Dogmatics in Outline.* New York: Harper & Row, 1949.
Bauman, Michael. "Interview with Thomas F. Torrance." In *Roundtable: Conversations with European Theologians*, by Michael Bauman, 111–18. Grand Rapids: Baker, 1990.
Becker, Ernest. *The Denial of Death.* New York: Free Press, 1973.
Berger, Peter L. *The Sacred Canopy: Elements of a Sociological Theory of Religion.* New York: Doubleday, 1969.
Berger, Peter L., and Thomas Luckmann. *The Social Construction of Reality: A Treatise in the Sociology of Knowledge.* Garden City, NY: Doubleday, 1966.
Berkhof, Hendrikus. *Christ and the Powers.* Translated by John Howard Yoder. 2nd ed. Scottdale, PA: Herald, 1977.
Berliner, Paul F. *Thinking in Jazz: The Infinite Art of Improvisation.* Chicago Studies in Ethnomusicology. Chicago: University of Chicago Press, 1994.
Braaten, Carl E. "Natural Law in Theology and Ethics." In *The Two Cities of God: The Church's Responsibility for the Earthly City*, edited by Carl E. Braaten and Robert W. Jenson, 42–58. Grand Rapids: Eerdmans, 1997.

Brunner, Emil, and Karl Barth. *Natural Theology: Comprising "Nature and Grace" by Professor Dr. Emil Brunner and the reply "No!" by Dr. Karl Barth.* London: Bles, 1946.

Clayton, Phillip D. *God and Contemporary Science.* Edinburgh Studies in Constructive Theology. Grand Rapids: Eerdmans, 1997.

Clifford, James. *The Predicament of Culture: Twentieth-Century Ethnography, Literature, and Art.* Cambridge: Harvard University Press, 1988.

Colyer, Elmer M. *How To Read T. F. Torrance: Understanding His Trinitarian & Scientific Theology.* Downers Grove, IL: InterVarsity, 2001.

———. *The Nature of Doctrine in T. F. Torrance's Theology.* Eugene, OR: Wipf & Stock, 2001.

———, editor. *The Promise of Trinitarian Theology: Theologians in Dialogue with T. F. Torrance.* Lanham, MD: Rowman & Littlefield, 2001.

———. "Review of Alister E. McGrath's *A Scientific Theology, Volume 1: Nature.*" *Pro Ecclesia* 12 (2003) 226–31.

———. "Review of Alister E. McGrath's *A Scientific Theology, Volume 2: Reality.*" *Pro Ecclesia* 12 (2003) 492–97.

———. "Review of Alister E. McGrath's *A Scientific Theology, Volume 3: Theory.*" *Pro Ecclesia* 13 (2004) 233–40.

Congar, Yves. *I Believe in the Holy Spirit.* Vol. 3, *The River of the Water of Life (Rev 22:1) Flows in the East and in the West.* New York: Seabury, 1983.

Csikszentmihalyi, Mihaly. *Flow: The Psychology of Optimal Experience.* New York: HarperPerennial, 1991.

Csikszentmihalyi, Mihaly, and Eugene Rochberg-Halton. *The Meaning of Things: Domestic Symbols and the Self.* Cambridge: Cambridge University Press, 1981.

Dawn, Marva J. "The Biblical Concept of 'the Principalities and Powers': John Yoder Points to Jacques Ellul." In *The Wisdom of the Cross: Essays in Honor of John Howard Yoder*, edited by Stanley Hauerwas, 168–86. Grand Rapids: Eerdmans, 1999.

Deddo, Gary W. "The Holy Spirit in T. F. Torrance's Theology." In *The Promise of Trinitarian Theology: Theologians in Dialogue with T. F. Torrance*, edited by Elmer M. Colyer, 81–114. Lanham, MD: Rowman & Littlefield, 2001.

Driver, Tom F. *The Magic of Ritual: Our Need for Liberating Rites That Transform Our Lives and Communities.* San Francisco: HarperSanFrancisco, 1991.

Dyrness, William A. *The Earth Is God's: A Theology of American Culture.* Faith and Cultures Series. Maryknoll, NY: Orbis, 1997.

Flett, Eric G. "Review of *Knowledge of the Self-Revealing God in the Thought of Thomas Forsyth Torrance*, by John Douglas Morrison." *Journal of the Evangelical Theological Society* 42 (1999) 548–49.

Geertz, Clifford. *The Interpretation of Cultures: Selected Essays.* New York: Basic Books, 1973.

Goudzwaard, Bob. *Aid for the Overdeveloped West.* Toronto: Wedge, 1975.

Gowan, Donald E. *Eschatology in the Old Testament.* 2nd ed. Edinburgh: T. & T. Clark, 2000.

Grenz, Stanley J. *Rediscovering the Triune God: The Trinity in Contemporary Theology.* Minneapolis: Fortress, 2004.

Grenz, Stanley J., and John R. Franke. *Beyond Foundationalism: Shaping Theology in a Postmodern Context.* Louisville: Westminster John Knox, 2001.

Gunton, Colin E. *Enlightenment and Alienation: An Essay towards a Trinitarian Theology*. Grand Rapids: Eerdmans, 1985.
———. *The Actuality of Atonement: A Study of Metaphor, Rationality and the Christian Tradition*. Edinburgh: T. & T. Clark, 1988.
———. "The Triune God and the Freedom of the Creature." In *Karl Barth: Centenary Essays*, edited by S. W. Sykes, 46–68. Cambridge: Cambridge University Press, 1989,
———. *Christ and Creation*. Grand Rapids: Eerdmans, 1992.
———. *The One, the Three and the Many: God, Creation, and the Culture of Modernity*. Cambridge: Cambridge University Press, 1993.
———. *The Triune Creator: A Historical and Systematic Study*. Edinburgh Studies in Constructive Theology. Edinburgh: Edinburgh University Press, 1998.
———. "Being and Person: T. F. Torrance's Doctrine of God." In *The Promise of Trinitarian Theology: Theologians in Dialogue with T. F. Torrance*, edited by Elmer M. Colyer, 115–37. Lanham, MD: Rowman & Littlefield, 2001.
Habets, Myk. *Theosis in the Theology of Thomas Torrance*. Ashgate New Critical Thinking in Religion, Theology, and Biblical Studies. Farnham, UK: Ashgate, 2009.
Hall, Douglas John. *Imaging God: Dominion as Stewardship*. 1986. Reprinted, Eugene, OR: Wipf & Stock, 2004.
Harrison, Lawrence E., and Samuel P. Huntington, editors. *Culture Matters: How Values Shape Human Progress*. New York: Basic Books, 2000.
Hendry, George S. *The Holy Spirit in Christian Theology*. Philadelphia: Westminster, 1956.
Hesselink, I. John. "A Pilgrimage in the School of Christ: An Interview with T. F. Torrance." *Reformed Review* 38 (1984) 49–64.
Hiebert, Paul G. *Cultural Anthropology*. Philadelphia: Lippincott, 1976.
———. *Anthropological Reflections on Missiological Issues*. Grand Rapids: Baker, 1994.
———. *The Missiological Implications of Epistemological Shifts: Affirming Truth in a Modern/Postmodern World*. Christian Mission and Modern Culture. Harrisburg, PA: Trinity, 1999.
Hunsinger, George. "The Dimension of Depth: Thomas F. Torrance on the Sacraments." In *The Promise of Trinitarian Theology: Theologians on Dialogue with T. F. Torrance*, edited by Elmer M. Colyer, 139–60. Lanham, MD: Rowman & Littlefield, 2001.
Jennings, Willie J. "Conformed to His Image: The *Imago Dei* as a Christological Vision." In *Incarnational Ministry: The Presence of Christ in Church, Society, and Family: Essays in Honor of Ray S. Anderson*, edited by Christian D. Kettler and Todd H. Speidell, 153–61. Colorado Springs: Helmers & Howard, 1990.
Jenson, Robert W. *Systematic Theology*. Vol. 2, *The Works of God*. New York: Oxford University Press, 1999.
Jüngel, Eberhard. "Humanity in Correspondence to God: Remarks on the Image of God as a Basic Concept in Theological Anthropology." In *Theological Essays*, 1:124–53. 2 vols. Edinburgh: T. & T. Clark, 1989.
Kang, Phee Seng. "The Epistemological Significance of *Homoousion* in the Theology of Thomas F. Torrance." *Scottish Journal of Theology* 45 (1992) 341–66.

Kimel, Alvin F., editor. *Speaking the Christian God: The Holy Trinity and the Challenge of Feminism.* Grand Rapids: Eerdmans, 1992.

Kirby, Richard Stephen. "The Theological Definition of Cosmic Disorder in the Writings of Thomas Forsyth Torrance." PhD diss., King's College, University of London, 1992.

Kraft, Charles H. *Christianity in Culture: A Study in Dynamic Biblical Theologizing in Cross-Cultural Perspective.* Maryknoll, NY: Orbis, 1979.

Kroeber, Alfred A., and Klyde Kluckhohn. *Culture: A Critical Review of Concepts and Definitions.* Papers of the Peabody Museum of American Archaeology and Ethnology, Harvard University, vol. 47, no. 1. Cambridge: The Museum, 1952.

LaCugna, Catherine Mowry. *God for Us: The Trinity and Christian Life.* San Francisco: HarperSanFrancisco, 1991.

Lee, Kye Won. *Living in Union with Christ: The Practical Theology of Thomas F. Torrance.* Issues in Systematic Theology 11. New York: Lang, 2002.

Luoma, Tapio. *Incarnation and Physics: Natural Science in the Theology of Thomas F. Torrance.* American Academy of Religion Academy Series. Oxford: Oxford University Press, 2002.

Mangina, Joseph L. "Mediating Theologies: Karl Barth between Radical and Neo-Orthodoxy." *Scottish Journal of Theology* 56 (2003) 427–43.

McGrath, Alister E. *Thomas F. Torrance: An Intellectual Biography.* Edinburgh: T. & T. Clark, 1999.

———. *A Scientific Theology.* Vol. 1, *Nature.* Grand Rapids: Eerdmans, 2002.

———. *A Scientific Theology.* Vol. 2, *Reality.* Grand Rapids: Eerdmans, 2002.

———. *A Scientific Theology.* Vol. 3, *Theory.* Grand Rapids: Eerdmans, 2003.

Molnar, Paul D. "Toward a Contemporary Doctrine of the Immanent Trinity: Karl Barth and the Present Discussion." *Scottish Journal of Theology* 49 (1996) 311–57.

Monson, Ingrid. *Saying Something: Jazz Improvisation and Interaction.* Chicago Studies in Ethnomusicology. Chicago: University of Chicago Press, 1996.

Morgan, David. *Visual Piety: A History and Theory of Popular Images.* Berkeley: University of California Press, 1998.

Morrison, John Douglas. *Knowledge of the Self-Revealing God in the Thought of Thomas Forsyth Torrance.* Issues in Systematic Theology 2. New York: Lang, 1997.

Mosser, Carl. "The Greatest Possible Blessing: Calvin and Deification." *Scottish Journal of Theology* 55 (2002) 36–57.

———. "The Earliest Patristic Interpretations of Psalm 82, Jewish Antecedents, and the Origin of Christian Deification." *Journal of Theological Studies* 56 (2005) 30–74.

Newbigin, Lesslie. *The Gospel in a Pluralist Society.* Grand Rapids: Eerdmans, 1989.

Niebuhr, H. Richard. *Christ and Culture.* London: Faber & Faber, 1952.

Niebuhr, Reinhold. *The Nature and Destiny of Man.* New York: Scribner, 1964.

Niedhardt, W. Jim. "Key Themes in Thomas F. Torrance's Integration of Judeo-Christian Theology and Natural Science." In *The Christian Frame of Mind: Reason, Order and Openness in Theology and Natural Science,* by Thomas F. Torrance, xi–xli. Colorado Springs: Helmers & Howard, 1989.

Pannenberg, Wolfhart. *Systematic Theology,* vol. 2. Translated by Geoffrey W. Bromiley. Grand Rapids: Eerdmans, 1994.

Peirce, Charles S. *Philosophical Writings of Peirce, Selected and Edited with an Introduction by Justus Buchler*. New York: Dover, 1955.
Peters, Ted. *God as Trinity: Relationality and Temporality in the Divine Life*. Louisville: Westminster, 1993.
Porter, Jean. *Natural and Divine Law: Reclaiming the Tradition for Christian Ethics*. Saint Paul University Series in Ethics. Grand Rapids: Eerdmans, 1999.
Rae, Murray A. "To Render Praise: Humanity in God's World." In *Science and Christianity: Festschrift in Honour of Harold Turner and John Morton*, edited by L. R. B. Mann, 177–201. Auckland: University of Auckland Centre for Continuing Education, 2001.
Rappaport, Roy A. *Ecology, Meaning, and Religion*. Richmond, CA: North Atlantic, 1979.
Richardson, Kurt Anders. "Revelation, Scripture, and Mystical Apprehension of Divine Knowledge." In *The Promise of Trinitarian Theology: Theologians in Dialogue with T. F. Torrance*, edited by Elmer M. Colyer, 185–203. Lanham, MD: Rowman & Littlefield, 2001.
Smail, Thomas A. *The Giving Gift: The Holy Spirit in Person*. London: Darton, Longman & Todd, 1994.
Smith, Christian. *Moral, Believing Animals: Human Personhood and Culture*. New York: Oxford University Press, 2003.
Spjuth, Roland. *Creation, Contingency and Divine Presence in the Theologies of Thomas F. Torrance and Eberhard Jungel*. Studia Theologica Lundensia 51. Lund: Lund University, 1995.
Tanner, Kathryn. *Theories of Culture: A New Agenda for Theology*. Guides to Theological Inquiry. Minneapolis: Fortress, 1997.
Taylor, John V. *The Go-Between God: The Holy Spirit and the Christian Mission*. New York: Oxford University Press, 1972.
Torrance, T. F. "The Word of God and the Nature of Man." In *Reformation Old and New: A Tribute to Karl Barth*, edited by F. W. Camfield, 121–41. London: Lutterworth, 1947.
———. *Calvin's Doctrine of Man*. London: Lutterworth, 1949.
———. *Kingdom and Church: A Study in the Theology of the Reformation*. Edinburgh: Oliver and Boyd, 1956.
———. *The Apocalypse Today*. Grand Rapids: Eerdmans, 1959.
———. *Conflict and Agreement in the Church*. Vol. 1, *Order and Disorder*. London: Lutterworth, 1959.
———, editor. *The School of Faith: The Catechisms of the Reformed Church*. London: James Clarke, 1959.
———. *Conflict and Agreement in the Church*. Vol. 2, *The Ministry and Sacraments of the Gospel*. London: Lutterworth, 1960.
———. *Theology in Reconstruction*. London: SCM, 1965.
———. "The Mission of the Church." *Scottish Journal of Theology* 19 (1966) 129–43.
———. "The Implications of *Oikonomia* for Knowledge and Speech of God in Early Christian Theology." In *Oikonomia: Heilsgeschichte als Thema der Theologie*, edited by Felix Christ, 223–38. Hamburg: Reich, 1967.
———. *Theological Science*. London: Oxford University Press, 1969.

———. "The Relevance of Orthodoxy." In *The Relevance of Orthodoxy*, by Thomas F. Torrance, 9–19. Edited with an introduction by John B. Logan. Stirling: Drummond, 1970.

———. *God and Rationality*. Oxford: Oxford University Press, 1971.

———. *Theology in Reconciliation: Essays towards Evangelical and Catholic Unity in East and West*. 1975. Reprinted, Eugene, OR: Wipf & Stock, 1996.

———. *Space, Time and Resurrection*. Grand Rapids: Eerdmans, 1976.

———. *The Ground and Grammar of Theology*. The Richard Lectures for 1978–1979 at the University of Virginia. Charlottesville: University Press of Virginia, 1980.

———. *Divine and Contingent Order*. Oxford: Oxford University Press, 1981.

———. *Juridical Law and Physical Law: Toward a Realist Foundation for Human Law*. Edinburgh: Scottish Academic, 1982.

———. *Reality and Evangelical Theology*. The 1981 Payton Lectures. Philadelphia: Westminster, 1982.

———. *Transformation & Convergence in the Frame of Knowledge: Explorations in the Interrelations of Scientific and Theological Enterprise*. Grand Rapids: Eerdmans, 1984.

———. *Reality and Scientific Theology*. Theology and Science at the Frontiers of Knowledge 1. Edinburgh: Scottish Academic, 1985.

———. *The Hermeneutics of John Calvin*. Monograph Supplements to the Scottish Journal of Theology. Edinburgh: Scottish Academic, 1988.

———. *The Trinitarian Faith: The Evangelical Theology of the Ancient Catholic Church*. Edinburgh: T. & T. Clark, 1988.

———, editor. *The Christian Frame of Mind: Reason, Order, and Openness in Theology and Natural Science*. 2nd ed. Colorado Springs: Helmers & Howard, 1989.

———. "Man, Mediator of Order." In *The Christian Frame of Mind: Reason, Order, and Openness in Theology and Natural Science*, edited by T. F. Torrance, 35–64. 2nd ed. Colorado Springs: Helmers & Howard, 1989.

———. "The Goodness and Dignity of Man in the Christian Tradition." In *Christ in Our Place: The Humanity of God in Christ for the Reconciliation of the World: Essays Presented to Professor James B. Torrance*, edited by Trevor A. Hart and Daniel P. Thimell, 369–87. Princeton Theological Monograph Series 25. Allison Park, PA: Pickwick, 1989.

———. "The Soul and Person, in Theological Perspective." In *Religion, Reason, and the Self*, edited by Stewart R. Sutherland and T. A. Roberts, 103–18. Cardiff: University of Wales Press, 1989.

———. *Karl Barth: Biblical and Evangelical Theologian*. Edinburgh: T. & T. Clark, 1990.

———. "Donor Insemination for the Single Woman: The Animalisation of the Human Race." *Ethics and Medicine* 7:3 (1991) 37–38.

———. "The Atonement: The Singularity of Christ and the Finality of the Cross: The Atonement and the Moral Order." In *Universalism and the Doctrine of Hell: Papers Presented and the Fourth Edinburgh Conference on Christian Dogmatics, 1991*, edited by Nigel M. de S. Cameron, 225–56. Scottish Bulletin of Evangelical Theology. Special Study 5. Grand Rapids: Baker, 1992.

———. "The Christian Apprehension of God the Father." In *Speaking the Christian God: The Holy Trinity and the Challenge of Feminism*, edited by Alvin F. Kimel, 120–43. Grand Rapids: Eerdmans, 1992.

———. *The Mediation of Christ*. 2nd ed. Edinburgh: T. & T. Clark, 1992.
———. *Royal Priesthood: A Theology of Ordained Ministry*. 2nd ed. Edinburgh: T. & T. Clark, 1993.
———. "The Transfinite Significance of Beauty in Science and Theology." In *L'Art, la Science et la Metaphysique: Etudes offertes a Andre Mercier*, edited by Luz García Alonzo et al., 393–418. Berne: Lang, 1993.
———. "The Ought and the Is: Moral and Natural Law." In *A Festschrift in Honor of George Stuart Heyer, Jr.* Special issue, *Insight: A Journal of the Faculty of Austin Seminary* Spring (1994) 49–59.
———. *The Christian Doctrine of God, One Being Three Persons*. Edinburgh: T. & T. Clark, 1996.
———. *The Soul and Person of the Unborn Child*. Edinburgh: Handsel, 1999.
———. *The Being and Nature of the Unborn Child*. Edinburgh: Handsel, 2000.
Volf, Miroslav. "The Final Reconciliation: Reflections on a Social Dimension of the Eschatological Transition." *Modern Theology* 16 (2000) 91–113.
Williams, Raymond. *The Sociology of Culture*. New York: Schocken, 1982.
Wink, Walter. *Naming the Powers: The Language of Power in the New Testament*. The Powers 1. Philadelphia: Fortress, 1984.
———. *Unmasking the Powers: The Invisible Forces That Determine Human Existence*. The Powers 2. Philadelphia: Fortress, 1986.
———. *Engaging the Powers: Discernment and Resistance in a World of Domination*. Minneapolis: Fortress, 1992.
Wolters, Albert M. *Creation Regained: Biblical Basics for a Reformational Worldview*. Grand Rapids: Eerdmans, 1985.
Wolterstorff, Nicholas. *Until Justice and Peace Embrace: The Kuyper Lectures for 1981*. Grand Rapids: Eerdmans, 1983.
Wuthnow, Robert et al. *Cultural Analysis: The Work of Peter L. Berger, Mary Douglas, Michel Foucault, and Jürgen Habermas*. London: Routledge & Kegan Paul, 1984.
Yeung, Jason Hing Kau. *Being and Knowing: An Examination of T.F. Torrance's Christological Science*. Jian Dao Dissertation Series 3. Theology and Culture 1. Hong Kong: Alliance Bible Seminary, 1996.
Yoder, John Howard. *The Politics of Jesus: Vicit Agnus Noster*. 2nd ed. Grand Rapids: Eerdmans, 1994.
Yu, Carver T. *Being and Relation: A Theological Critique of Western Dualism and Individualism*. Theology and Science at the Frontiers of Knowledge 8. Edinburgh: Scottish Academic, 1987.

www.ingramcontent.com/pod-product-compliance
Lightning Source LLC
Chambersburg PA
CBHW050437240426
43661CB00055B/2413